... Columbus—An Immense and
...usiastic Meeting.

...as arrived in Columbus on the
... on yesterday morning. A sub
... the committee on reception
...sers. CHITTENDEN and KELSEY)
...sburgh and accompanied him
...wark, where they were joined
... of the Committee, and by it
...to Columbus. At the depot a
...ere in readiness to receive the
...iams' Gun Squad announced
... Cars by a salute of thirteen
...was formed headed by Capt.
...litary company, who escorted
...his quarters at the American.
...ery direction brought
... people of the count

HON. ABE LINCOLN,

SEPTEMBER 17, 1859.

...KAT

...ET SPACE,

...Evening.

...ATTEND !!!

...Monster's Band, at

...P. M., and will be

...where he will ad-

...at 7½ o'clock.

Ohio State Journal.

SATURDAY MORNING, SEPT. 17, 1859.

SPEECH OF THE
HON. ABRAHAM LINCOLN

AT COLUMBUS,

Friday, September 15, 1859.

At the appointed hour, (8 o'clock,) yesterday
...ernoon, a very large audience assembled
...on the terrace at the eastern side of the
...ate House, to hear the eloquent Illinoisan.
...n. Geo. M. Parsons, Chairman of the Re-
...blican Central Committee, advanced in front
...the platform and said:

"Fellow citizens, a short t
...an Central Committee of
...st to the Hon. Abraham
...ddress the people of thi
...topics of the day. To
...ponded, and I now have
...to you.

"MR. LINCOLN'
...incoln came forw
...proceeded to spe
...w CITIZENS OF T
...ail to remember
...e before an audie
...audience that
...the Ch
...ferred

The Electioneering To...
Douglas.

This title, we regret to say, truly designates
the character of the movements of Mr. Senator Douglas. If it is not calculated to win
the respect of sober minded and well-inform-
ed men, the fault is his own. What a spectacle
would be exhibited to our country and to the
world if every gentleman who has been spok-
en to in connection with the Chief Magistracy
of the United States should follow his example.

THE SPEECHES OF SENATOR DOUGLAS.

The general love of literary merit, and the
deference to individual genius, have often led
men to yield to the orator of the hour not
only their admiration, but their convictions.—
But it is almost unanimously conceded that
while, in point of orato
equalled, if not excelled,
preceded him in the p
Magazine and his popu
sunk him to a very low p
tional lawyer and as a pop

THE DOUGLAS FOR

It is the general belief
...es of the metropolis

Senator Douglas at Wooster.
Senator Douglas appeared according to
announcement—as we learn by an exclusive
telegraphic dispatch—at Wooster, o' yesterday. The new feature of his speech was a bitter attack upon Attorney-General BLACK's review of his Harper's Magazine article. He is
reported to have accused the Attorney-General of falsifying, and of a deliberate attempt
to destroy the Democratic party and break
down all the leaders of the party in the Northern States. It must be conceded, how-
dull the pamphlet of the Atto
may be, that it is distin
nently courteous
lieve, con
"HARPER'S NEW MONTHLY MAGAZINE.

...er of the people leg
...es the people thereof perfectly
...regulate their domestic institu
...way, subject only to the Con
...nited States."

Those who believe that the Co
...shes slavery in the Territories
...om Congress and the Terri
...the power to control it; and
...n the event the Territorial L
...enact the requisite laws for i
...comes the imperative duty o

DAILY COMMERCIAL.

WEDNESDAY, SEPTEMBER 21, '59.

The Enquirer on Lincoln.

It would be difficult to compress more unfairness and more impudence into the com-
pass of a single article, than is done in an attempted criticism of the late speech of Hon.
ABRAM LINCOLN, in yesterday's Enquirer.
What is to be thought of an article, which begins with the statement that its author had
not read the speech, and then goes on to de-
nounce it in all its parts as made up of "trash,"
of "palpable lies," of "badinage and balder-
dash?" If any man, whose reasoning faculty
is not totally absorbed in partizan prejudice,
will read Mr. LINCOLN's speech, he will come
to the conclusion that it is the production of
an able and a logical intellect. We do not say
that any amount of reading would ever bring
to the admission of that fact, so unscrupulous
a party organ as the Enquirer. That journal
is not accustomed to admit any truth, when it
conflicts with the party exigencies. But to
put forth a violent and wholesale condemna-
tion of a political document, which, by its
confession, it had never read, is an exhibition
...ontery which, in any other journal,

THE Hon. ABE LINCOLN, of Illinois, is expected here this evening, and will be received
with becoming pomp and circumstance. His
political friends propose, we believe, to make
his reception equal to that given the Little
Giant by the ever faithful Democracy. As we
are in the way of lionizing the politicians of
Illinois, we see no reason why Mr. LINCOLN
should not have as big a turn out as DOUGLAS.
He is a very able man, and a droll one, full of
facts and a sort of odd wit that takes the
crowds immensely. He speaks to night at the
Fifth street market place, and will be well
worth hearing.

...soned re...
...er's own candid...
...delivered to what the Enqu...
..."a large and respect...
...must have an...
...stated
...

THE DIVIDING LINE BETWEEN FEDERAL AND LOCAL AUTHO
...POPULAR SOVEREIGNTY IN THE TERRITORIES.
...EN A. DOUGLAS

IN THE NAME OF THE PEOPLE

IN THE
NAME
OF THE
PEOPLE

*Speeches and Writings of Lincoln and Douglas
in the Ohio Campaign of 1859*

EDITED, WITH AN INTRODUCTION, BY

HARRY V. JAFFA AND
ROBERT W. JOHANNSEN

Published for
THE OHIO HISTORICAL SOCIETY
by
THE OHIO STATE UNIVERSITY PRESS
COLUMBUS

TO THE MEMORY OF THE GREAT DEBATERS

PREFACE

Last year, the University of Chicago Press, under the auspices of the Chicago Historical Society, published a handsome centennial edition of *The Complete Lincoln-Douglas Debates of 1858*, edited by the eminent scholar Paul M. Angle. The new edition is much more than a reprint of the speeches: it is a documentary account of the entire campaign that enables us to witness the debates in their living context. Only in one item does it fall below its 1860 predecessor: it omits Douglas' speech of July 16, 1858, at Bloomington, at which Lincoln was present, and which must have been very much in Lincoln's mind when he prepared his own speech for delivery at Springfield the next day.

It is not a defect of Professor Angle's edition, but a conspicuous difference nonetheless, that he decided not to reprint Lincoln's two Ohio speeches of 1859, both of which were included in the collection which played a historic role in Lincoln's rise to the Presidency. The reason for their original inclusion, of course, was that the Lincoln-Douglas debates were first brought out in 1860 in Columbus, Ohio, by Follett, Foster and Company—indeed, their publication may rate finally among the most important results of the Ohio campaign of 1859—and an Ohio publisher would naturally add Lincoln's Ohio speeches to the Illinois debates. It is appropriate, we feel, that the Ohio speeches, which were the direct cause of the publication of those in Illinois, should now receive their own distinctive tribute in this their centennial year, and that this should be done in Columbus by the Ohio State University Press for the Ohio Historical Society.

Ohio is naturally proud to celebrate its station upon the pathway to immortality of the Great Emancipator; it is a task of no less dignity to restore the proportions of the past by reviving, from the original records, speeches and writings of Stephen A. Douglas. Lincoln's Ohio speeches have always been available either in the *Debates* or in his *Collected Works*. Douglas' have been locked in the columns of the papers that first reported them. Perhaps more important is the failure, for a century, to reprint the great *Harper's* essay on "The Dividing Line between Federal and Local Authority." There have been countless thousands in the last hundred years who have read in the beginning of Lincoln's Cooper Union speech that he adopted "as a text" furnishing "a precise and agreed starting point for a discussion between Republicans and that wing of the Democracy headed by Senator Douglas," the proposition in Douglas' speech at Columbus, Ohio, that "Our fathers, when they framed the Government under which we live, understood this question just as well, and even better, than we do now." But almost none have read Douglas' Columbus speech, or the *Harper's* essay which is the fullest source of his understanding of the work of the founding fathers. The entire Ohio campaign is, in a sense, a commentary upon that essay. But neither

Lincoln's Ohio speeches nor the speech at Cooper Union are completely intelligible without knowing the arguments of Douglas he was encountering. The disregard of Lincoln's powerful antagonist has not served to enhance the appreciation of his own greatness.

Douglas' *Harper's* essay, the first piece printed in this volume, was directed against both the Republicans and the Democrats under the leadership of President Buchanan, whose "Directory" had fiercely and bitterly denounced Douglas ever since he broke with the administration over the Lecompton Constitution for Kansas. That branch of the Democratic party is represented in the present collection by the reprint of the September 10, 1859, article in the Washington *Constitution*, attacking Douglas' *Harper's* essay. It was published anonymously, but was almost immediately known to be the work of Jeremiah Sullivan Black, Buchanan's Attorney-General. The Black-Douglas controversy raged on after the Ohio campaign, but the main points in it are contained in Black's September 10th article, and in Douglas' Wooster speech, which is largely devoted to a counterattack upon his Democratic adversary. In Douglas' *Harper's* essay, in Black's attack upon it, and in Lincoln's and Douglas' speeches we have a collection of contemporary controversial pieces of unrivaled vividness and authority in portraying the three major party positions of 1860: Douglas Democracy, old-guard Southern Democracy, and Republicanism. No understanding of the election of 1860 is complete without a grasp of these positions; the speeches and writings incident to the Ohio campaign of 1859 convey the arguments es-

poused by the three groups of antagonists more clearly
than any other collection of equal length.

The planning of this volume has been a joint effort.
It has been the task of Professor Johannsen, of the University of Illinois, to contribute that part of the Introduction entitled "The Setting," and it has been mine
to interpret "The Issues." I think it only fair to add
that, as any interpretation of issues as controversial as
those of the Ohio campaign of 1858 is itself bound to
be controversial, the responsibility for the judgments
and opinions therein expressed is entirely my own.

The curious and the speculative may be interested
to know that the title chosen has been taken from
Coriolanus, Act III, scene iii, line 99.

HARRY V. JAFFA

Ohio State University
Columbus, Ohio
July 4, 1959

CONTENTS

Introduction
The Setting 1
The Issues 34

The Dividing Line between Federal and Local
Authority, *by Stephen A. Douglas*
Harper's Magazine, September, 1859 58

Speech of Stephen A. Douglas at Columbus, Ohio,
September 7, 1859 126

Speech of Stephen A. Douglas at Cincinnati, Ohio,
September 9, 1859 151

Observations on Senator Douglas' Views of Popular
Sovereignty, *by Jeremiah Black*
September 10, 1859 173

Speech of Stephen A. Douglas at Wooster, Ohio,
September 16, 1859 200

Speech of Abraham Lincoln at Columbus, Ohio,
September 16, 1859 231

Speech of Abraham Lincoln at Cincinnati, Ohio,
September 17, 1859 271

INTRODUCTION

The Setting

On September 1, 1859, the Columbus *Ohio States-man* announced that Senator Stephen A. Douglas, of Illinois, would address the people of Ohio at Columbus and Cincinnati during the ensuing week. The announcement was signed by George W. Manypenny, chairman of the Ohio Democratic State Central Committee and editor of the *Statesman*. Ohio was in the midst of a crucial election campaign, made doubly significant by the approaching Presidential election year of 1860. The Democratic party was desperate to place the state in the Democratic column, and it was to aid this purpose that Douglas consented to visit Ohio. At stake were the state offices and seats in the state legislature. The new state legislature would select a United States Senator, thus making the outcome of those races extremely important to both parties. Manypenny's invitation had been extended to Douglas as early as June, 1859, soon after the conclusion of the state conventions.[1] In the months that followed, Douglas received additional appeals for aid from other Ohio Democrats, including Samuel S. Cox and George E. Pugh, Representative and Senator respectively, the latter comment-

[1] George W. Manypenny to Stephen A. Douglas, June 27, 1859 (Stephen A. Douglas Papers, University of Chicago Library).

1

ing hopefully, "We have a chance in Ohio this year." [2]
The importance of the Ohio election to Democratic
prospects in the coming Presidential campaign was ap-
preciated by Douglas. "Ohio," he wrote, "should lead
the North West." [3]

Douglas' name, in the fall of 1859, was on everyone's lips. He was clearly the dominant figure in the
Democratic party and one of the most significant and
controversial in the politics of the time. Already famous
for his authorship of the Kansas-Nebraska Act in 1854,
he had achieved greater heights of notoriety in the years
that followed. His bold stand against the efforts of the
leadership in his own party to impose the proslavery
Lecompton Constitution on the people of Kansas, his
joint debates with Abraham Lincoln in Illinois in 1858
as he struggled to retain his Senate seat and his subsequent re-election to that body, his removal by a
Southern-dominated party caucus from the chairman-
ship of the Senate committee on Territories, a post he
had held for twelve years, for what was branded his
"Freeport heresy"—all had served to keep him before
the public notice. In 1859, he continued to defend his
conviction that the people of the Territories must be
allowed to decide the slavery question for themselves.
In spite of his unequivocal statement that he would
become a candidate only on a platform that was thoroughly consistent with his own position, Douglas had
emerged as the primary contender for the Democratic

[2] Samuel S. Cox to Douglas, August 26, 1859; George E. Pugh
to Douglas, August 13, 1859 (Douglas Papers, University of
Chicago Library).

[3] Douglas to Manypenny, October 1, 1859 (George W. Manypenny Papers, Library of Congress).

nomination in 1860.[4] A few days before the *Statesman's* announcement that he would visit Ohio, Douglas' noted essay on "The Dividing Line between Federal and Local Authority: Popular Sovereignty in the Territories," a formal exposition of his creed, was published by *Harper's Magazine*.[5] Douglas' participation in the Ohio campaign thus had a national as well as a local significance. To the editor of the *New York Times*, Douglas' visit signified the opening of the 1860 Presidential contest. "It is time," he wrote, "that we should begin to see whither the country is to drift in the approaching national canvass; and the responsible voice of a single statesman who does not fear to speak his mind, is of more importance just at this moment than an infinity of conventions, caucuses, conclaves and maneuvers in the dark." [6]

The announcement that Douglas would speak in Ohio took the state Republican organization by surprise. The challenge of Douglas' participation in the campaign could not go unanswered. On the same day on which the announcement appeared, September 1, William T. Bascom, secretary of the Republican State Central Committee, wrote to Abraham Lincoln, inviting him to make several speeches in Ohio "to head

[4] See Douglas to J. B. Dorr, June 22, 1859, *National Intelligencer* (Washington, D. C.), June 24, 1859. This letter, written to a Dubuque, Iowa, newspaper editor, made clear the terms on which Douglas would accept the Presidential nomination in 1860. It was reprinted widely in the press of the day.

[5] *Harper's Magazine*, XIV (September, 1859), 519-37. See Robert W. Johannsen, "Stephen A. Douglas, 'Harper's Magazine,' and Popular Sovereignty," *Mississippi Valley Historical Review*, XLV (March, 1959), 606-31. For the text of Douglas' essay, see pages 58-125 in this book.

[6] *New York Times*, September 6, 12, 1859.

off the little gentleman." [7] Almost simultaneously with
Bascom's invitation, a second appeal to Lincoln was
made. Peter Zinn, a member of the Central Committee,
invited Lincoln to speak in Cincinnati as soon after
Douglas' visit as possible.[8] Lincoln's reaction to the
invitations was favorable. On the same day that he accepted Zinn's appeal, he wrote, "I now have two invitations to go to Ohio. These last are prompted by
Douglas' going there; and I am really tempted to make
a flying trip to Columbus & Cincinnati." [9] On September 9, the *Ohio State Journal*, Columbus' Republican
organ, announced officially that the "Hon. Ab. Lincoln"
would visit Ohio.

In contrast to Douglas, Lincoln was but little known
in Ohio in 1859. His earlier contacts with the state
had been strictly legal and professional; he had never
made a political speech there. Nevertheless, his choice
by the Republican committee was a logical one. His
debates with Douglas in Illinois the year before had
proved his ability as a political campaigner, and his
attacks on Douglas' principle of popular sovereignty
had attracted nation-wide attention. More than any

[7] William T. Bascom to Lincoln, September 1, 1859 (Robert
Todd Lincoln Collection, Lincoln Papers, Library of Congress).
[8] Peter Zinn to Lincoln, September 2, 1859 (Robert Todd
Lincoln Collection, Lincoln Papers, Library of Congress).
[9] Lincoln to Hawkins Taylor, September 6, 1859, *The Col-
lected Works of Abraham Lincoln*, ed. Roy P. Basler (New
Brunswick, New Jersey: Rutgers University Press, 1953), III, 400.
Lincoln's new popularity as a campaign speaker since his de-
bates with Douglas brought him, in addition to the Ohio in-
vitation, bids to speak in Iowa, Pennsylvania, and New York
State in September, 1859: John A. Kasson to Lincoln, September
13, 1859; Russell Errett to Lincoln, September 13, 1859; Joshua
R. Giddings to Lincoln, September 12, 1859 (Robert Todd
Lincoln Collection, Lincoln Papers, Library of Congress).

other Republican, he had probed the meaning and implications of Douglas' doctrine. The appearance of Douglas' essay in *Harper's Magazine* on the eve of his arrival in Ohio seemed to indicate that the Illinois Senator's speeches would be an extension of the 1858 campaign. Who but Lincoln was better qualified to answer this new challenge? Certainly no Ohioan fit the bill quite so well. In his acknowledgment of Lincoln's acceptance, Bascom wrote, "There is no man in the Union who under the circumstances can do so much good in Central & Southern Ohio as you can, and more especially to follow Douglas." [10] The Republican committee also invited Douglas' Republican colleague in the Senate, Lyman Trumbull, to speak to the more radically antislavery audiences of northern Ohio. Sending the moderate Lincoln into the conservative Ohio River country was, in the words of a recent writer, "smart quarterbacking." [11]

Lincoln had kept in close touch with political developments in Ohio during 1859. The foremost issue in the state election compaign involved the Fugitive Slave Act of 1850. It was precipitated in the fall of 1858 by the rescue of an escaped slave who had been apprehended by federal authorities, for which thirty-seven citizens of Oberlin and Wellington were indicted for violation of the Fugitive Slave Act. On May 30, 1859, the Ohio state supreme court decided the case, upholding the constitutionality of the Act by a slim

[10] Bascom to Lincoln, September 9, 1859 (Robert Todd Lincoln Collection, Lincoln Papers, Library of Congress).
[11] Earl W. Wiley, "Behind Lincoln's Visit to Ohio in 1859," *Ohio State Archaeological and Historical Quarterly,* LX (January, 1951), 31.

three to two margin. The opinion was delivered by the chief justice, Joseph R. Swan, a leader in the early formation of the Republican party in Ohio, who also cast the crucial vote. The Democratic party in its convention, before the decision was known, upheld and endorsed the Fugitive Slave Act and condemned the Republicans for their opposition to it. Rufus P. Ranney, of Cuyahoga county, was nominated for the governorship. The Republicans, meeting after the decision, took a strong radical stand against the court's opinion, and especially against the chief justice who was up for renomination. William Dennison received the nomination for governor and Judge Swan was thrown over.

Lincoln watched these developments with interest and apprehension. To Samuel Galloway, an Ohio friend, he confided his fears. "Two things done by the Ohio Republican convention," he wrote, "the repudiation of Judge Swan, and the 'plank' for a repeal of the Fugitive Slave law—I very much regretted. These two things are of a piece; and they are viewed by many good men, sincerely opposed to slavery, as a struggle against, and in disregard of, the constitution itself. And it is the very thing that will greatly endanger our cause, if it be not be [sic] kept out of our national convention." [12] Earlier, Lincoln had warned Schuyler Colfax that "the point of danger is the temptation in different localities to 'platform' for something which will be popular just there, but which, nevertheless, will be a firebrand elsewhere," and had used the Ohio action as an example.[13] It was,

[12] Lincoln to Galloway, July 28, 1859, *The Collected Works of Abraham Lincoln*, ed. Basler, III, 394.
[13] Lincoln to Colfax, July 6, 1859, *ibid.*, III, 390-91.

perhaps, partly to offset the radicalism of the state convention that Lincoln consented to speak in Ohio. Galloway, who felt that the opposition to the Fugitive Slave Act might well defeat the party in the election, was confident that Lincoln's "programme of principles as set forth in your discussions with Judge Douglass, will suit all Republicans, and especially those of the old Whig stamp." [14]

Stephen A. Douglas had spent the summer of 1859 in the East working on his essay for *Harper's Magazine*. Following its publication, he had agreed to appear, with Kentucky's Senator John J. Crittenden, at the seventh annual fair of the United States Agricultural Society in Chicago beginning September 12. He consented to stop over in Ohio for speeches in Columbus and Cincinnati on his way west to Chicago. The news that Douglas would visit the state was greeted with mixed feelings by members of his own party in Ohio. Samuel Medary, former owner of the *Ohio Statesman* and an officeholder under James Buchanan, was disturbed at the news. Once an ardent Douglas supporter, Medary had sided with the Administration against the Little Giant on the Lecompton question. Writing to President Buchanan of Douglas' invitation to speak in Ohio, Medary commented:

I cannot see any good to result from this, but the chances of much evil. It is an unfortunate moment to spring the Presidential question into the other distracting questions involved in the elections here. In my humble opinion the State Central Committee has made a grand blunder. Some

[14] Galloway to Lincoln, July 23, 1859 (Robert Todd Lincoln Collection, Lincoln Papers, Library of Congress).

politicians seem never to know when to leave "well enough alone." [15]

The Republican press in Columbus, the *Ohio State Journal*, reported with undisguised glee that Douglas' invitation "has created no little consternation among the party wire-workers who have been constantly entreating the party to exclude all discussion of the claims of rival candidates for the Charleston nomination from the canvass, and who look upon Douglas as one whom they dare neither indorse nor repudiate." [16]

At the same time, concern was expressed lest Douglas alienate many of the Republicans who had sided with him in his war on the Administration. Washington McLean, a strong Douglas man and editor of the pro-Douglas *Cincinnati Enquirer,* advised Douglas against making extreme partisan addresses at Columbus and Cincinnati.

Do not . . . make any severe attacks on the Republicans. Tens of thousands of that party now stand well affected to you, and whose opinion will go far towards making up public opinion for or against you. Do not make the Territorial question, the principal feature of your speech. Your views on that subject are already known. Give a history of the Democratic party and show what it has accomplished for the country, make one of your lofty and national speeches.[17]

[15] Samuel Medary to James Buchanan, September 2, 1859 (James Buchanan Papers, Historical Society of Pennsylvania, Philadelphia).
[16] *Ohio State Journal* (Columbus), September 3, 1859.
[17] Washington McLean to Douglas, September 6, 1859 (Original in the possession of Martin F. Douglas, Greensboro, North Carolina).

In view of the deepening split between Douglas and the Buchanan administration, Douglas' presence in Ohio was thought to be fraught with danger by both wings of the distracted Democratic party. The day before Douglas' scheduled speech in Columbus, the *Ohio Statesman* printed an exchange of letters between William Dunbar, of Mt. Vernon, Ohio, and the Illinois Senator. Dunbar reviewed the controversy over the power of the Territories to legislate on slavery and asked Douglas a series of questions concerning his position on this issue. Douglas wisely declined to answer, referring Dunbar instead to his Congressional speeches and to his *Harper's* article.[18]

Douglas arrived in Columbus on the morning of September 7. His journey westward had been attended by enthusiastic receptions along the way. At Pittsburgh he was prevailed upon to address a large crowd before the St. Charles Hotel.[19] He was joined at Pittsburgh by two members of the Columbus reception committee; at Newark, Ohio, the remaining members of the committee joined the group to escort Douglas to the capital city. The arrival of Douglas' train in Columbus was greeted by "a mass of people" and a thirteen-gun salute by "Capt. Ijams' Gun Squad." A parade, headed by a military company, accompanied Douglas to his quarters at the American House. Trains, charging their passengers only half-fare, arrived at the Columbus depot during the morning bringing people from the out-

[18] William Dunbar to Douglas, August 18, 1859, and Douglas to Dunbar, August 31, 1859, *Ohio Statesman* (Columbus), September 7, 1859.
[19] *New York Times,* September 7, 1859.

lying countryside to hear Douglas' speech. The *Ohio
Statesman* described the events that followed.

Although Judge Douglas had lost his rest the two preceding nights, he was kept busy by calls from the yeomanry in
throngs until dinner, immediately after which he repaired
to the east portico of the State House where a stand had
been erected, and where Maier's Band were discoursing excellent music to the assembly in waiting, which covered as
compactly as people could stand the elevated flagged space,
which is about two hundred and fifty feet long by about
eighty feet wide. The vast steps and rotunda, the windows
and every nook and corner on the east side of the State
House, were also filled with ladies and gentlemen. A large
number of people could not get on the flagged space and
hence could not hear, and retired. Some five or six thousand people who were enabled to get in such a position as
to hear the speaker remained in the position they occupied
in the beginning until the end of the speech.[20]

Even taking into account the usual exaggeration of
newspaper editors on such occasions, Douglas' audience
was sizeable. Following his introduction by George W.
Manypenny, Douglas spoke for one hour and fifty minutes.

The speech, according to the *New York Times* correspondent, was received with "enthusiastic demonstrations of applause." [21] It, however, received scant notice in Columbus' Democratic press. Contrary to Mc-
Lean's advice, Douglas did review his position on the
Territorial question. Manypenny, who not only was
editor of the *Statesman* but also the chairman of the
state Democratic organization, was little inclined to

[20] *Ohio Statesman* (Columbus), September 8, 1859.
[21] *New York Times*, September 8, 1859.

notice at length this statement of Douglas' that was so at variance with the position of the Democratic Administration. Republicans were unimpressed with Douglas' performance. William T. Bascom wrote reassuringly to Lincoln that "Douglas had a large meeting here, but it had no effect. His speech was his Harpers Magazine article over again." [22] The *Ohio State Journal* was much less restrained in its reaction. The speech, wrote the editor, was "the heaviest morsel that has been forced on the press for a long time. A rehash of all the sophistries used to maintain untenable and dishonest positions, for the last five years, form the material." For Douglas himself, the paper, with characteristic invective, expressed even less respect.

He has betrayed the North, then the South, and now a political gambler, dead broke, he wants to make another raise out of the North to start the game again. . . . Can it be possible that this compound of cunning and impudence, this cast off tool of the South, who, while carrying out their bidding, disgraced the Senate with [the] vulgar, brutal insolence of the slave driver, or even to their disgust, an overbearing bully with them to back him, a fawning hypocrite now—can it be possible that such a person can ever be elevated to the head of this great nation? [23]

Douglas' Columbus speech, however, made journalistic history. Henry J. Raymond, editor of the *New York Times,* regarded the address as the "opening manifesto of the Presidential canvass" and as "an important document . . . which everyone at all interested in current

[22] Bascom to Lincoln, September 9, 1859 (Robert Todd Lincoln Collection, Lincoln Papers, Library of Congress).
[23] *Ohio State Journal* (Columbus), September 8, 1859.

political events would be anxious to see at the earliest moment." The entire speech, 7,100 words in length, was telegraphed verbatim to the New York newspaper at a cost of about $497, and appeared in its columns on the following morning. "By this power of the telegraph," Raymond noted, "the already gigantic power of the Press for good or ill must rapidly be increased in an almost illimitable degree. . . . If the public utterances of public men . . . are thus to be subjected to the criticism of the great centres of population and political activity in all their details, . . . the discourse of our statesmen must become of sheer necessity less provincial and less cunning—more statesmanlike, national and ample of view." [24] A vast stride in the dissemination of news had been accomplished.

Douglas left Columbus early on September 8, accompanied by Manypenny and Representatives Clement L. Vallandigham and Samuel S. Cox, for Cincinnati, where he was scheduled to speak that evening. At Dayton, he was expected to make a brief address to the assembled crowd but the pace of the previous days began to take its toll on his health. By the time he arrived in Dayton, he was suffering from a bad cold. After meeting and shaking hands with countless people in the lobby of the Phillips House, Douglas was taken to the home of Dr. Edwin Smith, where he spent the rest of the afternoon in bed. Because of his illness,

[24] *New York Times,* September 8, 9, 1859. The publication of Douglas' essay on popular sovereignty by *Harper's Magazine* and the verbatim telegraphic report of Douglas' Columbus speech are two indications of the appreciation for Douglas' leadership in American politics in 1859. Both events were unique in the history of political discussion in the United States and both were widely discussed by the national press.

Douglas' speaking engagement in Cincinnati was postponed until the following evening, disappointing hundreds of people who had gathered along the route of the train to greet the Little Giant and who had congregated in Cincinnati to hear his address.[25]

Douglas' reception in Cincinnati on September 9 was every bit as enthusiastic as his greeting in Columbus had been. He was no stranger to the "Queen City." Several years before he had visited the city for a speaking engagement but illness had forced him to cancel his address. In 1856, the Democratic National Convention met in Cincinnati; while Douglas did not personally attend the conclave, his supporters did, and through their efforts Cincinnatians became aware of the power of the Little Giant in American politics. Throughout the decade, Douglas was able to count on the staunch and loyal support of Washington McLean and his *Cincinnati Enquirer,* which now hailed the Illinois Senator as "the man of the times" and "the embodiment of the American Democracy." The *Enquirer* described Douglas' arrival in the city:

On his way to this city he was met by large crowds of people assembled at the various depots, and although the stopping of the train was but momentary at most of the stations, Mr. Douglas was compelled to show himself upon the platform, and was everywhere enthusiastically received. Upon the arrival of the train at Hamilton a salute was fired

[25] *Cincinnati Enquirer,* September 9, 1859; *New York Times,* September 9, 1859. Salmon P. Chase and William Dennison, the Republican candidate for governor, rode to Dayton, where Dennison and Rufus P. Ranney were to appear in a joint debate, on the same train as Douglas, but there is no evidence of any fraternization between the two groups [*Ohio Statesman* (Columbus), September 10, 1859].

by a military company, and Mr. D. was welcomed upon the
platform by several thousand persons who had assembled to
await his arrival. He briefly responded to the enthusiastic
greetings by a few words of thanks, which were necessarily
cut short by the brief time which the train could remain.
At Middletown the gathering was large and enthusiastic,
and the reception was an earnest, honest testimony of the
admiration which is felt by the people of the country.

.   .   .   .

On the arrival at the Cincinnati, Hamilton and Dayton
depot in this city, a large crowd, at least 4,000 people, had
assembled at the depot, and as the cars came in, cannon
were fired, and a great shout of welcome was raised.

.   .   .   .

A general desire was expressed to hear the distinguished
Senator speak, but as he was not well, suffering greatly from
a cold, the reception address was omitted, and he was escorted to a carriage and drawn by four horses up Sixty-
Street to Western-Row, down Western-Row to Fourth, up
Fourth to Vine and down Vine to the Burnet House, where
rooms had been engaged. As he passed through the streets,
ladies appeared at the windows and balconies waving their
handkerchiefs, and men cheered and huzzaed for "little
Doug" until the air rang with his name. The streets and
sidewalks were thronged, and a procession of carriages and
men on foot and horseback followed him to the hotel. Here
another effort was made to induce him to speak, but in his
then condition, he was compelled to decline, and retired
bowing to the multitude.[26]

Douglas spoke from a platform that had been erected
in the "Court-Street Market-Space" at eight o'clock that
evening to an audience that included citizens of Indiana and Kentucky as well as of Ohio. In his address,
Douglas again argued the "Territorial question," cov-

[26] *Cincinnati Enquirer,* September 8, 10, 1859.

ering much the same ground as in his Columbus speech. Although Douglas' voice was reported to be in bad condition, his speech was regarded by the *Enquirer* as "one of his most powerful efforts." "The boldness with which he enunciates his opinions with his voice and his pen," wrote the editor, "careless who or what they hit, is proof positive, that personal gain is with him subordinate to the public good. If the attainment of the Presidency was the great end and aim of his life, he would be more reserved and non-commital in his conduct."[27] To the Republican *Cincinnati Gazette*, however, the speech was "a rehash of the Harper copyright doctrine of Squatter Sovereignty, with but little dilution for weak Administration stomachs." The *Gazette's* editor felt the effect of the speech would be "to widen the breach between the two factions of the Democracy here, rather than to render any important aid in the present campaign."[28] In this he was probably correct.

Following his Cincinnati speech, Douglas resumed his journey to the West, arriving in Chicago on September 10 looking "quite cheerful and hopeful."[29] During the ensuing week, he participated in the national fair.

The announcement that Abraham Lincoln would speak in Ohio appeared in the columns of the *Ohio State Journal* on September 9, the same day that Douglas spoke in Cincinnati and just two days after Douglas had left Columbus. In discussing Lincoln's visit, it was impossible for Ohioans to avoid reference to the Illinois

[27] *Ibid.*, September 10, 11, 1859.
[28] *Cincinnati Gazette*, September 10, 1859.
[29] *New York Times*, September 15, 1859.

debates of the year before. The *Journal* was confident
that the reputation earned by Lincoln in the Illinois
campaign would lend a greater interest to his visit.[30] By
following closely on the heels of Douglas and by answer-
ing the Little Giant's speeches, Lincoln would attract
national attention to the Republican cause in Ohio.
The *Cincinnati Enquirer* commented that "the Illinois
fight is to be gone over again in Ohio."[31] Joseph Medill,
editor of the *Chicago Tribune,* advised Lincoln to use
the same argument he had used the year before in his
Chicago speech, when he had "made some strong points
. . . on the drift and tendency of the principles of the
Democr[ac]y, and the duty of patriots to resist the ag-
gressions of the oligarchy." From Medill came other
words of counsel:

Don't act on the defensive, but pitch hot shot into the
hulk of dough face and pro slavery democracy. Rake down
the swindling pretension of Douglas that his Kansas Nebraska bill guarantees or permits popular Sovrgnty [*sic*]. If
you will lay bare the fraud, delusion and shame of Squatter
Sovrignty, you will do our cause in Ohio much service, as
it will break the back of the Democratic pretenses. . . . Do
not fail to get off some of your "anecdotes & hits"—no people relish such things more than the Buckeyes.—I have one
word more of advice to offer viz: Go in boldly, strike
straight from the shoulder,—hit *below* the belt as well as
above, and kick like thunder.[32]

Lincoln's announced intention of following Douglas
with speeches at Columbus and Cincinnati, the publi-

[30] *Ohio State Journal* (Columbus), September 9, 1859.
[31] *Cincinnati Enquirer,* September 11, 1859.
[32] Joseph Medill to Lincoln, September 10, 1859 (Robert Todd
Lincoln Collection, Lincoln Papers, Library of Congress).

cation of Douglas' *Harper's* essay on popular sovereignty just before, and the Little Giant's defense of his own position on the "Territorial question" in his Ohio speeches signified that the Ohio campaign would be an extension of the hard-fought election in Illinois in 1858. Nor was the presence of Lincoln and Douglas in Ohio the only reminder of the Illinois campaign. The two contenders for Ohio's governorship, William Dennison and Rufus Ranney, appeared in several joint debates in the course of the struggle. Dennison further emphasized the close relationship between the two campaigns when he wrote to Lyman Trumbull for "valuable material" from the Lincoln-Douglas debates which he might use in his own meetings with Ranney.[33]

The Republicans in Columbus had only a week to prepare for Lincoln's visit before his scheduled speech in that city on September 16. The meeting was to be sponsored by the Young Men's Republican Club. In contrast to the preparations made in Columbus to receive Douglas, the Republicans seem to have gone about their task in a perfunctory manner. The usual arrangements were made with the railroads to run half-fare excursion trains into Columbus on the sixteenth, but the publicity given to the event left much to be desired. Lincoln arrived by train on the appointed day but found no such welcome as that which had greeted Douglas nine days before. No member of the Republican State Central Committee was on hand to take charge of the visitor. After disembarking from the train, Lincoln

[33] William Dennison to Lyman Trumbull, July 21, 1859 (Robert Todd Lincoln Collection, Lincoln Papers, Library of Congress).

made his way apparently unattended to his quarters in the Neil House, where he was received later by local Republican leaders.[34]

Lincoln spoke twice in Columbus, once in the afternoon from the east terrace of the State House and again in the evening before the Young Men's Republican Club in the City Hall. Neither speech was heavily attended. Through bad scheduling, the major afternoon address conflicted with the "great day" of the Franklin county agricultural fair, thus preventing "so large an audience as would have otherwise attended."[35] Introduced by George M. Parsons, chairman of the state Republican committee, Lincoln gave an able presentation of the Republican side of the "Territorial question," the first formal reply to Douglas' *Harper's* essay, and held Douglas' arguments up to close and careful criticism and analysis. The effort was widely discussed in the national press, but the local effect of the speech was somewhat mitigated by the circumstances surrounding Lincoln's visit. The *Ohio State Journal* reprinted the entire speech on the following morning although editorial comment on it was brief. "It is unnecessary for us to comment on the speech," wrote the editor, "as no one who has the opportunity will omit to read it."[36] Two days later the *Journal* described the speech briefly as an "unequaled, unrefutable expose of Judge Douglas' fallacies." The editor of a second Republican paper, the weekly *Columbus Gazette*, failed to attend the speech and devoted only a single paragraph to it.[37]

[34] Wiley, *op. cit.,* pp. 40-42, 46-47.
[35] *Ohio State Journal* (Columbus) , September 17, 1859.
[36] *Ibid.*
[37] Wiley, *op. cit.,* pp. 34-35.

The Democratic *Statesman* gave a full, though distorted, account of the event, concluding that Lincoln "is not an orator. He can hardly be classed as a third rate debater." The editor speculated that local Republicans must have felt that "they have burned their fingers, by bringing him here."[38] While relatively few people heard Lincoln speak, many Ohioans were apparently interested in reading his speech, for the reprint in the *Ohio State Journal* was soon exhausted and the paper was obliged to run it in both its triweekly and weekly editions to keep up with the demand. In advertising the speech, however, the paper pointedly remarked that a full report of the Franklin county fair, with the entire premium list, would be included with the address.[39]

A clue to Lincoln's rather cool reception in Columbus lies in Lincoln's conservative position on the issues of the state election, his criticism of the actions of the Republican state convention, and his relations with the radical state leader, Governor Salmon P. Chase. Chase was already being groomed as Ohio's favorite son candidate for the Republican nomination in 1860, and he may have considered Lincoln's presence in Ohio as a threat to that candidacy. Although Chase had been in the area several days before Lincoln's arrival, he was in northern Ohio at the time Lincoln spoke, thus avoiding what might have been an embarrassing situation. In addition, Chase made no move to congratulate Lincoln on his effort nor to express his regrets at not having been present until after Lincoln had written to him. Follow-

[38] *Ohio Statesman* (Columbus), September 17, 1859.
[39] *Ohio State Journal* (Columbus), September 19, 1859.

ing his return to Springfield, Lincoln wrote to Chase of his disappointment at not having met him during his Ohio visit, adding what might be construed as a word of caution in the election campaign:

It is useless for me to say to you (and yet I cannot refrain from saying it) that you must not let your approaching election in Ohio so result as to give encouragement to Douglasism. That ism is all which now stands in the way of an early and complete success of Republicanism; and nothing would help it or hurt us so much as for Ohio to go over or falter just now.[40]

Only then did Chase thank Lincoln for his Ohio speeches and express his deep regret that he could not have met Lincoln personally during the campaign.[41] The aloofness of John Greiner, the editor of the *Gazette* and one of the active supporters of Chase's candidacy for the Presidential nomination, added further evidence to the conclusion of one recent writer that Lincoln's Columbus visit was "blackballed by the Chase crowd."[42]

From Columbus, Lincoln followed Douglas' route through Dayton to Cincinnati, traveling in the company of Congressman John A. Gurley. At Dayton, he delivered a second major address at the Court House to a large and enthusiastic crowd of people. Commenting on the speech, the *Weekly Dayton Journal*, a Republican paper, described Lincoln as "remarkable for vigor of intellect, clearness of perception, and power of argu-

[40] Lincoln to Chase, September 21, 1859, *The Collected Works of Abraham Lincoln*, ed. Basler, III, 470-71.
[41] Chase to Lincoln, September 29, 1859 (Robert Todd Lincoln Collection, Lincoln Papers, Library of Congress).
[42] Wiley, *op. cit.*, p. 34.

mentation, and for fairness and honesty in the presentation of the facts." [43] To the opposition editor, he was simply "a very seductive reasoner" and his address "a network of fallacies and false assumptions."[44] After speaking for nearly two hours, he boarded the train for Cincinnati where he was scheduled to speak that evening. No contemporary verbatim report of Lincoln's Dayton speech was made but it was probably the same one he delivered later in Cincinnati.[45]

The enthusiasm of Lincoln's reception in Cincinnati on the evening of September 17 compensated for the coolness with which he was received in Columbus. The Republican *Cincinnati Gazette* reported:

Upon reaching the depot he was met by a large concourse of persons, who had assembled to greet the champion of Freedom in the "Sucker State." The reception must have reminded him of his tour through his own state when, as here, the guns thundered welcome, music greeted, and people cheered at each place of stopping.[46]

He was escorted by members of the reception committee to his quarters in the Burnet House, "where he shook many hands, and took his tea in very great haste." [47] Surprisingly, the most complete description of his reception

[43] September 20, 1859. Quoted in Daniel J. Ryan, "Lincoln and Ohio," *Ohio State Archaeological and Historical Quarterly,* XXXII (January, 1923), 64.

[44] *Dayton Daily Empire,* September 20, 1859, as quoted in Ryan, *op. cit.,* p. 65.

[45] See John H. Cramer, "Lincoln in Ohio; The Cincinnati Speech of September, 1859: Did Dayton Hear It First?" *Ohio State Achaeological and Historical Quarterly,* LIV (April-June, 1945), 149-60.

[46] *Cincinnati Gazette,* September 19, 1859.

[47] *Cincinnati Enquirer,* September 18, 1859.

in Cincinnati was provided by the pro-Douglas *Cincinnati Enquirer*:

At a quarter after eight o'clock he was driven to Fifthstreet Market-space in a carriage, accompanied by a number of persons on horseback (many others following on the sidewalks,) arrangements having been made for him to speak from the portico of E. & D. Kinsey's store and dwelling. Quite a crowd was assembled on the square, where bonfires were blazing, rockets whizzing, cannon firing and every effort making to give a show of enthusiasm to the scene.

The *Enquirer* also supplied an interesting and amazingly fair (for an opposition organ) sketch of Lincoln's appearance:

Hon. Mr. Lincoln is a tall, dark-visaged, angular, awkward, positive-looking sort of individual, with character written in his face and energy expressed in his every movement. He has the appearance of what is called in the Northeast a Western man—one who, without education or early advantages, has risen by his own exertions from an humble origin.[48]

However, the editor could not resist getting in a few licks for his own champion. Lincoln's reputation, he pointed out, rested on his opposition to Douglas the previous year. "He is the symbol of private and party enmity to the Senator of Illinois, accidentally endowed with voice and personality—owing his entire significance to that antagonism. Without Douglas Lincoln would be nothing."[49]

Some concern was expressed by local party leaders lest

48 *Ibid.*
49 *Ibid.*, September 20, 1859.

Lincoln deliver an address that was too partisan in tone
for conservative Cincinnati. A peculiar political situation existed in this river city and in Hamilton county.
The anti-Democratic organization did not use the
label "Republican" to describe itself but rather was
known simply as the "Opposition party." A strong effort
was being made by Republicans to woo the more conservative "American" element into its organization, and
there was a fear that a frankly partisan speech by Lincoln might jeopardize this move. Rutherford B. Hayes,
at that time Cincinnati's city solicitor, urged that Lincoln be informed of this situation and of the possibility
that injury might be done "if party names and party
doctrines" should be used. "I understand," wrote Hayes,
"Mr. Lincoln was an old Clay Whig, of Kentucky par-
entage, and with a wholesome dislike of Locofocoism.
These qualities with a word of caution as to our peculiar
position will enable him to make a fine impression." [50]
    In spite of this word of caution, Lincoln's address was
not non-partisan in its character and it seems to have
been well received by his audience. Again, Lincoln devoted most of his time to a review and criticism of
Douglas' position on the "Territorial question" as expounded in the *Harper's* essay. He displayed no reluc-
tance to brand himself as a "Black Republican" and to
declare his unequivocal opposition to the institution of
slavery. The *Gazette* felt that he had fully maintained
his reputation as a debater and praised the speech for
its logic and honesty. [51]

[50] Rutherford B. Hayes to Addison Peale Russell, September
14, 1859, as quoted in Ryan, *op. cit.*, pp. 70-71.
[51] *Cincinnati Gazette*, September 19, 1859.

Lincoln spent the following day, Sunday, resting in Cincinnati before his return to Illinois. On his way west, he stopped in Indianapolis, where he delivered another two hour speech, finally arriving in Springfield on September 20. His Ohio trip did not bring to a close his 1859 campaign efforts. He continued to receive invitations to speak in various parts of the North; at the end of September he was in Wisconsin, and in December he gave several speeches in Kansas.

Lincoln's visit to Ohio was generally received with enthusiasm by the rank and file, although his presence was not considered to be quite so important an event as was Douglas' several days before. Douglas, the foremost challenger for the Presidential nomination and a man who had been the center of national political controversy for at least five years, remained the more popular attraction during the campaign. This was a handicap Lincoln could not quite overcome. He was a newcomer on the political scene; his reputation outside of Illinois rested on his campaign against Douglas for the United States Senate in 1858, only the year before. Even then, Lincoln was not well known outside of his home state. The Illinois debates were not thoroughly reported in many parts of the country, and many people, including many Ohioans, had only a vague idea of Lincoln's position in the sectional conflict.[52] The editor of the *Cincinnati Commercial* summed up what must have been

---

[52] An exception would be the group of Mansfield, Ohio, citizens who met on November 5, 1858, and, on the strength of Lincoln's performance in the Illinois campaign, endorsed him for the next Republican candidate for President. *Sandusky Commercial-Register*, November 6, 1858, as quoted in Ryan, *op. cit.*, p. 104.

the attitude of many of Ohio's citizens following Lincoln's visit to the state:

> The republicans proposed that, as the democrats had made an immense lion of Mr. Douglas, they would cause Mr. Lincoln to play the lion on a scale equally extensive. But Mr. Douglas had a great advantage. He has become the most noted politician in the country. For some years he has been the central figure of American politics. There are thousands of persons who have an abiding faith that he is to be some day the president of the United States, and, animated by a lively sense of favors to come, they take every occasion to show their devotion to his person. Mr. Lincoln is not conspicuous as a presidential candidate.[53]

The fact that Lincoln was less well known than Douglas, the brief time between the announcement that he would visit Ohio and his first speech at Columbus, the conflict of his first address with the county fair, and the aloofness of the Chase faction all prevented Lincoln's Ohio campaign from being an unqualified success.

As Lincoln was delivering his two speeches in Columbus, Stephen A. Douglas had returned to the Buckeye State for a third and final public appearance. While in Ohio earlier, he had received several invitations to speak at various Ohio towns on his return to Washington from Chicago. Delegations visited him, and he received written invitations from such places as Mansfield (where Douglas had been burned in effigy in 1854) and Canton.[54] Before he left Columbus, Douglas agreed

---

[53] *Cincinnati Commercial*, as quoted in Ryan, *op. cit.*, p. 99.
[54] James Schrack to Douglas, September 9, 1859; B. Burns to Douglas, September 10, 1859; and J. D. Brown and S. Meyer to Douglas, September 10, 1859 (Douglas Papers, University of Chicago Library).

to address Wayne county Democrats at Wooster on September 16.

The same elaborate preparations were made at Wooster as at Columbus and Cincinnati earlier in the month. Three railroad lines ran special excursion trains, at half-fare, to the Ohio town. Douglas arrived at noon, about three hours late, and was greeted by a large and enthusiastic crowd at the depot. People had turned out at stations along the way to catch a glimpse of the Little Giant. At Mansfield, a brass fieldpiece mounted on a flatcar was attached to the train, which then "went literally booming through the country toward the point of destination." Following his arrival in Wooster, he was accompanied by a procession through the streets to the speaker's stand, "erected in a beautiful grove," where a large crowd had already gathered. Included in the parade was a wagon "composed of *hickory logs*, and filled with a crowd of people . . . drawn by ten horses, upon each one of which was a hard-fisted farmer." In the center stood a tall hickory tree flying the Stars and Stripes. Comparing Douglas with the "Hero of the Hermitage," the newspaper report enthusiastically declared that "everything looked as though the 'hickory' times were returning in good earnest." [55]

Douglas' Wooster speech was much more impassioned than his earlier efforts in Columbus and Cincinnati. Not only did he justify his position against Republican criticism, but he was also obliged to parry the thrusts of

[55] *Cincinnati Enquirer,* September 17, 20, 1859. For an interesting and unrestrained description of Douglas' reception along the route of the train from Crestline to Wooster by one who rode with the Illinois Senator, see "Privateer" to the Editor, *Ohio Statesman* (Columbus), September 22, 1859.

the Administration wing of his own party. While on the train en route to Wooster, he had been handed a copy of Attorney-General Jeremiah Black's attack on his *Harper's* essay. Black's attack, representing the views of President Buchanan and the Southern leaders in the Democratic party, was first published anonymously in the Washington *Constitution* on September 10, and later reprinted in pamphlet form. Although some attempt was made to conceal the identity of the author, Black's responsibility for the pamphlet became well known. The fact was revealed in the public press, and copies were sent broadcast throughout the United States under Black's frank. In the first portion of his address, Douglas repeated the arguments he had made earlier, but he soon launched into a bitter tirade against the Attorney-General. Black's answer to the *Harper's* article and Douglas' attack in his Wooster speech inaugurated a pamphlet war between the two men that was to continue for two months.[56]

The speech received the usual plaudits in the local Democratic press.[57] The *New York Times,* however, a paper which had reported Douglas' Ohio campaign with judiciousness, took great exception to the tone of his reply to Black at Wooster. "His reply," wrote the editor,

is personal, incomplete and undignified. He descends to the vulgarity of nicknaming the attorney general, and charges him half a dozen times in the course of his remarks with willful "falsehood." . . . Mr. Douglas may possibly have made a more marked impression for the moment upon the

[56] For the text of Black's attack on Douglas, see pages 173-99 in this book.

[57] *Cincinnati Enquirer,* September 17, 1859.

crowd he was addressing, by the use of epithets and vituper-
ation; but he gained nothing thereby either in reputation
or in argument with the people at large. However mistaken
in its assumptions, or in its argument, Judge Black's review
may have been, it was at least courteous in tone and respectful in its language; and Judge Douglas would have con-
sulted his true interest by responding to it in a similar
style.[58]

Douglas had obviously been aroused to anger by the
attack from his own party, and in the opinion of some
had overstepped the bounds of decency. Some journals,
both Republican and Democratic, according to an *Enquirer* report, now accused Douglas "of great impro-
priety in addressing public meetings, because . . . he
is a Presidential candidate." [59]

Although the speeches of Lincoln and Douglas in
Ohio in 1859 aroused national attention, their immedi-
ate purpose was to influence the outcome of a crucial
state election. Each man had labored hard on behalf of
his respective ticket, and in the process both had become
involved in factional disputes and splits within their
own parties. Their presence in Ohio was regarded in a
lukewarm fashion by significant groups in both party
organizations. The national split between Douglas and
the Buchanan administration and the coolness between
the conservative Lincoln and the more radical Chase
men in the state influenced the receptions accorded the
two speakers during the campaign. Both Lincoln and
Douglas were expected to walk tightropes between the
extremes; both had refused to do so, and instead

[58] *New York Times,* September 24, 1859.
[59] *Cincinnati Enquirer,* September 21, 1859.

presented their positions to the people in clear and unequivocal fashion.

But Lincoln and the Republicans had the advantage. Ohio had proved hospitable ground for the Republican party ever since its founding in the state in 1854. In the election of 1855, before the party had a national organization, it captured complete control of the state machinery, including majorities in both houses of the state legislature, and elected Salmon P. Chase to the governorship. This pattern of victory was repeated in later years. Although the Democrats assumed control of the legislature in 1857, Chase was re-elected to a second term. In the Congressional elections of 1856 and 1858, the Republicans were successful, and the state cast its electoral vote for John C. Fremont in the Presidential contest of 1856. After two terms in office, Chase stepped down from the governorship and divided his attention between the United States Senate seat that would be filled in 1860 and the Presidential nomination. George E. Pugh, Ohio's Democratic Senator, had been elected in 1854. His term would expire in 1860, but he was a candidate for re-election. The state legislative elections in 1859, then, were considered crucial; the results would determine whether Ohio would send a Republican or a Democrat to the United States Senate.

The October election resulted in a clear-cut and convincing Republican victory. The party swept the field, winning the governorship and all the state offices as well as both branches of the state legislature. The results were not altogether unanticipated. "There is no State where a change of opinion is less likely to happen," wrote the *New York Times*.[60] Republicans were jubilant, and in their happiness credited part of their success to Lincoln's efforts in the state.[61] At the same time, there were many who felt that Douglas' visit had actually injured Democratic chances. His speeches had highlighted the internal quarrel in the Democratic party; one correspondent had speculated that the principal effect of Douglas' visit might be to bring out Republican voters who would otherwise have stayed home.[62] Democrats found little consolation in the fact that they had carried the three counties in which Douglas had spoken. Franklin and Wayne counties, the sites of Douglas' Columbus and Wooster speeches, increased their Democratic majorities over the previous year, and Hamilton county and Cincinnati were wrested from Republican control. The last result may have been caused by the defection of the "Americans" from the Republican to the Democratic ranks over Lincoln's partisan address in Cincinnati.[63]

The impact of the Ohio election on the coming Presidential contest was significant. In view of Douglas' announced intention to seek the Democratic nomination on a platform avowing his position of popular sovereignty, his performance in Ohio was watched with considerable interest. The state election was a test of

[60] *New York Times,* October 4, 1859.

[61] William T. Bascom to Lincoln, October 13, 1859; and Samuel Galloway to Lincoln, October 13, 1859 (Robert Todd Lincoln Collection, Lincoln Papers, Library of Congress).

[62] *New York Times,* October 4, 1859.

[63] On the basis of these results, the *Cincinnati Enquirer* (October 16, 1859) commented that if Douglas had made ten or fifteen speeches in different parts of the state, Ohio could have been redeemed from Republican rule.

strength for the Little Giant's Presidential aspirations and for his solution to the problem of slavery in the Territories. A Democratic victory in Ohio would not only have enhanced Douglas' chances for the highest office in the land but would also have gone far toward settling the struggle for leadership within the Democratic party. But an Ohio defeat could spell disaster to both causes. Before the election, the *New York Times* made an observation that must have been in many minds: "If the democrats do not gain largely; nay, if they do not positively succeed, it will be proof positive in the minds of candid men that the Douglas dogma has brought no strength to the party, even in the Northwest." If Douglas could gain nothing in Ohio, "what can the Party gain by advancing his pretensions." [64] Douglas failed in his test of strength but the odds were against him from the beginning. The Democratic cause had not prospered in Ohio for five years and there was little reason to believe that 1859 would mark a reversal of that trend.

Postelection comments centered principally about the fate of Douglas and the Democratic party; Lincoln's stock, however, increased as a result of the successful Ohio campaign. Among the significant consequences of the election was the decision to publish the Illinois debates between Lincoln and Douglas as a campaign document for 1860. It was well known that Lincoln had prepared a scrapbook of the debates the year before and that he had carried it with him in Ohio. In fact, he had inadvertently left it behind in Columbus at the Neil House and it had had to be forwarded to him by the

[64] *New York Times*, October 4, 1859.

management.[65] In December, 1859, George M. Parsons, chairman of the Ohio Republican Committee, requested copies of the Illinois debates as well as of Lincoln's Ohio speeches, feeling that they would make "a document of great practical service to the Republican party in the approaching Presidential contest." [66] Parsons' request was concurred in by the members of the Republican committee and by Governor-elect Dennison. Not only would Lincoln's speeches prove invaluable to the Republican cause, but it was also thought that Douglas' statements might injure the prospect of Democratic unity in 1860. An effort had been made to publish the debates in Illinois earlier in the year, but nothing had come of the negotiations.[67] Lincoln was much more encouraged by Parsons' suggestion.[68] The scrapbook was sent on to Columbus, where it was turned over to the publishing house, Follett, Foster and Company. To Samuel Galloway, Lincoln wrote that he esteemed "the compliment paid me in this matter as the very highest I have ever received." [69] The result was the first publication of the debates in book form in 1860. Lincoln's Columbus and Cincinnati speeches were reprinted in the volume, although Douglas' Ohio speeches were not.

As a consequence of his Ohio trip and the subse-

[65] William T. Bascom to Lincoln, October 3, 1859 (Robert Todd Lincoln Collection, Lincoln Papers, Library of Congress).
[66] Quoted in Ryan, *op. cit.*, p. 107.
[67] Lincoln to William A. Ross, March 26, 1859, *The Collected Works of Abraham Lincoln*, ed. Basler, III, 372-74.
[68] Lincoln to George M. Parsons and Others, December 19, 1859, *ibid.*, III, 510.
[69] Lincoln to Samuel Galloway, December 19, 1859 (Copy in the possession of the Ohio Historical Society).

quent publication of the debates, Lincoln's stature as a contender for national political honors was increased.[70] His name became well known in the East. The importance of the participation of Lincoln and Douglas in the Ohio campaign cannot be minimized. The election provided the pretext for a further discussion of the issues that divided sections and parties during the years immediately preceding the Civil War. In a large sense, the Ohio speeches represent a continuation of the debates between Lincoln and Douglas in Illinois in 1858 and a testing ground for the crucial Presidential election of 1860, when the two protagonists were to face one another again.

[70] The exact publication date of the debates is not known. The publication was subject to delays, and it is possible that the books may have been kept off the market by Chase's supporters in order that Lincoln's chance for the Republican nomination might not be enhanced. See Robert S. Harper, "New Light from a Lincoln Letter on the Story of the Publication of the Lincoln-Douglas Debates," *Ohio Historical Quarterly*, LXVIII (April, 1959), 182-83. For the full story of the publication of the debates, see the introduction by David C. Mearns to *The Illinois Political Campaign of 1858: A Facsimile of the Printer's Copy of His Debates with Senator Stephen Arnold Douglas as Edited and Prepared for Press by Abraham Lincoln* (Washington 25, D. C.: Library of Congress, 1958).

The Issues

Lincoln's and Douglas' speeches in the Ohio campaign of 1859 continued the dialectical encounters of the celebrated Illinois campaign of the previous year, the canvass highlighted by the famous joint debates. The two men had, however, been political rivals for nearly a quarter of a century. Douglas, almost from the beginning of his career in Illinois politics, was the most prominent Jacksonian Democrat in the State. Lincoln was equally notable as a Clay Whig. The men clashed repeatedly, as the representative spokesmen of their parties. From the passage of Douglas' Kansas-Nebraska Act in 1854, however, the rivalry took a new and far more intense turn. Each man became, not a follower, but a leader. Neither was the spokesman of a party so much as he was the embodiment of a principle and a policy about which the structure of parties—and of political power in the nation—was to reshape itself. The joint debates of 1858 were only the dramatic culmination of exchanges that extended from the Illinois state fair in Springfield in October, 1854, until the Presidential year of 1860. The central practical question upon which the entire controversy turned, as defined by Lincoln at the outset, concerned "the repeal of the Missouri Compromise, and the propriety of its restoration." But this question, although never obscured, ultimately was subordinated to a theoretical question, upon whose resolution it was ever more clearly seen to depend: in what sense could it be said that all men are created equal.

The Kansas-Nebraska Act removed the federal prohibition of slavery which had been enacted in 1820. The Missouri Compromise had "forever prohibited" slavery in all the territory purchased from France north of the latitude 36 degrees 30 minutes which remained after the admission of Missouri as a slave State. The law withdrawing this prohibition opened to slavery, legally at least, a vast unorganized region between the Mississippi and the Rockies, from the Missouri line to the Canadian border, a region comprising all or most of the present states of Minnesota, Kansas, Nebraska, South Dakota, North Dakota, Colorado, Wyoming, and Montana. Its passage reopened with unprecedented violence the controversy over slavery that had threatened the Union in 1850, and had yielded to the compromise of that year only under the combined leadership of both major parties. The fiery struggle would not, alas, yield to compromise again; it would be quenched only in the blood of fratricidal war.

It is impossible to understand the Civil War without comprehending the motives which caused the repeal of the Missouri Compromise in 1854, or those which insisted upon its restoration thereafter. The story of the Kansas-Nebraska Act has been told often and well; unfortunately, there are hardly two accounts which do not differ significantly. What is important for us, however, is not the secret history of the legislation, but the principles by which it was openly justified and opposed in 1854 and afterwards. The leading doctrine identified with the measure was that of "popular sovereignty," as espoused and propounded by Stephen A. Douglas. As stated at the end of the famous *Harper's* article, this meant "that every distinct political Community, loyal to the Constitution and the Union, is entitled to all the rights, privileges, and immunities of self-government in respect to their local concerns and internal polity, subject only to the Constitution of the United States." What this meant, in practical language applied to the burning issue of the day, was that all questions pertaining to slavery in United States Territories should be left to the decision of the people residing therein, acting through their elected representatives. What it also meant, however, in theoretical language transcending time and place, was that the political judgment of popular majorities need not be controlled by any moral law "higher" than the procedural basis of majority rule as embodied in such a document as the Constitution. The substance of the Lincoln-Douglas debates thus involved, from their beginning in 1854, one of the major themes of political philosophy during two milleniums. Within the American tradition Jefferson had posed the question most distinctly when he said in his first inaugural address that it was a "sacred principle, that . . . the will of the majority is in all cases to prevail," but yet that "that will to be rightful must be reasonable; that the minority possess their equal rights, which equal law must protect, and to violate would be oppression." Jefferson never satisfactorily resolved the problem of how the law can be "equal" when its determination rests with the majority. The fragmentation of majorities into tentative coalitions of interest groups, and the dividing, checking, and balancing of governmental powers—the solution elaborated in the *Federalist*—was obviously in-

adequate when the minority in question was such as that
constituted by the Negroes in America. They were a
minority—an oppressed minority—in every State and
Territory of the Union they inhabited. What rights,
privileges, and immunities should be guaranteed to this
minority by law? Douglas said that, in accordance with
popular sovereignty, each Territory, like each State,
should be the sole judge of this question within its
borders. But he also said that Illinois had abolished
slavery *because it was not profitable,* and that wherever
soil, climate, and productions did make slavery profitable, it was expedient to treat at least one class of human
beings, one minority, as chattels. Douglas, of course,
thoroughly believed in the *inequality* of the races of
the world. It was right, according to him, for the white
man to legislate for the black man, but not vice versa.
Yet Lincoln maintained that such an acceptance of the
theory of inequality struck at the very basis of the idea
of popular self-government, an idea which owed its
origin and validity to a more fundamental truth. Lincoln believed that the problem of minority rights could
be solved only to the extent that both majority and
minority recognized and comprehended the basic
equality of all men. Douglas, by demanding the same
right for Territorial majorities that State majorities
possessed, actually argued for the equality of all *majorities* under the Constitution. Lincoln, in effect,
argued that no majority had a right to respect that did
not recognize the original equality of all men propounded in the Declaration of Independence. Whatever justification there was for slavery in the slave States
—where it had been introduced in the Colonial period
by the British without regard for the wishes of the

Colonists, and where the evil of rooting it out now might be greater than the evil of perpetuating it—there could be no justification for introducing it into new Territories, soon to become new States, where it did not already exist. In the empty (in 1854) lands of Kansas and Nebraska where the foundations of new societies were to be laid, there was no possible justification for permitting slavery to enter. No rights of majorities were denied to the inhabitants of Territories when they were forbidden to extend slavery since no one had the abstract right to enslave another man. Douglas' Nebraska Act, by repealing the slavery prohibition of 1820, expressed Douglas' own "Don't care" policy as to whether slavery should be voted up or voted down. This, Lincoln held, ignored the "father of all moral principle" for a free people, the principle for which States and Territories, Constitution and Union together existed, the principle "that all men are created equal."

It would be unfair to Douglas to judge him solely by the intrinsic theoretical merits of his doctrine of popular sovereignty. Douglas was not a theoretician, but a politician, in that ancient, honorable sense in which there is nothing invidious. After 1852, the Democratic party was the only truly national party remaining; it was the most powerful institutional bond that still survived to contain the forces of sectionalism. Douglas' task was to find a formula upon which the two wings of his party, North and South, might collaborate. The word is used advisedly: the party must work together, and support a single national ticket. It need not agree, as indeed Northerners and Southerners, no matter what their persuasion on other subjects, could

not agree, upon the merits of Negro slavery. But popular
sovereignty, in practical terms, was an agreement to dis-
agree: by leaving to the people of each Territory the
decision as to whether slavery would or would not be
established in that Territory, slavery would cease to be
a cause of contention in Congress. It would thereby
cease to be an issue in national politics; and as a result, the threats of disunion and civil war would also
come to an end. Douglas was convinced that once the
pressure of abolitionism and its allies upon the South
was relaxed, a pressure sustained by the Territorial
question, so would the pressure to force slavery into new
Territories abate. For Douglas believed that the
West theoretically opened to slavery by the repeal of
the Missouri Compromise would never prove eco-
nomically suited to it, and that the people of the Territories formed there, whether they came from North or
South, would never actually vote to introduce slavery.
Such tests of Douglas' expectations as the onrushing sectional crisis permitted, in particular the sequel to
Lecompton, would seem to bear him out. The theoretical weaknesses of Douglas' doctrine may, then, constitute its practical wisdom. Certainly they do not of
themselves gainsay the possibility that he, above any
man of his day, had formulated the policy that would
have enabled North and South to live peacefully together. Nor do they deny the possibility that that same
policy might have permitted slavery to die a natural
death, a death more fortunate for both the races in its
aftermath than the legacy of war and reconstruction.

To understand the struggle between Lincoln and
Douglas, as it moved into the pre-Presidential year of

1859, it is necessary to recall some high lights of the earlier phases. It is of particular importance to understand the difficulties created for both men by the Dred Scott decision of 1857. The *Harper's* essay, which provides the theme upon which controversy raged in 1859, is Douglas' laborious and definitive attempt to repair the damage done to popular sovereignty by that decision, damage that Lincoln exploited brilliantly in the joint debates.

The Kansas-Nebraska Act had declared that the Missouri Compromise restriction upon slavery was "inoperative and void" because "inconsistent with the principle of non-intervention by Congress with slavery in the States and Territories," i.e. inconsistent with popular sovereignty. It then went on to affirm that its true intent and meaning was "not to legislate slavery into any Territory or State, nor to exclude it therefrom, but to leave the people perfectly free to form and regulate their own domestic institutions in their own way, subject only to the Constitution of the United States." This declaration might sound sufficiently straightforward, but there were undoubtedly ambiguities in it: above all, how free did the Constitution leave the people in a United States Territory? Further, why was mention of "States" included in a law intended only for Territories? No responsible person had ever proposed that Congress had Constitutional power over slavery in "States." In the House Divided speech, which launched the Illinois campaign of 1858, Lincoln charged Douglas, together with Pierce, Taney, and Buchanan, with a plot to extend slavery into the free Territories and States alike. The first step, achieved in the Kansas-

Nebraska Act, was to secure the repeal of the Missouri restriction. The second, achieved in the Dred Scott decision, was to deny to the people of the Territories any power to keep slavery out. The third—the step that would come after the Republican cause met defeat at the polls—would be another decision of the Supreme Court, declaring that the people of the States might not exclude slavery. Whatever the truth of Lincoln's "conspiracy" charge, and whatever the probability of the future danger he anticipated, it certainly seemed that the opinion of the Chief Justice had reduced the freedom of the people of the Territories to form and regulate their domestic institutions to something a good deal less than "perfect," at least as regarded the institution of domestic slavery.

The Kansas-Nebraska Act had said that Congress *would* not, as a matter of policy, continue the Missouri slavery prohibition. In the case of Dred Scott, the Chief Justice had declared that Congress *could* not impose such a restriction, even if it would. The ground for this opinion was, in the main, the prohibition upon Congress in the Fifth Amendment to the Constitution, forbidding it to deprive any person "of life, liberty, or property, without due process of law." Slaves were property, and were recognized as such in the Constitution, said the Chief Justice, and for Congress to deprive a man of that species of property because he entered a United States Territory, a Territory purchased with the common treasure of the Union for the common benefit of its citizens, would certainly violate the Constitution. Thus far Taney's opinion would seem to accord with the idea of Congressional non-intervention,

proclaimed in the Kansas-Nebraska Act. But he went
farther: "And if Congress itself cannot do this [i.e., prohibit slavery in a Territory]—if it is beyond the powers
conferred on the Federal Government—it will be admitted, we presume, that it could not authorize a Territorial Government to exercise them. It could confer
no power on any local government established by its
authority, to violate the provisions of the Constitution."
Douglas had repeatedly endorsed the competence of the
Supreme Court to decide, and decide authoritatively,
for all three branches of the government, the questions
dealt with in Dred Scott. But how could he reconcile
the foregoing dicta with the notion that the people of
the Territories should and could decide for themselves
whether to introduce or exclude slavery? *Hoc opus, hic
labor est.*

At Freeport, Illinois, on August 27, 1858, at the
second joint debate, Lincoln had asked Douglas the
famous question: "Can the people of a United States
Territory, in any lawful way, against the wish of any
citizen of the United States, exclude slavery from its
limits prior to the formation of a State constitution?"
When Lincoln propounded his "interrogatory" he had
no doubt what Douglas' answer would be. Douglas had
already said several times before, in substance, what he
said now at Freeport:

It matters not what way the Supreme Court may hereafter
decide as to the abstract question whether slavery may or
may not go into a Territory under the Constitution, the
people have the lawful means to introduce it or exclude it

as they please, for the reason that slavery cannot exist a day or an hour anywhere, unless it is supported by local police regulations. Those police regulations can only be established by the local legislature, and if the people are opposed to slavery they will elect representatives to that body who will by unfriendly legislation effectually prevent the introduction of it in their midst. If, on the contrary, they are for it, their legislation will favor its extension. Hence, no matter what the decision of the Supreme Court may be . . . the right of the people to make a slave Territory or a free Territory is perfect and complete under the Nebraska bill.

It has been a commonplace of the textbooks that Lincoln showed uncommon acumen in framing the question we have quoted. According to legend, he forced Douglas to offend either his Northern or Southern supporters, thereby assuring that he could not be the nominee of a united Democratic party in 1860. But Lincoln knew, or at least believed, that Douglas had already lost all popular support in the South: his leadership of the coalition in Congress that defeated the fraudulent Lecompton proslavery constitution for Kansas had already assured that. As Lincoln wrote to a friend on July 31, 1858, a month before Freeport:

He [Douglas] cares nothing for the South—he knows he is already dead there. He only leans Southward now to keep the Buchanan party from growing in Illinois. You shall have hard work to get him directly to the point whether a territorial Legislature has or has not the power to exclude slavery. But if you succeed in bringing him to it, though he will be compelled to say it possesses no such power; he will instantly take ground that slavery can not actually exist in the territories, unless the people desire it, and so give it protective territorial legislation. If this offends the South he

will let it offend them; as at all events he means to hold on
to his chances in Illinois.

Lincoln's great strategic aim, both in the Illinois campaign of 1858 and the Ohio campaign of 1859, was to
destroy Douglas' credentials as a free-soil champion,
credentials which he had gained in large measure because of his leadership of the fight against Lecompton,
in which the Republican Congressional delegation had
been his followers. It was because of this leadership—
albeit under the banner of popular sovereignty—that
Horace Greeley and other eastern Republican poten-
tates had urged the Republicans of Illinois to support,
not oppose Douglas, in 1858. The heat of the fight in
Illinois in 1858 virtually destroyed any chance of a new
free-soil coalition combining the forces of the Republicans and Douglas Democracy. The great electoral danger of 1860, as both Lincoln and Douglas must have
seen it, was that the vote in the free States would be so
divided that the Presidential contest would be thrown
into the House, where the South might have controlled
the result. Strangely, Douglas' remaining chance to
bend the South to the yoke of his leadership now depended mainly upon his ability to command free-soil
votes. It should be remembered that, in 1860, Lincoln's
victory in the free States was such that he would have
been elected even if the votes in favor of all his opponents had been combined in favor of any one of them.
In 1856 it was the division of the free-State vote—which
was mainly a free-soil vote—between Fremont and Fillmore that permitted the election of Buchanan. Douglas
knew very well, by 1858, that the 1860 contest would
be decided largely by the manner in which the Northern

Whigs and "Americans" who had voted for Fillmore abandoned their now archaic loyalties. The issue would be whether the Republicans or a free-soil Democracy would benefit mainly from the "break." These Whigs and Americans were, as has been said, mostly free-soilers; but they were free-soilers mainly in the sense that they were opposed to the extension of slavery into the Territories, where they bitterly detested the idea of finding Negroes, free or slave. They were not antislavery in any other sense; indeed, most of them would not have wanted slavery abolished, if that would have meant emancipating Negroes to enter free States and Territories. Douglas' doctrine was appealing to them just because it seemed a safe way of keeping slavery out of Kansas and Nebraska without raising the specter of the ultimate, even if gradual, extinction of slavery that was fundamental to Lincoln. If Douglas could gain any large number of these conservative free-soil votes he might win the Presidential contest as the candidate of a united Democratic party. If his free-soil strength had given him the political odor of a winner, it is much less likely that the Southern Democrats would have bolted a convention determined to nominate Douglas, as happened in 1860. After all, Douglas *had* been the principal instrument in the repeal of the Missouri Compromise, and if he had attacked Lecompton, he had also insisted that he would defend equally the right of Kansans to have a slave constitution if that were their honestly and lawfully expressed will. More important, possibly, was Douglas' expansionist foreign policy, which undoubtedly would have played a major role in his Presidency. The acquisition of Cuba would almost certainly have come rapidly; and other islands of the Caribbean, more of Mexico, and parts of Central America may not have been far behind. All these lands were far more likely outlets for the expansion of slavery than Kansas or Nebraska. Had Douglas been able to be elected President at all, he would have had a good chance of carrying the grumbling South with him. We cannot, of course, know that; but it is evident that, in 1858-60, the only chance Douglas did have to become President would be won or lost in the contest for the free-soil vote, uncommitted as yet to the Republicans or Democrats. In this connection, the situation of Ohio is notable. Ohio's 23 electoral votes—the third largest number in the country after New York's 35 and Pennsylvania's 27—had gone in 1856 to Fremont. But Fillmore's twenty-eight thousand votes was eleven thousand five hundred more than the sixteen thousand five hundred separating Fremont and Buchanan. The challenge to Douglas Democracy in Ohio, to cut into the Fillmore vote, represented in compact form the challenge of 1860.

Lincoln attacked Douglas' Freeport doctrine over and again. He was to give that doctrine its verbal coup de grâce at Columbus when he reduced it to the proposition that "a thing may be lawfully driven away from where it has a lawful right to be." To make plain the strategy leading up to the Columbus coup, which set the problem for the *Harper's* article, we give the following passage from Lincoln's reply to Douglas at Alton. These were Lincoln's last words in the joint debates:

I suppose most of us . . . believe that the people of the Southern States are entitled to a Congressional fugitive slave law—that it is a right fixed in the Constitution. But it cannot be made available to them without Congressional legislation. In the Judge's language, it is a "barren right" which needs legislation before it can become efficient and valuable to the persons to whom it is guaranteed. And as the right is constitutional I agree that the legislation shall be granted to it . . . not that we like the institution of slavery. . . . And if I believed that the right to hold a slave in a Territory was equally fixed in the Constitution with the right to reclaim fugitives [Taney's opinion declared that "the right of property in a slave is distinctly and expressly affirmed in the Constitution," and that the only power over slavery granted the Congress by the Constitution "is the power, coupled with the duty, of guarding and protecting the owner in his rights"], I should be bound to give it the legislation necessary to support it. . . . I say if that Dred Scott decision is correct, then the right to hold slaves in a Territory is equally a constitutional right with the right of a slaveholder to have his runaway returned. . . . And the man who argues that by unfriendly legislation, in spite of that constitutional right, slavery may be driven from the Territories, cannot avoid furnishing an argument by which Abolitionists may deny the obligation to return fugitives, and claim the power to pass laws unfriendly to the right of the slaveholder to reclaim his fugitive. . . . I defy any man to make an argument that will justify unfriendly legislation to deprive a slaveholder of his right to hold his slave in a Territory, that will not equally, in all its length, breadth, and thickness furnish an argument for nullifying the fugitive slave law. Why, there is not such an Abolitionist in the nation as Douglas, after all.

We shall not explore here the validity of Lincoln's powerful assault. Strategically, however, Lincoln's design was to turn the tables on Douglas, who throughout the campaign hammered at the radicalism of Lincoln's theme of the divided house, and who attempted to identify Lincoln with abolitionism. That Douglas had to some extent succeeded is shown by the opening remarks of Lincoln in his Columbus speech, in which he is at pains to deny the report in the *Ohio Statesman* of that morning that he had declared in favor of Negro suffrage in the Illinois campaign of the previous year— a report that was, incidentally, the exact opposite of the truth. For Lincoln to call Douglas an abolitionist was, of course, ironical. What he really meant was that Douglas, by his acceptance of the Dred Scott decision, conceded all the ground needed to justify the Southern radicals' demand for a Congressional slave code, which alone could fertilize the "barren right" to hold slaves in the Territories. What made the Dred Scott decision such dynamite was that, in addition to denying to Congress the lawful power to exclude slavery from the Territories, it appeared to make the right to hold slaves in the Territories as positive as the right to reclaim fugitives. Now the conservative, middle-ground opinion of the North, for whom Lincoln and Douglas were now competing, on the whole venerated the Supreme Court, the great defender of the sanctity of property; but the same opinion was aghast at the idea of a federal Territorial slave code. Lincoln's argument, vis-à-vis the Court, was simple: we shall never interfere with any disposition of property in accordance with a Court decision; who the Court decides is a slave shall be a slave. But the dicta of the Court shall not determine the policy of the Congress and the President, it shall not nullify the will of the American people, deliberately expressed through free elections. If there is no present way of giving effect to a Congressional enactment forbidding slavery in the Territories, then, (such was the inference Lincoln intended) the people should employ the political means open to them to change the composition of the Court. Judges should be appointed to enable the Court to decide in favor of such an enactment. Douglas, in virtue of his long record of Democratic party orthodoxy, had repeatedly committed himself to accept as the true meaning of the Constitution what the present Southern-dominated Court decided. As such, he was no trustworthy repository of free-soil interests. Only a Republican President, who firmly denied that the Constitution "expressly affirmed" any right to hold slaves, could be entrusted with the task of making appointments to the Supreme Court. Such a President, reading the prohibition in the Fifth Amendment that "no person . . . shall be deprived of . . . liberty . . . without due process of law," and knowing that Negroes, even slaves, are counted as persons in the Constitution, would read the Constitution as a free-soil document. Fundamental to the whole Republican position was the view that the Constitution, *ex vi termini,* made the soil under federal control free-soil. The apparent exception to this, the District of Columbia, could be explained by the fact that the land there was ceded by slave States, and the permission of slavery was a condition implied in the acceptance of the land. But if, by the Fifth Amendment, no person could, by the Congress, be deprived of his liberty except for the commission of crime, whereof he should have been duly convicted (the meaning here of "due process of law"), then Negroes should, in principle, be automatically free in United States Territories. The passage of such slavery restrictions as that in the Missouri Compromise only made effective what, in the abstract, the Constitution already implied. Such was the Republican view of the fundamental law of the land. It positively contradicted the Southern ultra view which said that, as the Fifth Amendment forbade the arbitrary taking of property by Congress, federal Territories must be as automatically open to the ingress of slavery as the Republicans held it to be closed. The truth of the matter is that the Fifth Amendment, taken on its face, is entirely compatible with these absolutely contradictory interpretations. If a Negro can be regarded as nothing more than a chattel, then there can hardly be any justification for depriving an owner of this species of property simply because he has migrated to a federal Territory. But if a Negro is a man, and hence susceptible of the human rights enumerated in the Declaration of Independence, then it must be at least as wrong to countenance his enslavement as to countenance another man's expropriation. There really was no logical middle ground between the two positions. The vote of the people of a Territory could not decide it. In truth, no vote of any kind could decide whether there were rights which all men, simply as men, were entitled to enjoy; nor could it decide whether, in the full and proper sense of the term, the Negro was a man. Yet it was upon answers to these questions that the political and constitutional questions depended. Whether the introduction of such ultimate, philosophical issues into political debate makes politics more or less humane, whether it makes democratic politics more or less feasible, are further questions for the readers of this volume to ponder.

The heart of Douglas' problem, when he sat down

to write the essay for *Harper's* magazine, was to discover an argument showing that the language used by the Chief Justice in his opinion in the Dred Scott case did not create any obligation, either upon the Territorial legislature or upon the United States Congress, to enact a slave code that contravened the wishes and desires of the people of a Territory. We have already quoted the crucial passage in which Taney said that to prohibit slavery "is beyond the powers conferred on the Federal Government," and that it could not "authorize a Territorial Government to exercise" powers denied to it by the Constitution. Douglas met this difficulty with a highly ingenious distinction. There were, said Douglas, powers which the Congress may *exercise* but may not confer; and powers which it may *confer* but may not exercise. Examples of the former class are all the enumerated powers: Congress may coin money, declare war, establish tribunals inferior to the Supreme Court, etc. All of these Congress may exercise but may not confer upon any other body to exercise. On the other hand, Congress may not hear and determine the cases it may assign to the courts it establishes. It "may institute governments for the Territories, composed of an executive, judicial, and legislative department . . . without having the right to exercise any one of those powers or functions itself." Just as Congress may confer judicial powers upon federal or Territorial courts, without itself possessing the right to exercise judicial powers, so it may confer legislative powers upon a Territorial legislature which it may not itself possess any right to exercise. And the rights which it "may thus *confer* but can not *exercise,* are such as relate to the domestic affairs and internal polity of the Territory." Thus did Douglas finally formulate his famous dividing line between federal and local authority.

The bulk of the *Harper's* essay is a laborious search for precedents, an insistent effort to show that the dividing line thus conceived was the basis for the entire Revolutionary cause, and of the work of the framers of the Constitution. To say that the Revolution was fought for local self-government, without any reference to the relation of such self-government to the rights of man under "the laws of nature and of nature's God," gives the entire historical brief an air of speciousness. Lincoln, in the Columbus speech, fastens upon Douglas' entire omission of reference to the antislavery provision in the Northwest Ordinance, and argues that this crucial historical instance entirely destroys Douglas' case. Whether or not the Northwest Ordinance really contradicts Douglas' historical brief we will not here attempt to decide. Lincoln himself never explained adequately why, if it was the policy of the founding fathers to exclude slavery from the Territories, as indicated by the exclusion *north* of the Ohio River, no similar attempt was made to exclude it from the territory *south* of the Ohio River. Lincoln also ridiculed Douglas' analytical distinction with respect to the powers of the federal government. It was absurd, Lincoln said, to assert that the dividing line between federal and local authority was such that the

general government may give to the Territories governors, judges, marshals, secretaries, and all the other chief men to govern them, but . . . must not touch upon this other question. Why? The question of who shall be governor of a Territory for a year or two . . . is a question of vast national magnitude. It is so much opposed in its nature to locality, that the nation itself must decide it; while this other matter of planting slavery upon a soil—a thing which once planted cannot be eradicated by the succeeding millions who have as much right there as the first comers . . . he considers the power to prohibit it, as one of these little, local, trivial things that the nation ought not to say a word about. . . .

In speaking thus, however, Lincoln made an unwarranted assumption not justified by Douglas' text, viz., that local things are trivial, that the questions assigned to the general government are more important than the questions reserved to the local governments by the Constitution. But Douglas belonged to the party of Jackson and, more remote and more fundamental, the party of Jefferson. And it belonged to the republicanism of the Virginia sage to regard local government as inherently of greater dignity because inherently more concerned with those daily matters that shape the characters and lives of the citizens. The primary function of the general government was to provide the strength that would make the union of states proof against foreign depredations, to enable the people in their states and home communities to work out their destinies unafraid. But the business of creating the conditions of a good life for the citizens was primarily a matter of local government. Self-government was both a moral and political right; but the general government, by reason of the fact that it was more remote, was less able to be a vehicle of self-government. Lincoln's insistence that the general government, more than local governments, was the vehicle of the central moral idea of popular government was a departure

from the pristine Jeffersonian faith. It was not less so because Jefferson himself, both by the Louisiana Purchase
and the Embargo—but particularly the latter—had de-
parted from it in practice.

One further comment on Douglas' theory of the
nature of the Union. The *Harper's* essay develops the
idea that the legislative powers of a Territory, as they
relate to internal polity, are only given legal recognition
by the Congress but are not derived from or delegated
by Congress. This implies that such powers inhere in
the people of the Territories as an individual, collective
personality. Thus, according to Douglas, any people
capable of legislating for themselves have an inherent
right of self-legislation. The act of establishing Territorial government is analogous to (although not
identical with) the act of recognizing a new government under international law. To Douglas the very
basis of State rights (and hence of federalism) lay in the
inalienability of the indefeasible legislative right of any
people capable of forming a political community. If
this right were not recognized in the Territories, it
would be undermined in the States. Douglas' argument
here parallels Lincoln's: "all men are created equal"
meant that no man, by nature, has a political superior,
that all men are, by nature, autonomous. Douglas'
popular sovereignty meant that all communities are
autonomous. Of course Lincoln recognized that men,
although by nature equal, institute governments which
set up inequalities, inequalities they consent to in order
to better secure their originally equal rights. So too do
communities, in Douglas' view, accept alienation of
some autonomy; but such alienation can refer only to
those common purposes which cannot be achieved by

the communities separately. Douglas insisted upon the unalienable rights of communities to manage their domestic affairs in the same way that Lincoln insisted upon the unalienable rights of man. Douglas' record on Territorial self-government was not always entirely consistent with the foregoing analysis; he came to it gradually but steadily, and in the end he was thoroughgoing and rock-bound in his fidelity to it. As a political theory, it did not always fit perfectly with the constitutional practices of the past, including some of his own. It was meant rather to mold constitutional practice in the future; but like every politician he had to pretend that his own creative thinking was not his own, but his ancestors'. This, however, is a familiar paradox: in politics, one must generally pretend never to do anything for the first time. There is irony in the fact that such a theory as Douglas', to be effective, would have had to be adopted by the general government first, quite as much as Lincoln's opposing doctrine.

Douglas' doctrine of popular sovereignty, although an ingenious and original development within the context of the politics of the 1850's, stands in the mainstream of the ideas of Jeffersonian democracy. Although neither Jefferson or any other American ever doubted the legitimacy of representative government as such, yet there is a suspicion of representation—a device of government feudal in origin—running through the American democratic tradition, a suspicion which helps to account for the never-fading vitality of the idea of State rights. Despite the fact that the governmental problems of Americans have, from the beginning, been increasingly national and federal, yet there has been the persistent feeling that true legislative power, democratic legislative power, legislative power properly so-called, is that which most nearly approximates the decisions of an assembly of the governed. It survives today in the passionate belief, in some circles, that when the federal government does something the States could have done, it is less democratically done. It accounts for at least some of the contemporary popularity of public opinion polls. Perhaps the greatest irony that one confronts in Douglas' career—but one that also runs through to him from Jefferson—is that he would have elevated foreign policy to a much more active concern of government than his Whig or Republican antagonists. Although firmly advocating the exclusive rights of local governments in matters of internal polity, his foreign ventures would of necessity have swept most of the business of government into the hands of the central institutions.

In his belief that the most important sphere of government is that which regulates the social condition of men in their daily lives, and that this government must be so close to the lives of men as faithfully to reflect their opinions, feelings, and desires, Douglas was faithful to main tenets of Jeffersonian democracy. But Lincoln, in his insistence that every free community must recognize the fundamental equality of all men, and that no community could justly claim as a democratic right a right which constituted a denial of that equality, was no less true to that same tradition. Perhaps there is no greater integrity in the idea and tradition of popular self-government than the debate which reminds us so acutely of the inner conflict in the elements of

which it is comprised. The great debaters have passed
into history. But the great debate can never end.

BIBLIOGRAPHICAL NOTE

The entire Lincoln-Douglas debates revolve around the question of the propriety of the repeal of the Missouri Compromise.
An excellent guide to the literature on this question, with a
fresh discussion of the issue, is "The Kansas-Nebraska Act: A
Century of Historiography," by Roy F. Nichols, in the *Mississippi
Valley Historical Review* of September, 1956. The only full-length
study of the debates is Harry V. Jaffa's *Crisis of the House Divided: An Interpretation of the Issues in the Lincoln-Douglas
Debates* (New York: Doubleday & Company, Inc., 1959). This
includes, incidentally, four chapters on the repeal of the Missouri Compromise; but it does not interpret, except paren-
thetically, that part of the controversy that came after 1858. The
only recent scholarly account of Douglas' *Harper's* essay is
"Stephen A. Douglas, 'Harper's Magazine,' and Popular Sovereignty," by Robert W. Johannsen, in the *Mississippi Valley
Historical Review* of March, 1959. This article is valuable not
only for its full exposition of the setting in which the *Harper's*
essay occurred, but for its documented account of the peripheral
controversies which it engendered among the lesser champions
of the three main positions. On the 1858 conflict between the
Illinois Republicans and the eastern Republicans, a conflict
which is of fundamental importance to keep in mind when
studying events in 1859, see Don E. Fehrenbacher, "The Nomination of Abraham Lincoln in 1858," in the *Abraham Lincoln
Quarterly* of March, 1950. Of the great recent syntheses of historical knowledge dealing with the period, most notable is Allan
Nevins' *Ordeal of Union* (New York: Charles Scribner's Sons,
1947). The second volume contains an account of the Kansas-
Nebraska Act, and the third volume, appearing as the first of
two entitled *The Emergence of Lincoln* (New York: Charles
Scribner's Sons, 1950), contains a chapter on the Lincoln-Douglas debates within the framework of the nation's history. No less
important are the chapters "North and South" and "Lincoln
and Douglas" in the first volume of James G. Randall's *Lincoln
the President* (New York: Dodd, Mead & Co., 1945). A brilliant
guide to the literature dealing with the Civil War period is
Thomas J. Pressly's *Americans Interpret Their Civil War*
(Princeton, N. J.: Princeton University Press, 1954). This work
ably documents the thesis, which many have long suspected to
be true, that American historiography consists, in large measure,
of the Civil War "continued by other means."

THE DIVIDING LINE BETWEEN FEDERAL AND LOCAL AUTHORITY

Popular Sovereignty in the Territories [1]

By Stephen A. Douglas

Under our complex system of government it is the first duty of American statesmen to mark distinctly the dividing line between Federal and Local authority. To do this with accuracy involves an inquiry, not only into the powers and duties of the Federal Government under the Constitution, but also into the rights, privileges, and immunities of the people of the Territories, as well as of the States composing the Union. The relative powers and functions of the Federal and State governments have become well understood and clearly defined by their practical operation and harmonious action for a long series of years; while the disputed question—involving the right of the people of the Territories to govern themselves in respect to their local affairs and internal polity—remains a fruitful source of partisan strife and sectional controversy. The political organization which was formed in 1854, and has assumed the name of the Republican Party, is based on the theory that African slavery, as it exists in this country, is an evil of such magnitude—social, moral, and political—as to justify and require the exertion of the entire power and influence of the Federal Government to the full extent that the Constitution, according to their inter-

[1] *Harper's Magazine,* XIV (September, 1859), 519-37.

pretation, will permit for its ultimate extinction. In the platform of principles adopted at Philadelphia by the Republican National Convention in 1856, it is affirmed:

That the Constitution confers upon Congress sovereign power over the Territories of the United States for their government, and that in the exercise of this power it is both the right and the duty of Congress to prohibit in the Territories those twin relics of barbarism, polygamy and slavery.

According to the theory of the Republican party there is an irrepressible conflict between freedom and slavery, free labor and slave labor, free States and slave States, which is irreconcilable, and must continue to rage with increasing fury until the one shall become universal by the annihilation of the other. In the language of the most eminent and authoritative expounder of their political faith,

It is an irrepressible conflict between opposing and enduring forces; and it means that the United States must and will, sooner or later, become either entirely a slaveholding nation or entirely a free labor nation. Either the cotton and rice fields of South Carolina, and the sugar plantations of Louisiana, will ultimately be tilled by free labor, and Charleston and New Orleans become marts for legitimate merchandise alone, or else the rye fields and wheat fields of Massachusetts and New York must again be surrendered by their farmers to slave culture and to the production of slaves, and Boston and New York become once more markets for trade in the bodies and souls of men.

In the Illinois canvass of 1858 the same proposition was advocated and defended by the distinguished Republican standard-bearer in these words:

In my opinion it [the slavery agitation] will not cease until a crisis shall have been reached and passed. "A house divided against itself can not stand." I believe this government can not endure permanently half slave and half free. I do not expect the house to fall, but I do expect it will cease to be divided. It will become all one thing or all the other. Either the opponents of slavery will arrest the further spread of it, and place it where the public mind shall rest in the belief that it is in the course of ultimate extinction, or its advocates will push forward till it shall become alike lawful in all the States—old as well as new, North as well as South.

Thus it will be seen, that under the auspices of a political party, which claims sovereignty in Congress over the subject of slavery, there can be no peace on the slavery question—no truce in the sectional strife—no fraternity between the North and South, so long as this Union remains as our fathers made it—divided into free and slave States, with the right on the part of each to retain slavery so long as it chooses, and to abolish it whenever it pleases.

On the other hand, it would be uncandid to deny that, while the Democratic party is a unit in its irreconcilable opposition to the doctrines and principles of the Republican party, there are radical differences of opinion in respect to the powers and duties of Congress, and the rights and immunities of the people of the Territories under the Federal Constitution, which seriously disturb its harmony and threaten its integrity. These differences of opinion arise from the different interpretations placed on the Constitution by persons who belong to one of the following classes:

First.—Those who believe that the Constitution of

the United States neither establishes nor prohibits slavery in the States or Territories beyond the power of the people legally to control it, but "leaves the people thereof perfectly free to form and regulate their domestic institutions in their own way, subject only to the Constitution of the United States."

Second.—Those who believe that the Constitution establishes slavery in the Territories, and withholds from Congress and the Territorial Legislature the power to control it; and who insist that, in the event the Territorial Legislature fails to enact the requisite laws for its protection, it becomes the imperative duty of Congress to interpose its authority and furnish such protection.

Third.—Those who, while professing to believe that the Constitution establishes slavery in the Territories beyond the power of Congress or the Territorial Legislature to control it, at the same time protest against the duty of Congress to interfere for its protection; but insist that it is the duty of the Judiciary to protect and maintain slavery in the Territories without any law upon the subject.

By a careful examination of the second and third propositions, it will be seen that the advocates of each agree on the theoretical question, that the Constitution establishes slavery in the Territories, and compels them to have it whether they want it or not; and differ on the practical point, whether a right secured by the Constitution shall be protected by an act of Congress when all other remedies fail. The reason assigned for not protecting by law a right secured by the Constitution is, that it is the duty of the Courts to protect slavery in the

Territories without any legislation upon the subject. How the Courts are to afford protection to slaves or any other property, where there is no law providing remedies and imposing penalties and conferring jurisdiction upon the Courts to hear and determine the cases as they arise, remains to be explained.

The acts of Congress, establishing the several Territories of the United States, provide that: "The jurisdiction of the several Courts herein provided for, both appellate and original, and that of the Probate Courts and Justices of the Peace, shall be as limited by law"— meaning such laws as the Territorial Legislatures shall from time to time enact. It will be seen that the judicial tribunals of the Territories have just such jurisdiction, and only such, in respect to the rights of persons and property pertaining to the citizens of the Territory as the Territorial Legislature shall see fit to confer; and consequently, that the Courts can afford protection to persons and property no further than the Legislature shall, by law, confer the jurisdiction, and prescribe the remedies, penalties, and modes of proceeding.

It is difficult to conceive how any person who believes that the Constitution confers the right of protection in the enjoyment of slave property in the Territories, regardless of the wishes of the people and of the action of the Territorial Legislature, can satisfy his conscience and his oath of fidelity to the Constitution in withholding such Congressional legislation as may be essential to the enjoyment of such right under the Constitution. Under this view of the subject it is impossible to resist the conclusion that, if the Constitution does establish slavery in the Territories, beyond the power of the people to control it by law, it is the imperative duty of Congress to supply all the legislation necessary to its protection; and if this proposition is not true, it necessarily results that the Constitution neither establishes nor prohibits slavery anywhere, but leaves the people of each State and Territory entirely free to form and regulate their domestic affairs to suit themselves, without the intervention of Congress or of any other power whatsoever.

But it is urged with great plausibility by those who have entire faith in the soundness of the proposition, that "a Territory is the mere creature of Congress; that the creature can not be clothed with any powers not possessed by the creator; and that Congress, not possessing the power to legislate in respect to African slavery in the Territories, can not delegate to a Territorial Legislature any power which it does not itself possess."

This proposition is as plausible as it is fallacious. But the reverse of it is true as a general rule. Congress can not delegate to a Territorial Legislature, or to any other body of men whatsoever, any power which the Constitution has vested in Congress. In other words: *Every power conferred on Congress by the Constitution must be exercised by Congress in the mode prescribed in the Constitution.*

Let us test the correctness of this proposition by reference to the powers of Congress as defined in the Constitution:

The Congress shall have power—
To lay and collect taxes, duties, imposts, and excises, etc.;

To borrow money on the credit of the United States;
To regulate commerce with foreign nations, etc.;
To establish a uniform rule of naturalization, etc.;
To coin money, and regulate the value thereof;
To establish post-offices and post-roads;
To constitute tribunals inferior to the Supreme Court;
To declare war, etc.;
To provide and maintain a navy.

This list might be extended so as to embrace all the powers conferred on Congress by the Constitution; but enough has been cited to test the principle. Will it be contended that Congress can delegate any one of these powers to a Territorial Legislature or to any tribunal whatever? Can Congress delegate to Kansas the power to "regulate commerce," or to Nebraska the power "to establish uniform rules of naturalization," or to Illinois the power "to coin money and regulate the value thereof," or to Virginia the power "to establish post-offices and post-roads"?

The mere statement of the question carries with it the emphatic answer, that Congress can not delegate any power which it does possess; but that every power conferred on Congress by the Constitution must be exercised by Congress in the manner prescribed in that instrument.

On the other hand, there are cases in which Congress may establish tribunals and local governments, and invest them with powers which Congress does not possess and can not exercise under the Constitution. For instance, Congress may establish courts inferior to the Supreme Court, and confer upon them the power to hear and determine cases, and render judgments affecting the life, liberty, and property of the citizen, without itself having the power to hear and determine such causes, render judgments, or revise or annul the same. In like manner Congress may institute governments for the Territories, composed of an executive, judicial, and legislative department; and may confer upon the Governor all the executive powers and functions of the Territory, without having the right to exercise any one of those powers or functions itself.

Congress may confer upon the judicial department all the judicial powers and functions of the Territory, without having the right to hear and determine a cause, or render a judgment, or to revise or annul any decision made by the courts so established by Congress. Congress may also confer upon the legislative department of the Territory certain legislative powers which it can not itself exercise, and only such as Congress can not exercise under the Constitution. The powers which Congress may thus *confer* but can not *exercise*, are such as relate to the domestic affairs and internal polity of the Territory, and do not affect the general welfare of the Republic.

This dividing line between Federal and Local authority was familiar to the framers of the Constitution. It is clearly defined and distinctly marked on every page of history which records the great events of that immortal struggle between the American Colonies and the British Government, which resulted in the establishment of our national independence. In the beginning of that struggle the Colonies neither contemplated nor desired independence. In all their addresses to the Crown, and to the Parliament, and to the people of

Great Britain, as well as to the people of America, they averred that as loyal British subjects they deplored the causes which impelled their separation from the parent country. They were strongly and affectionately attached to the Constitution, civil and political institutions and jurisprudence of Great Britain, which they proudly claimed as the birthright of all Englishmen, and desired to transmit them unimpaired as a precious legacy to their posterity. For a long series of years they remonstrated against the violation of their inalienable rights of self-government under the British Constitution, and humbly petitioned for the redress of their grievances.

They acknowledged and affirmed their allegiance to the Crown, their affection for the people, and their devotion to the Constitution of Great Britain; and their only complaint was that they were not permitted to enjoy the rights and privileges of self-government, in the management of their internal affairs and domestic concerns in accordance with the guaranties of that Constitution and the Colonial charters granted by the Crown in pursuance of it. They conceded the right of the Imperial government to make all laws and perform all acts concerning the Colonies, which were in their nature *Imperial* and not *Colonial*—which affected the general welfare of the Empire, and did not interfere with the "internal polity" of the Colonies. They recognized the right of the Imperial government to declare war and make peace; to coin money and determine its value; to make treaties and conduct intercourse with foreign nations; to regulate commerce between the several colonies, and between each colony and the parent country, and with foreign countries; and in general they recognized the right of the Imperial government of Great Britain to exercise all the powers and authority which, under our Federal Constitution, are delegated by the people of the several States to the Government of the United States.

Recognizing and conceding to the Imperial government all these powers—*including the right to institute governments for the Colonies,* by granting charters under which the inhabitants residing within the limits of any specified Territory might be organized into a political community, with a government consisting of its appropriate departments, executive, legislative, and judicial; conceding all these powers, the Colonies emphatically denied that the Imperial government had any rightful authority to impose taxes upon them without their consent, or to interfere with their internal polity; claiming that it was the birthright of all Englishmen—inalienable when formed into a political community—to exercise and enjoy all the rights, privileges, and immunities of self-government in respect to all matters and things, which were Local and not General —Internal and not External—Colonial and not Imperial —as fully as if they were inhabitants of England, with a fair representation in Parliament.

Thus it appears that our fathers of the Revolution were contending, not for Independence in the first instance, but for the inestimable right of Local Self-Government under the British Constitution; the right of every distinct political community—dependent Colonies, Territories, and Provinces, as well as sovereign States— to make their own local laws, form their own domestic institutions, and manage their own internal affairs in their own way, subject only to the Constitution of Great Britain as the paramount law of the Empire.

The government of Great Britain had violated this inalienable right of local self-government by a long series of acts on a great variety of subjects. The first serious point of controversy arose on the slavery question as early as 1699, which continued a fruitful source of irritation until the Revolution, and formed one of the causes for the separation of the colonies from the British Crown.

For more than forty years the Provincial Legislature of Virginia had passed laws for the protection and encouragement of African slavery within her limits. This policy was steadily pursued until the white inhabitants of Virginia became alarmed for their own safety, in view of the numerous and formidable tribes of Indian savages which surrounded and threatened the feeble white settlements, while shiploads of African savages were being daily landed in their midst. In order to check and restrain a policy which seemed to threaten the very existence of the Colony, the Provincial Legislature enacted a law imposing a tax upon every slave who should be brought into Virginia. The British merchants, who were engaged in the African slave trade, regarding this legislation as injurious to their interests and in violation of their rights, petitioned the King of England and his Majesty's ministers to annul the obnoxious law and protect them in their right to carry their slaves into Virginia and all other British Colonies which were the common property of the Empire—acquired by the common blood and common treasure—and from which a few adventurers who had settled on the Imperial do-

main by his Majesty's sufferance, had no right to exclude them or discriminate against their property by a
mere Provincial enactment. Upon a full consideration
of the subject the King graciously granted the prayer of
the petitioners; and accordingly issued peremptory
orders to the Royal Governor of Virginia, and to the
Governors of all the other British Colonies in America,
forbidding them to sign or approve any Colonial or
Provincial enactment injurious to the African Slave
Trade, unless such enactment should contain a clause
suspending its operation until his Majesty's pleasure
should be made known in the premises.

Judge Tucker, in his Appendix to Blackstone, refers
to thirty-one acts of the Provincial Legislature of Virginia, passed at various periods from 1662 to 1772, upon
the subject of African slavery, showing conclusively that
Virginia always considered this as one of the questions
affecting her "internal polity," over which she, in common with the other colonies, claimed "the right of exclusive legislation in their Provincial Legislatures"
within their respective limits. Some of these acts, particularly those which were enacted prior to the year
1699, were evidently intended to foster and encourage,
as well as to regulate and control African slavery, as one
of the domestic institutions of the Colony. The act of
1699, and most of the enactments subsequent to that
date, were as obviously designed to restrain and check
the growth of the institution with the view of confining
it within the limit of the actual necessities of the community, or its ultimate extinction, as might be deemed
most conducive to the public interests, by a system of
unfriendly legislation, such as imposing a tax on all

slaves introduced into the colony, which was increased and renewed from time to time, as occasion required, until the period of the Revolution. Many of these acts never took effect, in consequence of the King withholding his assent, even after the Governor had approved the enactment, in cases where it contained a clause suspending its operation until his Majesty's pleasure should be made known in the premises.

In 1772 the Provincial Legislature of Virginia, after imposing another tax of five per cent on all slaves imported into the Colony, petitioned the King to remove all those restraints which inhibited his Majesty's Governors assenting to such laws as might check so very pernicious a commerce as slavery. Of this petition Judge Tucker says:

The following extract from a petition to the Throne, presented from the House of Burgesses of Virginia, April 1st, 1772, will show the sense of the people of Virginia on the subject of slavery at that period:
"The importation of slaves into the colony from the coast of Africa hath long been considered as a trade of great inhumanity; and under its present encouragement we have too much reason to fear will endanger the very existence of your Majesty's American dominions."

Mark the ominous words! Virginia tells the King of England in 1772, four years prior to the Declaration of Independence, that his Majesty's American dominions are in danger: Not because of the Stamp duties—not because of the tax on Tea—not because of his attempts to collect revenue in America! These have since been deemed sufficient to justify rebellion and revolution.

But none of these are referred to by Virginia in her address to the Throne—there being another wrong which, in magnitude and enormity, so far exceeded these and all other causes of complaint that the very existence of his Majesty's American dominions depended upon it! That wrong consisted in forcing African slavery upon a dependent Colony without her consent, and in opposition to the wishes of her own people!

The people of Virginia at that day did not appreciate the force of the argument used by the British merchants, who were engaged in the African slave trade, and which was afterward indorsed, at least by implication, by the King and his Ministers; that the Colonies were the common property of the Empire—acquired by the common blood and treasure—and therefore all British subjects had the right to carry their slaves into the Colonies and hold them in defiance of the local law and in contempt of the wishes and safety of the Colonies.

The people of Virginia not being convinced by this process of reasoning, still adhered to the doctrine which they held in common with their sister Colonies, that it was the birthright of all freemen—inalienable when formed into political communities—to exercise exclusive legislation in respect to all matters pertaining to their internal polity—slavery not excepted; and rather than surrender this great right they were prepared to withdraw their allegiance from the Crown.

Again referring to this petition to the King, the same learned Judge adds:

This petition produced no effect, as appears from the first clause of our [Virginia] Constitution, where, among other

acts of misrule, the inhuman use of the Royal negative refusing us [the people of Virginia] permission to exclude
slavery from us by law, is enumerated among the reasons
for separating from Great Britain.

This clause in the Constitution of Virginia, referring
to the inhuman use of the Royal negative, in refusing
the Colony of Virginia permission to exclude slavery
from her limits by law as one of the reasons for separating from Great Britain, was adopted on the 12th day of
June, 1776, three weeks and one day previous to the
Declaration of Independence by the Continental Congress; and after remaining in force as a part of the Constitution for a period of fifty-four years, was re-adopted,
without alteration, by the Convention which framed the
new Constitution in 1830, and then ratified by the people as a part of the new Constitution; and was again re-
adopted by the Convention which amended the Constitution in 1850, and again ratified by the people as a
part of the amended Constitution, and at this day remains a portion of the fundamental law of Virginia—
proclaiming to the world and to posterity that one of
the reasons for separating from Great Britain was "the
inhuman use of the Royal negative in refusing us [the
Colony of Virginia] permission to exclude slavery from
us by law"!

The legislation of Virginia on this subject may be
taken as a fair sample of the legislative enactments of
each of the thirteen Colonies, showing conclusively that
slavery was regarded by them all as a domestic question
to be regulated and determined by each Colony to suit
itself, without the intervention of the British Parliament
or "the inhuman use of the Royal negative." Each

Colony passed a series of enactments, beginning at an early period of its history and running down to the commencement of the Revolution, either protecting, regulating, or restraining African slavery within its respective limits and in accordance with their wishes and supposed interests. North and South Carolina, following the example of Virginia, at first encouraged the introduction of slaves, until the number increased beyond their wants and necessities, when they attempted to check and restrain the further growth of the institution, by imposing a high rate of taxation upon all slaves which should be brought into those Colonies; and finally, in 1764, South Carolina passed a law imposing a penalty of one hundred pounds (or five hundred dollars) for every negro slave subsequently introduced into that Colony.

The Colony of Georgia was originally founded on strict antislavery principles, and rigidly maintained this policy for a series of years, until the inhabitants became convinced by experience, that, with their climate and productions, slave labor, if not essential to their existence, would prove beneficial and useful to their material interests. Maryland and Delaware protected and regulated African slavery as one of their domestic institutions. Pennsylvania, under the advice of William Penn, substituted fourteen years' service and perpetual adscript to the soil for hereditary slavery, and attempted to legislate, not for the total abolition of slavery, but for the sanctity of marriage among slaves, and for their personal security. New Jersey, New York, and Connecticut, recognized African slavery as a domestic institution lawfully existing within their respective limits, and passed the requisite laws for its control and regulation.

Rhode Island provided by law that no slave should serve more than ten years, at the end of which time he was to be set free; and if the master should refuse to let him go free, or sold him elsewhere for a longer period of service, he was subject to a penalty of forty pounds, which was supposed at that period to be nearly double the value of the slave.

Massachusetts imposed heavy taxes upon all slaves brought into the Colony, and provided in some instances for sending the slaves back to their native land; and finally prohibited the introduction of any more slaves into the Colony under any circumstances.

When New Hampshire passed laws which were designed to prevent the introduction of any more slaves, the British Cabinet issued the following order to Governor Wentworth: "You are not to give your assent to, or pass any law imposing duties upon Negroes imported into New Hampshire."

While the legislation of the several Colonies exhibits dissimilarity of views, founded on a diversity of interests, on the merits and policy of slavery, it shows conclusively that they all regarded it as a domestic question affecting their internal polity in respect to which they were entitled to a full and exclusive power of legislation in the several Provincial Legislatures. For a few years immediately preceding the American Revolution the African Slave Trade was encouraged and stimulated by the British Government and carried on with more vigor by the English merchants than at any other period in the history of the Colonies; and this fact, taken in connection with the extraordinary claim asserted in the Memorable Preamble to the act repealing the Stamp duties, that "Parliament possessed the right to bind the Colonies in all cases whatsoever," not only in respect to all matters affecting the general welfare of the empire, but also in regard to the domestic relations and internal polity of the Colonies—produced a powerful impression upon the minds of the colonists, and imparted peculiar prominence to the principle involved in the controversy.

Hence the enactments by the several Colonial Legislatures calculated and designed to restrain and prevent the increase of slaves; and, on the other hand, the orders issued by the Crown instructing the Colonial Governors not to sign or permit any legislative enactment prejudicial or injurious to the African Slave Trade, unless such enactment should contain a clause suspending its operation until the royal pleasure should be made known in the premises; or, in other words, until the King should have an opportunity of annulling the acts of the Colonial Legislatures by the "inhuman use of the Royal negative."

Thus the policy of the Colonies on the slavery question had assumed a direct antagonism to that of the British Government; and this antagonism not only added to the importance of the principle of local self-government in the Colonies, but produced a general concurrence of opinion and action in respect to the question of slavery in the proceedings of the Continental Congress, which assembled at Philadelphia for the first time on the 5th of September, 1774.

On the 14th of October the Congress adopted a Bill of Rights for the Colonies, in the form of a series of resolutions, in which, after conceding to the British Government the power to regulate commerce and do such other things as affected the general welfare of the empire without interfering with the internal polity of the Colonies, they declared "That they are entitled to a free and exclusive power in their several provincial Legislatures, where their right of representation can alone be preserved, in all cases of taxation and internal polity." Having thus defined the principle for which they were contending, the Congress proceeded to adopt the following "Peaceful Measures," which they still hoped would be sufficient to induce compliance with their just and reasonable demands. These "Peaceful Measures" consisted of addresses to the King, to the Parliament, and to the people of Great Britain, together with an Association of Non-Intercourse to be observed and maintained so long as their grievances should remain unredressed.

The second article of this Association, which was adopted without opposition and signed by the delegates from all the Colonies, was in these words:

That we will neither import nor purchase any slave imported after the first day of December next; after which time we will wholly discontinue the Slave-Trade, and will neither be concerned in it ourselves, nor will we hire our vessels, nor sell our commodities or manufactures to those who are engaged in it.

This Bill of Rights, together with these articles of association, were subsequently submitted to and adopted by each of the thirteen Colonies in their respective Provincial Legislatures.

Thus was distinctly formed between the Colonies and the parent country that issue upon which the Declaration of Independence was founded and the battles of the Revolution were fought. It involved the specific claim on the part of the Colonies—denied by the King and Parliament—to the exclusive right of legislation touching all local and internal concerns, *slavery included.* This being the principle involved in the contest, a majority of the Colonies refused to permit their Delegates to sign the Declaration of Independence except upon the distinct condition and express reservation to each Colony of the exclusive right to manage and control its local concerns and police regulations without the intervention of any general Congress which might be established for the United Colonies.

Let us cite one of these reservations as a specimen of all, showing conclusively that they were fighting for the inalienable right of local self-government, with the clear understanding that when they had succeeded in throwing off the despotism of the British Parliament, no Congressional despotism was to be substituted for it:

We, the Delegates of Maryland, in convention assembled, do declare that the King of Great Britain has violated his compact with this people, and that they owe no allegiance to him. We have therefore thought it just and necessary to empower our Deputies in Congress to join with a majority of the United Colonies in declaring them free and independent States, in framing such further confederation between them, in making foreign alliances, and in adopting such other measures as shall be judged necessary for the preservation of their liberties:

Provided, the sole and exclusive right of regulating the

internal polity and government of this Colony be reserved to the people thereof.

We have also thought proper to call a new convention for the purpose of establishing a government in this Colony.

No ambitious views, no desire of independence, induced the people of Maryland to form an union with the other Colonies. To procure an exemption from Parliamentary taxation, and to continue to the Legislatures of these Colonies the sole and exclusive right of regulating their Internal Polity, was our original and only motive. To maintain inviolate our liberties, and to transmit them unimpaired to posterity, was our duty and first wish; our next, to continue connected with and dependent on Great Britain. For the truth of these assertions we appeal to that Almighty Being who is emphatically styled the Searcher of hearts, and from whose omniscience none is concealed. Relying on his Divine protection and assistance, and trusting to the justice of our cause, we exhort and conjure every virtuous citizen to join cordially in defense of our common rights, and in maintenance of the freedom of this and her sister Colonies.

The first Plan of Federal Government adopted for the United States was formed during the Revolution, and is usually known as "The Articles of Confederation." By these Articles it was provided that "Each State retains its Sovereignty, Freedom, and Independence, and every power, jurisdiction, and right which is not by this Confederation expressly delegated to the United States in Congress assembled."

At the time the Articles of Confederation were adopted—July 9, 1778—the United States held no lands or territory in common. The entire country—including all the waste and unappropriated lands—embraced within or pertaining to the Confederacy, belonged to

and was the property of the several States within whose
limits the same was situated.

On the 6th day of September, 1780, Congress "recom-
mended to the several States in the Union having claims
to waste and unappropriated lands in the Western country, a liberal cession to the United States of a portion
of their respective claims for the common benefit of
the Union."

On the 20th day of October, 1783, the Legislature of
Virginia passed an act authorizing the Delegates in Congress from that State to convey to the United States
"the territory or tract of country within the limits of
the Virginia Charter, lying and bearing to the Northwest of the River Ohio"—which grant was to be made
upon the "condition that the territory so ceded shall be
laid out and formed into States"; and that "the States
so formed shall be distinct republican States, and admitted members of the Federal Union, having the same
rights of Sovereignty, Freedom, and Independence as
the other States."

On the 1st day of March, 1784, Thomas Jefferson and
his colleagues in Congress executed the deed of cession
in pursuance of the act of the Virginia Legislature,
which was accepted and ordered to "be recorded and
enrolled among the acts of the United States in Congress
assembled." This was the first territory ever acquired,
held, or owned by the United States. On the same day
of the deed of cession Mr. Jefferson, as chairman of a
committee which had been appointed, consisting of Mr.
Jefferson of Virginia, Mr. Chase of Maryland, and Mr.
Howell of Rhode Island, submitted to Congress "a plan
for the temporary government of the territory ceded or

to be ceded by the individual States to the United States."

It is important that this Jeffersonian Plan of government for the Territories should be carefully considered for many obvious reasons. It was the first plan of government for the Territories ever adopted in the United States. It was drawn by the author of the Declaration of Independence, and revised and adopted by those who shaped the issues which produced the Revolution, and formed the foundations upon which our whole American system of governments rests. It was not intended to be either local or temporary in its character, but was designed to apply to all "territory ceded or to be ceded," and to be universal in its application and eternal in its duration, wherever and whenever we might have territory requiring a government. It ignored the right of Congress to legislate for the people of the Territories without their consent, and recognized the inalienable right of the people of the Territories, when organized into political communities, to govern themselves in respect to their local concerns and internal polity. It was adopted by the Congress of the Confederation on the 23d day of April, 1784, and stood upon the Statute Book as a general and permanent plan for the government of all territory which we then owned or should subsequently acquire, with a provision declaring it to be a "Charter of Compact," and that its provisions should "stand as fundamental conditions between the thirteen original States and those newly described, unalterable but by the joint consent of the United States in Congress assembled, and of the particular State within which such alteration is proposed to be made." Thus this Jeffersonian Plan for the government of the Territories—this "Charter of Compact"—"these fundamental conditions," which were declared to be "unalterable" without the consent of the people of "the particular State [Territory] within which such alteration is proposed to be made," stood on the Statute Book when the Convention assembled at Philadelphia in 1787 and proceeded to form the Constitution of the United States.

Now let us examine the main provisions of the Jeffersonian Plan:

First.—That the territory ceded or to be ceded by the individual States to the United States, whenever the same shall have been purchased of the Indian inhabitants and offered for sale by the United States, shall be formed into *additional States,* etc., etc.

The Plan proceeds to designate the boundaries and territorial extent of the proposed "additional States," and then provides:

Second.—That the settlers within the territory so to be purchased and offered for sale shall, either on their own petition or on the order of Congress, receive authority from them, with appointments of time and place, for their free males of full age to meet together for the purpose of establishing a temporary government to adopt the Constitution and laws of any one of these States [the original States], so that such laws nevertheless shall be subject to alteration by their ordinary legislature; and to erect, subject to like alteration, counties or townships for the election of members for their Legislature.

Having thus provided a mode by which the first in-

habitants or settlers of the Territory may assemble together and choose for themselves the Constitution and
laws of some one of the original thirteen States, and
declare the same in force for the government of their
Territory temporarily, with the right on the part of the
people to change the same, through their local Legislature, as they may see proper, the Plan then proceeds to
point out the mode in which they may establish for
themselves "a permanent Constitution and government," whenever they shall have twenty thousand inhabitants, as follows:

Third.—That such temporary government only shall continue in force in any *State* until it shall have acquired
twenty thousand free inhabitants, when, giving due proof
thereof to Congress, they shall receive from them authority,
with appointments of time and place, to call a Convention
of Representatives to establish a permanent Constitution
and government for themselves.

Having thus provided for the first settlers "a temporary government" in these "additional States," and
for "a permanent Constitution and government" when
they shall have acquired twenty thousand inhabitants,
the Plan contemplates that they shall continue to govern
themselves *as States,* having, as provided in the Virginia
deed of cession, "the same rights of sovereignty, freedom, and independence," in respect to their domestic
affairs and internal polity, "as the other States," until
they shall have a population equal to the least numerous
of the original thirteen States; and in the mean time
shall keep a sitting member in Congress, with a right of
debating but not of voting, when they shall be admitted

into the Union on an equal footing with the other States, as follows:

Fourth.—That whenever any of the said States shall have of free inhabitants as many as shall then be in any one of the least numerous of the thirteen original States, such *State* shall be admitted by its delegates into the Congress of the United States on an equal footing with the said original States. . . .

And—

Until such admission by their delegates into Congress any of the said *States,* after the establishment of their temporary government, shall have authority to keep a sitting member in Congress, with the right of debating, but not of voting.

Attached to the provision which appears in this paper under the "third" head is a proviso, containing five propositions, which, when agreed to and accepted by the people of said additional States, were to "be formed into a charter of compact," and to remain forever "unalterable," except by the consent of such States as well as of the United States—to wit:

Provided that both the temporary and permanent governments be established on these principles as their basis:

1st.—That they shall forever remain a part of the United States of America.

2d.—That in their persons, property, and territory they shall be subject to the government of the United States in Congress assembled, and to the Articles of Confederation in all those cases in which the original States shall be so subject.

3d.—That they shall be subject to pay a part of the federal debts contracted, or to be contracted—to be apportioned on them by Congress according to the same common rule and measure by which apportionments thereof shall be made on the other States.

4th.—That their respective governments shall be in republican form, and shall admit no person to be a citizen who holds any hereditary title.

The fifth article, which relates to the prohibition of slavery after the year 1800, having been rejected by Congress, never became a part of the Jeffersonian Plan of Government for the Territories, as adopted April 23, 1784.

The concluding paragraph of this Plan of Government, which emphatically ignores the right of Congress to bind the people of the Territories without their consent, and recognizes the people therein as the true source of all legitimate power in respect to their internal polity, is in these words:

That all the preceding articles shall be formed into a *charter of compact,* shall be duly executed by the President of the United States, in Congress assembled, under his hand and the seal of the United States, shall be promulgated, and shall stand as fundamental conditions between the thirteen original States and those newly described, unalterable but by the joint consent of the United States in Congress assembled, and of the particular State within which such alteration is proposed to be made.

This Jeffersonian Plan of Government embodies and carries out the ideas and principles of the fathers of the Revolution—that the people of every separate political community (dependent Colonies, Provinces, and

Territories as well as sovereign States) have an inalienable right to govern themselves in respect to their internal polity, and repudiates the dogma of the British Ministry and the Tories of that day that all Colonies, Provinces, and Territories were the property of the Empire, acquired with the common blood and common treasure, and that the inhabitants thereof have no rights, privileges, or immunities except such as the Imperial government should graciously condescend to bestow upon them. This Plan recognizes by law and irrevocable "compact" the existence of two distinct classes of States under our American system of government—the one being members of the Union, and consisting of the original thirteen and such other States, having the requisite population, as Congress should admit into the Federal Union, with an equal vote in the management of Federal affairs as well as the exclusive power in regard to their internal polity respectively—the other, not having the requisite population for admission into the Union, could have no vote or agency in the control of the Federal relations, but possessed the same exclusive power over their domestic affairs and internal policy respectively as the original States, with the right, while they have less than twenty thousand inhabitants, to choose for their government the Constitution and laws of any one of the original States; and when they should have more than twenty thousand, but less than the number required to entitle them to admission into the Union, they were authorized to form for themselves "a permanent Constitution and government"; and in either case they were entitled to keep a delegate in Congress with the right of debating, but not of voting. This "Charter of Compact," with its "fundamental conditions," which were declared to be "unalterable" without "the joint consent" of the people interested in them, as well as of the United States, thus stood on the statute book unrepealed and irrepealable—furnishing a complete system of government for all "the territory ceded or to be ceded" to the United States, without any other legislation upon the subject, when, on the 14th day of May, 1787, the Federal Convention assembled at Philadelphia and proceeded to form the Constitution under which we now live. Thus it will be seen that the dividing line between Federal and Local authority, in respect to the rights of those political communities which, for the sake of convenience and in contradistinction to the States represented in Congress, we now call Territories, but which were then known as *"States,"* or *"new States,"* was so distinctly marked at that day that no intelligent men could fail to perceive it.

It is true that the government of the Confederation had proved totally inadequate to the fulfillment of the ends for which it was devised, not because of the relations between the Territories, or new States, and the United States, but in consequence of having no power to enforce its decrees on the Federal questions which were clearly within the scope of its expressly delegated powers. The radical defects in the Articles of Confederation were found to consist in the fact that it was a mere league between sovereign States, and not a Federal Government with its appropriate departments—Executive, Legislative, and Judicial—each clothed with authority to perform and carry into effect its own peculiar functions. The Confederation having no power to enforce compliance with its resolves, "the consequence was, that though in theory the Resolutions of Congress were equivalent to laws, yet in practice they were found to be mere recommendations, which the States, like other sovereignties, observed or disregarded according to their own good-will and gracious pleasure." Congress could not impose duties, collect taxes, raise armies, or do any other act essential to the existence of government, without the voluntary consent and co-operation of each of the States. Congress could resolve, but could not carry its resolutions into effect—could recommend to the States to provide a revenue for the necessities of the Federal Government, but could not use the means necessary to the collection of the revenue when the States failed to comply—could recommend to the States to provide an army for the general defense, and apportion among the States their respective quotas, but could not enlist the men and order them into the Federal service. For these reasons a Federal Government, with its appropriate departments, acting directly upon the individual citizens, with authority to enforce its decrees to the extent of its delegated powers, and not dependent upon the voluntary action of the several States in their corporate capacity, became indispensable as a substitute for the government of the Confederation.

In the formation of the Constitution of the United States the Federal Convention took the British Constitution, as interpreted and expounded by the Colonies during their controversy with Great Britain, for their model—making such modifications in its structure and principles as the change in our condition had rendered necessary. They intrusted the Executive functions to a President in the place of a King; the Legislative functions to a Congress composed of a Senate and House of Representatives, in lieu of the Parliament consisting of the Houses of Lords and Commons; and the Judicial functions to a Supreme Court and such inferior Courts as Congress should from time to time ordain and establish.

Having thus divided the powers of government into the three appropriate departments, with which they had always been familiar, they proceeded to confer upon the Federal Government substantially the same powers which they as Colonies had been willing to concede to the British Government, and to reserve to the States and to the people the same rights and privileges which they as Colonies had denied to the British Government during the entire struggle which terminated in our Independence, and which they had claimed for themselves and their posterity as the birthright of all freemen, inalienable when organized into political communities, and to be enjoyed and exercised by Colonies, Territories, and Provinces as fully and completely as by sovereign States. Thus it will be seen that there is no organic feature or fundamental principle embodied in the Constitution of the United States which had not been familiar to the people of the Colonies from the period of their earliest settlement, and which had not been repeatedly asserted by them when denied by Great Britian during the whole period of their colonial history.

Let us pause at this point for a moment, and inquire whether it be just to those illustrious patriots and sages who formed the Constitution of the United States, to assume that they intended to confer upon Congress that unlimited and arbitrary power over the people of the American Territories, which they had resisted with their blood when claimed by the British Parliament over British Colonies in America? Did they confer upon Congress the right to bind the people of the American Territories in all cases whatsoever, after having fought the battles of the Revolution against a "Preamble" declaring the right of Parliament "to bind the Colonies in all cases whatsoever?"

If, as they contended before the Revolution, it was the birthright of all Englishmen, inalienable when formed into political communities, to exercise exclusive power of legislation in their local legislatures in respect to all things affecting their internal polity—slavery not excepted—did not the same right, after the Revolution, and by virtue of it, become the birthright of all Americans, in like manner inalienable when organized into political communities—no matter by what name, whether Colonies, Territories, Provinces, or new States?

Names often deceive persons in respect to the nature and substance of things. A signal instance of this kind is to be found in that clause of the Constitution which says:

Congress shall have power to dispose of, and make all needful rules and regulations respecting the territory or other property belonging to the United States.

This being the only clause of the Constitution in which the word "territory" appears, that fact alone has doubtless led many persons to suppose that the right of

Congress to establish temporary governments for the Territories, in the sense in which the word is now used, must be derived from it, overlooking the important and controlling facts that at the time the Constitution was formed the word "territory" had never been used or understood to designate a political community or government of any kind in any law, compact, deed of cession, or public document; but had invariably been used either in its geographical sense to describe the superficial area of a State or district of country, as in the Virginia deed of cession of the "territory or *tract of country*" northwest of the River Ohio; or as meaning land in its character as property, in which latter sense it appears in the clause of the Constitution referred to, when providing for the disposition of the "territory or other property belonging to the United States." These facts, taken in connection with the kindred one that during the whole period of the Confederation and the formation of the Constitution the temporary governments which we now call "Territories," were invariably referred to in the deeds of cession, laws, compacts, plans of government, resolutions of Congress, public records, and authentic documents as "States," or "new States," conclusively show that the words "territory and other property" in the Constitution were used to designate the unappropriated lands and other property which the United States owned, and not the people who might become residents on those lands, and be organized into political communities after the United States had parted with their title.

It is from this clause of the Constitution alone that Congress derives the power to provide for the surveys and sale of the public lands and all other property belonging to the United States, not only in the Territories, but also in the several States of the Union. But for this provision Congress would have no power to authorize the sale of the public lands, military sites, old ships, cannon, muskets, or other property, real or personal, which belong to the United States and are no longer needed for any public purpose. It refers exclusively to property in contradistinction to persons and communities. It confers the same power "to make all needful rules and regulations" in the States as in the Territories, and extends wherever there may be any land or other property belonging to the United States to be regulated or disposed of; but does not authorize Congress to control or interfere with the domestic institutions and internal polity of the people (either in the States or the Territories) who may reside upon lands which the United States once owned. Such a power, had it been vested in Congress, would annihilate the sovereignty and freedom of the States as well as the great principle of self-government in the Territories, wherever the United States happen to own a portion of the public lands within their respective limits, as, at present, in the States of Alabama, Florida, Mississippi, Louisiana, Arkansas, Missouri, Illinois, Indiana, Ohio, Michigan, Wisconsin, Iowa, Minnesota, California, and Oregon, and in the Territories of Washington, Nebraska, Kansas, Utah, and New Mexico. The idea is repugnant to the spirit and genius of our complex system of government, because it effectually blots out the dividing line between Federal and Local authority which forms an essential barrier for the defense of the independence of the States and the liberties of the people against Federal invasion. With one anomalous exception, all the powers conferred on Congress are *Federal,* and not *Municipal,* in their character—affecting the general welfare of the whole country without interfering with the internal polity of the people—and can be carried into effect by laws which apply alike to States and Territories. The exception, being in derogation of one of the fundamental principles of our political system (because it authorizes the Federal Government to control the municipal affairs and internal polity of the people in certain specified, limited localities), was not left to vague inference or loose construction, nor expressed in dubious or equivocal language; but is found plainly written in that section of the Constitution which says:

Congress shall have power to exercise exclusive legislation in all cases whatsoever, over such district (not exceeding ten miles square) as may, by cession of particular States, and the acceptance of Congress, become the seat of the government of the United States, and to exercise like authority over all places purchased by the consent of the Legislature of the State in which the same shall be, for the erection of forts, magazines, arsenals, dock-yards, and other needful buildings.

No such power "to exercise exclusive legislation in all cases whatsoever," nor indeed any legislation in any case whatsoever, is conferred on Congress in respect to the municipal affairs and internal polity, either of the States or of the Territories. On the contrary, after the Constitution had been finally adopted, with its Federal powers delegated, enumerated, and defined, in order to guard in all future time against any possible infringement of the reserved rights of the States, or of the people, an amendment was incorporated into the Constitution which marks the dividing line between Federal and Local authority so directly and indelibly that no lapse of time, no partisan prejudice, no sectional aggrandizement, no frenzied fanaticism can efface it. The amendment is in these words:

The powers not delegated to the United States by the Constitution, nor prohibited by it to the States, are reserved to the States respectively, or to the people.

This view of the subject is confirmed, if indeed any corroborative evidence is required, by reference to the proceedings and debates of the Federal Convention, as reported by Mr. Madison. On the 18th of August, after a series of resolutions had been adopted as the basis of the proposed Constitution and referred to the Committee of Detail for the purpose of being put in proper form, the record says:

Mr. Madison submitted, in order to be referred to the Committee of Detail, the following powers, as proper to be added to those of the General Legislature (Congress):

To dispose of the unappropriated lands of the United States.

To institute temporary governments for the new States arising therein.

To regulate affairs with the Indians, as well within as without the limits of the United States.

To exercise exclusively legislative authority at the seat of the general government, and over a district around the same not exceeding —— square miles, the consent of the

Legislature of the State or States comprising the same being first obtained.

Here we find the original and rough draft of these several powers as they now exist, in their revised form, in the Constitution. The provision empowering Congress "to dispose of the unappropriated lands of the United States" was modified and enlarged so as to include "other property belonging to the United States," and to authorize Congress to "make all needful rules and regulations" for the preservation, management, and sale of the same.

The provision empowering Congress "to institute temporary governments for the new States arising in the unappropriated lands of the United States," taken in connection with the one empowering Congress "to exercise exclusively legislative authority at the seat of the general government, and over a district of country around the same," clearly shows the difference in the extent and nature of the powers intended to be conferred in the new States or Territories on the one hand, and in the District of Columbia on the other. In the one case it was proposed to authorize Congress "to institute temporary governments for the new States," or Territories, as they are now called, just as our Revolutionary fathers recognized the right of the British Crown to institute local governments for the Colonies, by issuing charters, under which the people of the Colonies were "entitled (according to the Bill of Rights adopted by the Continental Congress) to a free and exclusive power of legislation, in their several Provincial Legislatures, where their right of representation can alone be

preserved, in all cases of taxation and internal polity";
while, in the other case, it was proposed to authorize
Congress to exercise, exclusively, legislative authority
over the municipal and internal polity of the people residing within the district which should be ceded for
that purpose as the seat of the general government.

Each of these provisions was modified and perfected
by the Committees of Detail and Revision, as will appear by comparing them with the corresponding clauses
as finally incorporated into the Constitution. The provision to authorize Congress to institute temporary governments for the new States or Territories, and to provide for their admission into the Union, appears in the
Constitution in this form:

New States may be admitted by the Congress into this
Union.

The power to admit *"new States,"* and "to make all
laws which shall be necessary and proper" to that end,
may fairly be construed to include the right to institute
temporary governments for such new States or Territories, the same as Great Britain could rightfully institute similar governments for the Colonies; but certainly not to authorize Congress to legislate in respect
to their municipal affairs and internal concerns, without
violating that great fundamental principle in defense of
which the battles of the Revolution were fought.

If judicial authority were deemed necessary to give
force to principles so eminently just in themselves, and
which form the basis of our entire political system, such
authority may be found in the opinion of the Supreme

Court of the United States in the Dred Scott case. In that case the Court say:

This brings us to examine by what provision of the Constitution the present Federal Government, under its delegated and restricted powers, is authorized to acquire territory outside of the original limits of the United States, and what powers it may exercise therein over the person or property of a citizen of the United States, while it remains a Territory, and until it shall be admitted as one of the States of the Union.

There is certainly no power given by the Constitution to the Federal Government to establish or maintain Colonies, bordering on the United States or at a distance, to be ruled and governed at its own pleasure; nor to enlarge its territorial limits in any way except by the admission of new States. . . .

The power to expand the territory of the United States by the admission of new States is plainly given; and in the construction of this power by all the departments of the Government, it has been held to authorize the acquisition of territory, not fit for admission at the time, but to be admitted as soon as its population and situation would entitle it to admission. It is acquired to become a State, and not to be held as a Colony and governed by Congress with absolute authority; and as the propriety of admitting a new State is committed to the sound discretion of Congress, the power to acquire territory for that purpose, to be held by the United States until it is in a suitable condition to become a State upon an equal footing with the other States, must rest upon the same discretion.

Having determined the question that the power to acquire territory for the purpose of enlarging our territorial limits and increasing the number of States is included within the power to admit new States and

conferred by the same clause of the Constitution, the
Court proceed to say that "the power to acquire necessarily carries with it the power to preserve and apply to
the purposes for which it was acquired." And again, referring to a former decision of the same Court in respect
to the power of Congress to institute governments for
the Territories, the Court say:

> The power stands firmly on the latter alternative put by
> the Court—that is, as "the inevitable consequence of the
> right to acquire territory."

The power to acquire territory, as well as the right, in
the language of Mr. Madison, "to institute temporary
governments for the new States arising therein" (or
Territorial governments, as they are now called), having
been traced to that provision of the Constitution which
provides for the admission of "new States," the Court
proceed to consider the nature and extent of the power
of Congress over the people of the Territories:

> All we mean to say on this point is, that, as there is no
> express regulation in the Constitution defining the power
> which the general Government may exercise over the per-
> son or property of a citizen in a Territory thus acquired,
> the Court must necessarily look to the provisions and prin-
> ciples of the Constitution, and its distribution of powers,
> for the rules and principles by which its decision must be
> governed.
>
> Taking this rule to guide us, it may be fairly assumed
> that citizens of the United States, who emigrate to a Ter-
> ritory belonging to the people of the United States, can
> not be ruled as mere colonists, dependent upon the will of
> the general Government, and to be governed by any laws it
> may think proper to impose. . . . The Territory being a

part of the United States, the Government and the citizen both enter it under the authority of the Constitution, with their respective rights defined and marked out; and the Federal Government can exercise no power over his person or property beyond what that instrument confers, nor lawfully deny any right which it has reserved.

Hence, inasmuch as the Constitution has conferred on the Federal Government no right to interfere with the property, domestic relations, police regulations, or internal polity of the people of the Territories, it necessarily follows, under the authority of the Court, that Congress can rightfully exercise no such power over the people of the Territories. For this reason alone, the Supreme Court were authorized and compelled to pronounce the eighth section of the Act approved March 6, 1820 (commonly called the Missouri Compromise), inoperative and void—there being no power delegated to Congress in the Constitution authorizing Congress to prohibit slavery in the Territories.

In the course of the discussion of this question the Court gave an elaborate exposition of the structure, principles, and powers of the Federal Government; showing that it possesses no powers except those which are delegated, enumerated, and defined in the Constitution; and that all other powers are either *prohibited* altogether or are *reserved* to the States, or to the people. In order to show that the prohibited, as well as the delegated powers are enumerated and defined in the Constitution, the Court enumerated certain powers which can not be exercised either by Congress or by the Territorial Legislatures, or by any other authority whatever, for the simple reason that they are forbidden by the Constitution.

Some persons who have not examined critically the opinion of the Court in this respect have been induced to believe that the *slavery question* was included in this class of prohibited powers, and that the Court had decided in the Dred Scott case that the Territorial Legislature could not legislate in respect to slave property the same as all other property in the Territories. A few extracts from the opinion of the Court will correct this error, and show clearly the class of powers to which the Court referred, as being forbidden alike to the Federal Government, to the States, and to the Territories. The Court say:

A reference to a few of the provisions of the Constitution will illustrate this proposition. For example, no one, we presume, will contend that Congress can make any law in a Territory respecting the establishment of religion, or the free exercise thereof, or abridging the freedom of speech or of the press, or the right of the people of the Territory peaceably to assemble, and to petition the Government for the redress of grievances.

Nor can Congress deny to the people the right to keep and bear arms, nor the right to trial by jury, nor compel any one to be a witness against himself in a criminal proceeding. . . . So too, it will hardly be contended that Congress could by law quarter a soldier in a house in a Territory without the consent of the owner in a time of peace; nor in time of war but in a manner prescribed by law. Nor could they by law forfeit the property of a citizen in a Territory who was convicted of treason, for a longer period than the life of the person convicted, nor take private property for public use without just compensation.

The powers over persons and property, of which we speak, are not only not granted to Congress, but are in express terms denied, and they are forbidden to exercise them. And this prohibition is not confined to the States, but the words are general, and extend to the whole territory over which the Constitution gives it power to legislate, including those portions of it remaining under Territorial Governments, as well as that covered by States.

It is a total absence of power, everywhere within the dominion of the United States, and places the citizens of a Territory, so far as these rights are concerned, on the same footing with citizens of the States, and guards them as firmly and plainly against any inroads which the general Government might attempt, under the plea of implied or incidental powers. And if Congress itself can not do this —if it is beyond the powers conferred on the Federal Government—it will be admitted, we presume, that it could not authorize a Territorial government to exercise them. It could confer no power on any local government, established by its authority, to violate the provisions of the Constitution.

Nothing can be more certain than that the Court were here speaking only of *forbidden powers,* which were denied alike to Congress, to the State Legislatures, and to the Territorial Legislatures, and that the prohibition extends "everywhere within the dominion of the United States," applicable equally to States and Territories, as well as to the United States.

If this sweeping prohibition—this just but inexorable restriction upon the powers of government—Federal, State, and Territorial—shall ever be held to include the slavery question, thus negativing the right of the people of the States and Territories, as well as the Federal Government, to control it by law (and it will be observed that in the opinion of the Court "the citizens of a Territory, so far as these rights are concerned, are on the same footing with the citizens of the States"), then, in-

deed, will the doctrine become firmly established that
the principles of law applicable to African slavery are
uniform throughout the dominion of the United States,
and that there "is an irrepressible conflict between opposing and enduring forces, which means that the
United States must and will, sooner or later, become
either entirely a slaveholding nation or entirely a free
labor nation."

Notwithstanding the disastrous consequences which
would inevitably result from the authoritative recognition and practical operation of such a doctrine, there are
those who maintain that the Court referred to and included the slavery question within that class of forbidden powers which (although the same in the Territories as in the States) could not be exercised by the
people of the Territories.

If this proposition were true, which fortunately for
the peace and welfare of the whole country it is not, the
conclusion would inevitably result, which they logically
deduce from the premises—that the Constitution by the
recognition of slavery establishes it in the Territories
beyond the power of the people to control it by law, and
guarantees to every citizen the right to go there and be
protected in the enjoyment of his slave property; and
when all other remedies fail for the protection of such
rights of property, it becomes the imperative duty of
Congress (to the performance of which every member is
bound by his conscience and his oath, and from which
no consideration of political policy or expediency can
release him) to provide by law such adequate and complete protection as is essential to the full enjoyment of
an important right secured by the Constitution. If the

proposition be true, that the Constitution establishes slavery in the Territories beyond the power of the people legally to control it, another result, no less startling, and from which there is no escape, must inevitably follow. The Constitution is uniform "everywhere within the dominions of the United States"—is the same in Pennsylvania as in Kansas—and if it be true, as stated by the President in a special Message to Congress, "that slavery exists in Kansas by virtue of the Constitution of the United States," and that "Kansas is therefore at this moment as much a slave State as Georgia or South Carolina," why does it not exist in Pennsylvania by virtue of the same Constitution?

If it be said that Pennsylvania is a sovereign State, and therefore has a right to regulate the slavery question within her own limits to suit herself, it must be borne in mind that the sovereignty of Pennsylvania, like that of every other State, is limited by the Constitution, which provides that:

This Constitution, and all laws of the United States which shall be made in pursuance thereof, and all treaties made, or which shall be made, under the authority of the United States, shall be the *supreme law of the land,* and the judges in every State shall be bound thereby, *anything in the Constitution or laws of any State to the contrary notwithstanding.*

Hence, the State of Pennsylvania, with her Constitution and laws, and domestic institutions, and internal policy, is subordinate to the Constitution of the United States, in the same manner, and to the same extent, as the Territory of Kansas. The Kansas-Nebraska Act says that the Territory of Kansas shall exercise legislative power over "all rightful subjects of legislation consistent with the Constitution," and that the people of said Territory shall be left "perfectly free to form and regulate their domestic institutions in their own way, subject only to the Constitution of the United States." The provisions of this Act are believed to be in entire harmony with the Constitution, and under them the people of Kansas possess every right, privilege, and immunity, in respect to their internal polity and domestic relations which the people of Pennsylvania can exercise under their Constitution and laws. Each is invested with full, complete, and exclusive powers in this respect, "subject only to the Constitution of the United States."

The question recurs then, if the Constitution does establish slavery in Kansas or any other Territory beyond the power of the people to control it by law, how can the conclusion be resisted that slavery is established in like manner and by the same authority in all the States of the Union? And if it be the imperative duty of Congress to provide by law for the protection of slave property in the Territories upon the ground that "slavery exists in Kansas" (and consequently in every other Territory), "by virtue of the Constitution of the United States," why is it not also the duty of Congress, for the same reason, to provide similar protection to slave property in all the States of the Union, when the Legislatures fail to furnish such protection?

Without confessing or attempting to avoid the inevitable consequences of their own doctrine, its advocates endeavor to fortify their position by citing the Dred Scott decision to prove that the Constitution recognizes property in slaves—that there is no legal distinction between this and every other description of property— that slave property and every other kind of property stand on an equal footing—that Congress has no more power over the one than over the other—and, consequently, can not discriminate between them.

Upon this point the Court say:

> Now as we have already said in an earlier part of this opinion, upon a different point, the right of property in a slave is distinctly and expressly affirmed in the Constitution. . . . And if the Constitution recognizes the right of property of the master in a slave, and makes no distinction between that description of property and other property owned by a citizen, no tribunal acting under the authority of the United States, whether it be legislative, executive, or judicial, has a right to draw such a distinction, or deny to it the benefit of the provisions and guarantees which have been provided for the protection of private property against the encroachments of the government. . . . And the government in express terms is pledged to protect it in all future time, *if the slave escapes from his owner*. This is done in plain words—too plain to be misunderstood. And no word can be found in the Constitution which gives Congress a *greater* power over slave property, or which entitles property of that kind to *less* protection than property of any other description. The only power conferred is the power coupled with the duty of guarding and protecting the owner in his rights.

The rights of the owner which it is thus made the duty of the Federal Government to guard and protect are those expressly provided for in the Constitution, and defined in clear and explicit language by the Court— that "the government, in express terms, is pledged to protect it (slave property) in all future time, *if the slave escapes from his owner."* This is the only contingency, according to the plain reading of the Constitution as authoritatively interpreted by the Supreme Court, in which the Federal Government is authorized, required, or permitted to interfere with slavery in the States or Territories; and in that case only for the purpose "of guarding and protecting the owner in his rights" to reclaim his slave property. In all other respects slaves stand on the same footing with all other property—"the Constitution makes no distinction between that description of property and other property owned by a citizen"; and "no word can be found in the Constitution which gives Congress a greater power over slave property, or which entitles property of that kind to less protection than property of any other description." This is the basis upon which all rights pertaining to slave property, either in the States or the Territories, stand under the Constitution as expounded by the Supreme Court in the Dred Scott case.

Inasmuch as the Constitution has delegated no power to the Federal Government in respect to any other kind of property belonging to the citizen—neither introducing, establishing, prohibiting, nor excluding it anywhere within the dominion of the United States, but leaves the owner thereof perfectly free to remove into any State or Territory and carry his property with him, and hold the same subject to the local law, and relying upon the local authorities for protection, it follows, according to the decision of the Court, that slave property stands on the same footing, is entitled to the same rights and immunities, and in like manner is dependent upon the local authorities and laws for protection.

The Court refer to that clause of the Constitution

which provides for the rendition of fugitive slaves as
their authority for saying that "the right of property in
slaves is distinctly and expressly affirmed in the Constitution." By reference to that provision it will be seen
that, while the word "slaves" is not used, still the Constitution not only recognizes the right of property in
slaves, as stated by the Court, but explicitly states what
class of persons shall be deemed slaves, and under what
laws or authority they may be held to servitude, and
under what circumstances fugitive slaves shall be restored to their owners, all in the same section, as follows:

No person held to service or labor in one State, *under
the laws thereof,* escaping into another, shall, in consequence of any law or regulation therein, be discharged
from such service or labor, but shall be delivered up on
claim of the party to whom such service or labor may be
due.

Thus it will be seen that a slave, within the meaning
of the Constitution, is a "person held to service or labor
in one State, *under the laws thereof"*—not under the
Constitution of the United States, nor by the laws
thereof, nor by virtue of any Federal authority whatsoever, but under the laws of the particular State where
such service or labor may be due.

It was necessary to give this exact definition of slavery
in the Constitution in order to satisfy the people of the
South as well as of the North. The slaveholding States
would never consent for a moment that their domestic
relations—and especially their right of property in their
slaves—should be dependent upon Federal authority, or
that Congress should have any power over the subject—

either to extend, confine, or restrain it; much less to
protect or regulate it—lest, under the pretense of protection and regulation, the Federal Government, under
the influence of the strong and increasing antislavery
sentiment which prevailed at that period, might destroy
the institution, and divest those rights of property in
slaves which were sacred under the laws and constitutions of their respective States so long as the Federal
Government had no power to interfere with the subject.

In like manner the non-slaveholding States, while
they were entirely willing to provide for the surrender
of all fugitive slaves—as is conclusively shown by the
unanimous vote of all the States in the Convention for
the provision now under consideration—and to leave
each State perfectly free to hold slaves under its own
laws, and by virtue of its own separate and exclusive authority, so long as it pleased, and to abolish it when it
chose, were unwilling to become responsible for its
existence by incorporating it into the Constitution as
a national institution, to be protected and regulated,
extended and controlled by Federal authority, regardless of the wishes of the people, and in defiance of the
local laws of the several States and Territories. For these
opposite reasons the Southern and Northern States
united in giving a unanimous vote in the Convention
for that provision of the Constitution which recognizes
slavery as a local institution in the several States where
it exists, "under the laws thereof," and provides for the
surrender of fugitive slaves.

It will be observed that the term "State" is used in
this provision, as well as in various other parts of the
Constitution, in the same sense in which it was used by

Mr. Jefferson in his plan for establishing governments for the new States in the territory ceded and to be ceded to the United States, and by Mr. Madison in his proposition to confer on Congress power "to institute temporary governments for the *new States* arising in the unappropriated lands of the United States," to designate the political communities, Territories as well as States, within the dominion of the United States. The word "States" is used in the same sense in the Ordinance of the 13th July, 1787, for the government of the territory northwest of the River Ohio, which was passed by the remnant of the Congress of the Confederation, sitting in New York while its most eminent members were at Philadelphia, as delegates to the Federal Convention, aiding in the formation of the Constitution of the United States.

In this sense the word "States" is used in the clause providing for the rendition of fugitive slaves, applicable to all political communities under the authority of the United States, including the Territories as well as the several States of the Union. Under any other construction the right of the owner to recover his slave would be restricted to the *States* of the Union, leaving the Territories a secure place of refuge for all fugitives. The same remark is applicable to the clause of the Constitution which provides that "a person charged in any *State* with treason, felony, or other crime, who shall flee from justice, and be found in *another State,* shall, on the demand of the executive authority of the *State* from which he fled, be delivered up to be removed to the State having jurisdiction of the crime." Unless the term State, as used in these provisions of the Constitution, shall be construed to include every distinct political community under the jurisdiction of the United States, and to apply to Territories as well as to the States of the Union, the Territories must become a sanctuary for all the fugitives from service and justice, for all the felons and criminals who shall escape from the several *States* and seek refuge and immunity in the *Territories*.

If any other illustration were necessary to show that the political communities, which we now call Territories (but which, during the whole period of the Confederation and the formation of the Constitution, were always referred to as "States" or "New States"), are recognized as "States" in *some* of the provisions of the Constitution, they may be found in those clauses which declare that "no *State*" shall enter into any "treaty, alliance, or confederation; grant letters of marque and reprisal; coin money; emit bills of credit; make any thing but gold and silver coin a tender in payment of debts; pass any bill of attainder, *ex post facto* law, or law impairing the obligation of contracts; or grant any title of nobility."

It must be borne in mind that in each of these cases where the power is not expressly delegated to Congress the prohibition is not imposed upon the Federal Government, but upon the *States*. There was no necessity for any such prohibition upon Congress or the Federal Government, for the reason that the omission to delegate any such powers in the Constitution was of itself a prohibition, and so declared in express terms by the 10th Amendment, which declares that "the powers not delegated to the United States by the Constitution, nor prohibited by it to the States, are reserved to the States respectively, or to the people."

Hence it would certainly be competent for the States

and Territories to exercise these powers but for the prohibition contained in those provisions of the Constitution; and inasmuch as the prohibition only extends to the "States," the people of the "Territories" are still at liberty to exercise them, unless the Territories are included within the term *States,* within the meaning of these provisions of the Constitution of the United States.

It only remains to be shown that the Compromise Measures of 1850 and the Kansas-Nebraska Act of 1854 are in perfect harmony with, and a faithful embodiment of the principles herein enforced. A brief history of these measures will disclose the principles upon which they are founded.

On the 29th of January, 1850, Mr. Clay introduced into the Senate a series of resolutions upon the slavery question which were intended to form the basis of the subsequent legislation upon that subject. Pending the discussion of these resolutions the chairman of the Committee on Territories prepared and reported to the Senate, on the 25th of March, two bills—one for the admission of California into the Union of States, and the other for the organization of the Territories of Utah and New Mexico, and for the adjustment of the disputed boundary with the State of Texas—which were read twice and printed for the use of the Senate. On the 19th of April a select committee of thirteen was appointed, on motion of Mr. Foote, of Mississippi, of which Mr. Clay was made chairman, and to which were referred all pending propositions relating to the slavery question. On the 8th of May, Mr. Clay, from the select committee of thirteen, submitted to the Senate an elaborate report covering all the points in controversy, accompanied by a bill, which is usually known as the "Omnibus Bill." By reference to the provisions of this bill, as it appears on the files of the Senate, it will be seen that it is composed of the two printed bills which had been reported by the Committee on Territories on the 25th of March previous; and that the only material change in its provisions, involving an important and essential principle, is to be found in the tenth section, which prescribes and defines the powers of the Territorial Legislature. In the bill, as reported by the Committee on Territories, the legislative power of the Territories extended to "all rightful subjects of legislation consistent with the Constitution of the United States," *without excepting African slavery;* while the bill, as reported by the committee of thirteen, conferred the same power on the Territorial Legislature, *with the exception of African slavery.* This portion of the section in its original form read thus:

And be it further enacted that the legislative power of the Territory shall extend to all rightful subjects of legislation consistent with the Constitution of the United States and the provisions of this act; but no law shall be passed interfering with the primary disposition of the soil.

To which the committee of thirteen added these words: *"Nor in respect to African slavery."* When the bill came up for action on the 15th of May, Mr. Davis, of Mississippi, said:

I offer the following amendment. To strike out, in the sixth line of the tenth section, the words *"in respect to African slavery,"* and insert the words *"with those rights of property growing out of the institution of African slavery*

as it exists in any of the States of the Union." The object of
the amendment is to prevent the Territorial Legislature
from legislating against the rights of property growing out
of the institution of slavery. . . . It will leave to the Territorial Legislatures those rights and powers which are es-
sentially necessary, not only to the preservation of property, but to the peace of the Territory. It will leave the
right to make such police regulations as are necessary to
prevent disorder, and which will be absolutely necessary
with such property as that to secure its beneficial use to its
owner. With this brief explanation I submit the amendment.

Mr. Clay, in reply to Mr. Davis, said:

I am not perfectly sure that I comprehend the full meaning of the amendment offered by the Senator from Mississippi. If I do, I think he accomplishes nothing by striking
out the clause now in the bill and inserting that which he
proposes to insert. The clause now in the bill is, that the
Territorial legislation shall not extend to anything respecting African slavery within the Territory. The effect of retaining the clause as reported by the Committee will be
this: That if in any of the Territories slavery now exists, it
shall not be abolished by the Territorial Legislature; and
if in any of the Territories slavery does not now exist, it
can not be introduced by the Territorial Legislature. The
clause itself was introduced into the bill by the Committee
for the purpose of tying up the hands of the Territorial
Legislature in respect to legislating at all, one way or the
other, upon the subject of African slavery. It was intended
to leave the legislation and the law of the respective Territories in the condition in which the Act will find them. I
stated on a former occasion that I did not, in Committee,
vote for the amendment to insert the clause, though it was
proposed to be introduced by a majority of the Committee.
I attached very little consequence to it at the time, and I

attach very little to it at present. It is perhaps of no particular importance whatever. Now, Sir, if I understand the
measure proposed by the Senator from Mississippi, it aims
at the same thing. I do not understand him as proposing
that if anyone shall carry slaves into the Territory—although by the laws of the Territory he can not take them
there—the legislative hands of the Territorial government
should be so tied as to prevent it saying he shall not enjoy
the fruits of their labor. If the Senator from Mississippi
means to say that—

Mr. Davis:

I do mean to say it.

Mr. Clay:

If the object of the Senator is to provide that slaves may
be introduced into the Territory contrary to the *lex loci*,
and, being introduced, nothing shall be done by the Legislature to impair the rights of owners to hold the slaves thus
brought contrary to the local laws, *I certainly can not vote
for it.* In doing so I shall repeat again the expression of
opinion which I announced at an early period of the
session.

Here we find the line distinctly drawn between those
who contended for the right to carry slaves into the
Territories and hold them in defiance of the local law,
and those who contended that such right was subject to
the local law of the Territory. During the progress of
the discussion on the same day Mr. Davis, of Mississippi,
said:

We are giving, or proposing to give, a government to a
Territory, which act rests upon the basis of our right to

make such provision. We suppose we have a right to confer power. If so, we may mark out the limit to which they may legislate, and are bound not to confer power beyond that which exists in Congress. If we give them power to legislate beyond that we commit a fraud or usurpation, as it may be done openly, covertly, or indirectly.

To which Mr. Clay replied:

Now, Sir, I only repeat what I have had occasion to say before, that while I am willing to stand aside and make no legislative enactment one way or the other—to lay off the Territories without the Wilmot Proviso, on the one hand, with which I understand we are threatened, or without an attempt to introduce a clause for the introduction of slavery into the Territories. While I am for rejecting both the one and the other, I am content that the law as it exists shall prevail; and if there be any diversity of opinion as to what it means, I am willing that it shall be settled by the highest judicial authority of the country. While I am content thus to abide the result, I must say that I can not vote for any express provision recognizing the right to carry slaves there.

To which Mr. Davis rejoined, that—

It is said our Revolution grew out of a Preamble; and I hope we have something of the same character of the hardy men of the Revolution who first commenced the war with the mother country—something of the spirit of that bold Yankee who said he had a right to go to Concord, and that go he would; and who, in the maintenance of that right, met his death at the hands of a British sentinel. Now, Sir, if our right to carry slaves into these Territories be a constitutional right, it is out first duty to maintain it.

Pending the discussion which ensued Mr. Davis, at

the suggestion of friends, modified his amendment from time to time, until it assumed the following shape:

Nor to introduce or exclude African slavery. Provided that nothing herein contained shall be construed so as to prevent said Territorial Legislature from passing such laws as may be necessary for the protection of the rights of property of every kind which may have been, or may be hereafter, comformably to the Constitution of the United States, held in or introduced into said Territory.

To which, on the same day, Mr. Chase, of Ohio, offered the following amendment:

Provided further, That nothing herein contained shall be construed as authorizing or permitting the introduction of slavery or the holding of persons as property within said Territory.

Upon these amendments—the one affirming the proslavery and the other the antislavery position, in opposition to the right of the people of the Territories to decide the slavery question for themselves—Mr. Douglas said:

The position that I have ever taken has been, that this, and all other questions relating to the domestic affairs and domestic policy of the Territories, ought to be left to the decision of the people themselves; and that we ought to be content with whatever way they may decide the question, because they have a much deeper interest in these matters than we have, and know much better what institutions suit them than we, who have never been there, can decide for them. I would therefore have much preferred that that portion of the bill should have remained as it was reported from the Committee on Territories, with no provision on the subject of slavery, the one way or the other. And I do hope yet that that clause will be stricken out. I am satisfied, Sir, that it gives no strength to the bill. I am satisfied, even if it did give strength to it, that it ought not to be there, *because it is a violation of principle*—a violation of that principle upon which we have all rested our defense of the course we have taken on this question. I do not see how those of us who have taken the position we have taken— that of *non-intervention*—and have argued in favor of the right of the people to legislate for themselves on this question, can support such a provision without abandoning all the arguments which we used in the Presidential campaign in the year 1848, and the principles set forth by the honorable Senator from Michigan (Mr. Cass) in that letter which is known as the "Nicholson Letter." We are required to abandon that platform; we are required to abandon those principles, and to stultify ourselves, and to adopt the opposite doctrine—and for what? In order to say, that *the people of the Territories shall not have such institutions as they shall deem adapted to their condition and their wants.* I do not see, Sir, how such a provision can be acceptable either to the people of the North or the South.

Upon the question, how many inhabitants a Territory should contain before it should be formed into a political community with the rights of self-government, Mr. Douglas said:

The Senator from Mississippi puts the question to me as to what number of people there must be in a Territory before this right to govern themselves accrues. Without determining the precise number, I will assume that the right ought to accrue to the people at the moment they have enough to constitute a government; and, Sir, the bill assumes that there are people enough there to require a government, and enough to authorize the people to govern themselves. . . . Your bill concedes that a representative government is necessary—a government founded upon the

principles of popular sovereignty and the right of a people
to enact their own laws; and for this reason you give them
a Legislature composed of two branches, like the Legislatures of the different States and Territories of the Union.
You confer upon them the right to legislate on "all rightful
subjects of legislation," except negroes. Why except negroes?
Why except African slavery? If the inhabitants are competent to govern themselves upon all other subjects, and in
reference to all other descriptions of property—if they are
competent to make laws and determine the relations between husband and wife, and parent and child, and municipal laws affecting the rights and property of citizens generally, they are competent also to make laws to govern
themselves in relation to slavery and negroes.

With reference to the protection of property in slaves,
Mr. Douglas said:

I have a word to say to the honorable Senator from Mississippi (Mr. Davis). He insists that I am not in favor of
protecting property, and that his amendment is offered for
the purpose of protecting property under the Constitution.
Now, Sir, I ask you what authority he has for assuming
that? Do I not desire to protect property because I wish to
allow the people to pass such laws as they deem proper
respecting their rights to property without any exception?
He might just as well say that I am opposed to protecting
property in merchandise, in steamboats, in cattle, in real
estate, as to say that I am opposed to protecting property
of any other description; for I desire to put them all on an
equality, and allow the people to make their own laws in
respect to the whole of them.

Mr. Cass said (referring to the amendments offered
by Mr. Davis and Mr. Chase):

Now with respect to the amendments. I shall vote against
them both; and then I shall vote in favor of striking out

the restriction in the Bill upon the power of the Territorial governments. I shall do so upon this ground. I was opposed, as the honorable Senator from Kentucky has declared he was, to the insertion of this prohibition by the committee. I consider it inexpedient and unconstitutional. I have already stated my belief that the rightful power of internal legislation in the Territories belongs to the people.

After further discussion the vote was taken by yeas and nays on the amendment of Mr. Chase, and decided in the negative: Yeas, 25; Nays, 30. The question recurring on the amendment of Mr. Davis, of Mississippi, it was also rejected: Yeas, 25; Nays, 30. Whereupon Mr. Seward offered the following amendment:

Neither slavery nor involuntary servitude, otherwise than by conviction for crime, shall ever be allowed in either of said Territories of Utah and New Mexico.

Which was rejected—Yeas, 23; Nays, 33.

After various other amendments had been offered and voted upon—all relating to the power of the Territorial Legislature over slavery—Mr. Douglas moved to strike out all relating to African slavery, so that the Territorial Legislature should have the same power over that question as over all other rightful subjects of legislation consistent with the Constitution—which amendment was rejected. After the rejection of this amendment, the discussion was renewed with great ability and depth of feeling in respect to the powers which the Territorial Legislature should exercise upon the subject of slavery. Various propositions were made, and amendments offered and rejected—all relating to this one controverted point—when Mr. Norris, of New Hampshire, renewed the motion of Mr. Douglas, to strike out the restriction on the Territorial Legislature in respect to African slavery. On the 31st of July this amendment was adopted by a vote of 32 to 19—restoring this section of the bill to the form in which it was reported from the Committee on Territories on the 25th of March, and conferring on the Territorial Legislature power over "all rightful subjects of legislation consistent with the Constitution of the United States," *without excepting African slavery.*

Thus terminated this great struggle in the affirmance of the principle, as the basis of the Compromise Measures of 1850, so far as they related to the organization of the Territories, *that the people of the Territories should decide the slavery question for themselves through the action of their Territorial Legislatures.*

This controverted question having been definitely settled, the Senate proceeded on the same day to consider the other portions of the bill, and after striking out all except those provisions which provided for the organization of the Territory of Utah, ordered the bill to be engrossed for a third reading, and on the next day —August 1, 1850—the bill was read a third time, and passed.

On the 14th of August the bill for the organization of the Territory of New Mexico was taken up, and amended so as to conform fully to the provisions of the Utah Act in respect to the power of the Territorial Legislature over "all rightful subjects of legislation consistent with the Constitution," without excepting African slavery, and was ordered to be engrossed for a third reading without a division; and on the next day the bill was passed—Yeas, 27; Nays, 10.

These two bills were sent to the House of Representatives, and passed that body without any alteration in respect to the power of the Territorial Legislatures over the subject of slavery, and were approved by President Fillmore, September 9, 1850.

In 1852, when the two great political parties—Whig and Democratic—into which the country was then divided, assembled in National Convention at Baltimore for the purpose of nominating candidates for the Presidency and Vice-Presidency, each Convention adopted and affirmed the principles embodied in the Compromise Measures of 1850 as rules of action by which they would be governed in all future cases in the organization of Territorial governments and the admission of new States.

On the 4th of January, 1854, the Committee on Territories of the Senate, to which had been referred a bill for the organization of the Territory of Nebraska, reported the bill back, with an amendment, in the form of a substitute for the entire bill, which, with some modifications, is now known on the statute book as the "Kansas-Nebraska Act," accompanied by a Report explaining the principles upon which it was proposed to organize those Territories, as follows:

The principal amendments which your Committee deem it their duty to commend to the favorable action of the Senate, in a special report, are those in which the principles established by the Compromise Measures of 1850, so far as they are applicable to territorial organizations, are proposed to be affirmed and carried into practical operation within the limits of the new Territory. The wisdom of those measures is attested, not less by their salutary and beneficial effects in allaying sectional agitation and restoring peace and harmony to an irritated and distracted people, than by the cordial and almost universal approbation with which they have been received and sanctioned by the whole country.

In the judgment of your Committee, those measures were intended to have a far more comprehensive and enduring effect than the mere adjustment of the difficulties arising out of the recent acquisition of Mexican territory. They were designed to establish certain great principles, which would not only furnish adequate remedies for existing evils, but, in all time to come, avoid the perils of a similar agitation, by withdrawing the question of slavery from the Halls of Congress and the political arena, and committing it to the arbitrament of those who were immediately interested in and alone responsible for its consequences. With a view of conforming their action to the settled policy of the Government, sanctioned by the approving voice of the American people, your Committee have deemed it their duty to incorporate and perpetuate, in their Territorial bill, the principles and spirit of those measures.

After presenting and reviewing certain provisions of the bill, the Committee conclude as follows:

From these provisions it is apparent that the Compromise Measures of 1850 affirm and rest upon the following propositions:

"*First.*—That all questions pertaining to slavery in the Territories, and in the new States to be formed therefrom, are to be left to the decision of the people residing therein, by their appropriate representatives to be chosen by them for that purpose.

"*Second.*—That all cases involving title to slaves and questions of personal freedom, are referred to the adjudication of the local tribunals, with the right of appeal to the Supreme Court of the United States.

"Third.—That the provision of the Constitution of the United States in respect to fugitives from service, is to be carried into faithful execution in all the organized Territories, the same as in the States. The substitute for the bill which your Committee have prepared, and which is commended to the favorable action of the Senate, proposes to carry these propositions and principles into practical operation, in the precise language of the Compromise Measures of 1850."

By reference to that section of the "Kansas-Nebraska Act" as it now stands on the statute book, which prescribed and defined the power of the Territorial Legislature, it will be seen that it is, "in the precise language of the Compromise Measures of 1850," extending the legislative power of the Territory "to all rightful subjects of legislation consistent with the Constitution," without excepting African slavery.

It having been suggested, with some plausibility during the discussion of the bill, that the act of Congress of March 6, 1820, prohibiting slavery north of the parallel of 36° 30′ would deprive the people of the Territory of the power of regulating the slavery question to suit themselves while they should remain in a Territorial condition, and before they should have the requisite population to entitle them to admission into the Union as a State, an amendment was prepared by the chairman of the Committee, and incorporated into the bill to remove this obstacle to the free exercise of the principle of popular sovereignty in the Territory, while it remained in a Territorial condition, by repealing the said act of Congress, and declaring the true intent and meaning of all the friends of the bill in these words:

That the Constitution and all laws of the United States
which are not locally inapplicable, shall have the same force
and effect within the said Territory as elsewhere within the
United States, except the eighth section of the act preparatory to the admission of Missouri into the Union, approved
March 6, 1820, which being inconsistent with the principle
of non-intervention by Congress with slavery in the States
and Territories, as recognized by the legislation of 1850,
commonly called the "Compromise Measures," is hereby declared inoperative and void—*it being the true intent and
meaning of this act not to legislate slavery into any Territory or State, nor to exclude it therefrom, but to leave the
people thereof perfectly free to form and regulate their
domestic institutions their own way, subject only to the
Constitution of the United States.*

To which was added, on motion of Mr. Badger, the
following:

Provided, That nothing herein contained shall be construed to revive or put in force any law or regulation which
may have existed prior to the act of the sixth of March,
1820, either protecting, establishing, or abolishing slavery.

In this form, and with this distinct understanding of
its "true intent and meaning," the bill passed the two
houses of Congress, and became the law of the land by
the approval of the President, May 30, 1854.

In 1856, the Democratic party, assembled in National
Convention at Cincinnati, declared by a unanimous
vote of the delegates from every State in the Union, that

The American Democracy recognize and adopt the principles contained in the organic laws establishing the Territories of Kansas and Nebraska as embodying the only
sound and safe solution of the "slavery question," upon

which the great national idea of the people of this whole country can repose in its determined conservatism of the Union—non-interference by Congress with slavery in State and Territory, or in the District of Columbia;

That this was the basis of the Compromises of 1850, confirmed by both the Democratic and Whig parties in National Conventions—ratified by the people in the election of 1852—and rightly applied to the organization of the Territories in 1854; That by the uniform application of this Democratic principle to the organization of Territories and to the admission of new States, with or without domestic slavery as they may elect, the equal rights of all will be preserved intact—the original compacts of the Constitution maintained inviolate—and the perpetuity and expansion of this Union insured to its utmost capacity of embracing in peace and harmony any future American State that may be constituted or annexed with a Republican form of government.

In accepting the nomination of this Convention, Mr. Buchanan, in a letter dated June 16, 1856, said:

The agitation on the question of domestic slavery has too long distracted and divided the people of this Union, and alienated their affections from each other. This agitation has assumed many forms since its commencement, but it now seems to be directed chiefly to the Territories; and judging from its present character, I think we may safely anticipate that it is rapidly approaching a "finality." The recent legislation of Congress respecting domestic slavery, derived, as it has been, from the original and pure fountain of legitimate political power, the will of the majority, promises, ere long, to allay the dangerous excitement. This legislation is founded upon principles as ancient as free government itself, and in accordance with them has simply declared that the people of a Territory, like those of a

State, *shall decide for themselves whether slavery shall or shall not exist within their limits.*

This exposition of the history of these measures shows conclusively that the authors of the Compromise Measures of 1850, and of the Kansas-Nebraska Act of 1854, as well as the members of the Continental Congress of 1774, and the founders of our system of government subsequent to the Revolution, regarded the people of the Territories and Colonies as political communities which were entitled to a free and exclusive power of legislation in their Provincial Legislatures, where their representation could alone be preserved, in all cases of taxation and internal polity. This right pertains to the people collectively as a law-abiding and peaceful community, and not to the isolated individuals who may wander upon the public domain in violation of law. It can only be exercised where there are inhabitants sufficient to constitute a government, and capable of performing its various functions and duties—a fact to be ascertained and determined by Congress. Whether the number shall be fixed at ten, fifteen, or twenty thousand inhabitants does not affect the principle.

The principle, under our political system, is *that every distinct political community, loyal to the Constitution and the Union, is entitled to all the rights, privileges, and immunities of self-government in respect to their local concerns and internal polity, subject only to the Constitution of the United States.*

SPEECH OF STEPHEN A. DOUGLAS

at Columbus, Ohio, September 7, 1859 [1]

Fellow Citizens of Ohio: In compliance with the invitation of your State Central Committee, I appear before you today for the purpose of discussing some of those great leading topics which now agitate the public mind of this country. It is not my intention to enter into an examination of any one question pertaining to the local and domestic policy of your own State, because, in regard to the interests and concerns of your State, I hold my political action bound by that great principle of the Nebraska bill which tells every political community to regulate its own affairs and mind its own business, and not to interfere with those of its neighbors. [Cheers, and cries of "Good."] But there are certain great principles, of universal application, which it is proper to discuss in all parts of the Confederation in the same way, and to enforce by the same arguments. I maintain any political creed to be unsound which cannot be avowed in Chicago the same as in New Orleans. If the Democratic creed cannot be avowed and practiced in Ohio the same as in Kentucky, in the North as well as in the South, there must be something radically wrong. So long as we live under a common Constitution, which is the supreme law of the entire public, our political creed should be as broad as the Republic and as universal as that Constitution. I wish to invite your attention today to those great principles

[1] *New York Times,* September 8, 1859.

126

which underlie the Democratic creed, and draw the dividing line between the Democracy and all the other political parties in this country upon this vexed question of slavery, which for the last few years seems to have absorbed all other questions. The Democratic party hold that it is the right of the people of every State, of every Territory, and every political community within this Confederacy to decide that question to suit themselves. We not only apply that principle to the question of slavery, but we extend it to all the local and domestic institutions of all the States and all the Territories of the Union. On the other hand, we are told by the leaders of the Republican party that there is an irrepressible conflict between freedom and slavery, free labor and slave labor, free States and slave States, and that it is their intention to continue to excite, agitate and divide the country until slavery shall be abolished or established throughout the country. In other words, the Republican party hold that there must be uniformity in the local institutions of all the States and Territories of the Union. Mr. Seward, in his Rochester speech, says that it is an irrepressible conflict between enduring forces, that must last until uniformity shall be established. Mr. Lincoln, in the Illinois canvass of last year, compared it to a house divided against itself which could not stand, and said that this Union could not permanently endure divided into free and slave States, as our fathers made it. Hence you find that in the platform of the Republican party, adopted in Philadelphia in 1856, it is declared that Congress possesses sovereign powers over all the Territories of the Union, and that it is both their right and their duty to exercise that power for the abolishment and prohibition of African slavery. Here you find at once the line of conflict between the Republicans and the Democratic party. The Republican party hold that the federal government can decide the slavery question for the people of the Territories and the new States. We Democrats maintain that the federal government has no right to interfere with the question, either to establish, to protect, to abolish, or to prohibit slavery; but that the people in each State, and each Territory, shall be left entirely free to decide it for themselves. ["Hear, hear," and applause.] This question of the right of the people in their local legislatures to decide all internal questions to suit themselves is not a new doctrine. It is as old as the principles of free government on the American continent. It was the first question that seriously divided the American Colonies from the British Government, and out of which the first serious cause of quarrel arose. The American Colonies claimed the right in their Colonial legislatures to regulate the slavery question, and all other matters affecting their internal policy, to suit themselves, without the interference of the British Parliament, or any other power on earth. In accordance with that right, as early as 1699, the Colonial legislature of Virginia passed a law imposing heavy penalties upon all slaves brought into that Colony subsequently to the date of that act. Virginia did not pass that law because of her hostility to African slavery, but she did it as a matter of domestic policy, affecting her own interests and her own safety. The Colony of Virginia was a feeble settlement, surrounded by formidable savage tribes of Indians, and the large number of

African savages poured into her midst made her feel alarmed for the safety of her firesides, and stimulated her to the enactment of a law for her own preservation, by which a tax was imposed upon all African slaves subsequently brought into the Colony. So soon as that tax was levied, the British merchants who were engaged in the African slave trade petitioned the King of England to annul that law of Virginia, upon the ground that the Colonies were the common property of the Empire, that every British subject had a right to move into them, carry his slaves and other property with him, and hold it there in defiance of the local law, and that Virginia had no right to exclude them or their property by a mere legislative enactment. It strikes me that I have heard that argument substantially urged since 1699. It strikes me that I have heard a very similar argument advanced in the American Congress, and that in modern days that same proposition has found its advocates in America. The British king, after mature consideration, decided in favor of the British slave trader, and against the right of the people of Virginia to exclude slavery from their limits by law. Virginia immediately passed another act, intended to keep slavery out, and then another, and still another, until she had passed thirty-one laws, each designed to enforce the right of the Colony to decide the slavery question for itself. In 1772, four years before the Declaration of Independence, Virginia passed another act, imposing a 5 per cent tax upon all slaves brought into the territory, and, in addition, petitioned the King to remove the restrictions upon the right of the Colony to decide the question to suit themselves, and notified him in that memorial that if he did not grant that right, his dominions in America were in danger, intimating to the King that our fathers would fight for the right of each Colony to decide the slavery question for itself. Each of the Colonies claimed the same right. Read the history of the Colonies up to the time of the Revolution, and you will find upon the statute books of every one of the thirteen enactments regulating and controlling this slavery question. Assembled for the first time, in 1774, they for their first act adopted a Bill of Rights for the Colonies. Look into that Bill of Rights, and you will find the great foundation principles upon which all of our institutions have been based since in that Bill of Rights. The Colonies first declared that they were willing to grant to Great Britain the right to regulate commerce and decide all their questions of a general character, but they said that they claimed for themselves the free and exclusive power of legislation in their Provincial legislatures upon all subjects of internal policy. There is the principle, distinctly asserted, for which they went to war. It was the principle that every Colony has a right to decide for itself, in its own legislature, all questions of taxation and internal policy. That was a reply to the preamble to the Stamp Act, in which the Parliament of England had declared its right to bind the Colonies in all cases whatsoever. It will be seen, therefore, that the Tories of the Revolution held at that day that the imperial Parliament had a right to govern the Territories as it pleased, not only in general matters, but in matters affecting their local interests, slavery included. The Colonies, on the other hand, denied that pretension of the Tories, and said that they as Colonies had the exclusive right to decide all questions of Territorial policy, slavery included, to suit themselves. The Declaration of Independence was put forth, and all the battles of the Revolution were fought in vindication of that great principle. Our fathers did not at first desire independence—they protested that they did not wish to separate from Great Britain; but what they contended for was the right of local self-government in their internal affairs, without the interference of Parliament; and if they could not obtain that right under the British government, they would declare their independence and fight for the right. They did fight the battle out nobly, for seven long years. They carried in triumph the flag of local self-government for the Colonies, until at last Great Britain recognized their independence, and the war ceased. After the independence was established, the different States ceded to the federal government the land which they held in the western country to the north of the Ohio River. This country, where we are now assembled, belonged to the State of Virginia, and she ceded it to the Government—first for the common benefit of the Union, on condition that it should be formed into States and admitted into the Union on an equal footing with the original States. That deed of cession was accepted on the 1st day of March, 1784, and on the same day Thomas Jefferson, the author of the Declaration of Independence, reported his plan for the government of the new Territories or new States [north]west of the Ohio River. By that plan the Territories were recognized as States, the people having the right to decide all international [internal] questions to suit themselves. It is true that Mr. Jefferson proposed to obtain their consent to a proposition prohibiting slavery—not that the present Government had the right or power—but he asked for their consent to such a compact, and Congress struck out the clause and passed the plan of Mr. Jefferson recognizing these Territories as States and the right of the people inhabiting them to decide the slavery question to suit themselves, without the interference of Congress or of any other State or power on earth. Thus you find that up to the time the Constitution was adopted this great principle of local self-government was maintained in the government of the new Territories, or new States as they were then called. Now let me ask you, is it reasonable to suppose, after our fathers had fought the battles of the Revolution in behalf of the right of each Colony to govern itself in respect to its local and domestic concerns, that then they conferred upon Congress the arbitrary sovereign power which they had refused to the British Parliament? [Cries of "Never."] The Republican party, in their Philadelphia National Convention, affirmed that Congress has sovereign power over the Territories for their government, and that it is their duty to prohibit slavery. This is precisely the principle asserted by the British Parliament over the American Colonies. That Parliament and the Tories of King George's time asserted that the former had sovereign power for the government of the Colonies, and the Republican party now repeat that Congress possesses sovereign power for the government of the Territories. Washington, Jefferson, Hancock, Franklin, and the sages of the Revolution decided that the Colonies, Provinces, and Territories,

when organized as political communities, had the inalienable right to govern themselves in respect to their
local and domestic concerns. That is precisely what
I now assert on behalf of the Territories. Let me ask
you, as American citizens, whether the people of the
American Territories under our Constitution are not
entitled to as many rights as the inhabitants of the
British Colonies were before the Revolution. Our
fathers, previous to the Revolution, declared that it
was the inalienable birthright of Englishmen, when
forming political communities, to govern themselves
in their internal polity. Now if that was the birthright
of Englishmen before the Revolution, did it not become
the birthright of all Americans after the Revolution?—
and by virtue of it to govern themselves without the
interference of the American Congress? I only claim
for the people of the Territories those same rights for
which our fathers fought for the American Colonies.
Remember, the Revolution was not fought for the
rights of sovereign States. Our fathers were contending
for the rights of Colonies, of Provinces, of dependent
Territories, when they asserted this inalienable right
of local self-government; and we are asserting now, in
behalf of the people of the American Territories, the
same great inalienable right. Why should it not be
granted? The Republicans tell us that they are willing
to grant this right of self-government in the Territories
in all cases excepting the negro. They do not deny
that the people of the Territories are capable of making
all laws to regulate the relations of husband and wife,
parent and child, and guardian and ward, or all laws
affecting white men; but there is something so sacred

in the rights of the negro that they will not trust them
to the same legislature that controls yours and mine.
[Laughter and cheers.] Then, down south in Kentucky
and a few other States, there are a number of gentlemen calling themselves the Opposition party, who say
that they are not willing to trust their right of property
in negro slaves to the protection of the local law. Bear
in mind that Congress never passed a law for the protection of any kind of property whatever in the Territories of the United States. Congress never passed a
criminal code for any organized Territory. If any man
steals your horse, you do not look to Congress, but
to the local law, for protection. If he robs your house
or your store you cannot apply to Congress, but must
go to the local law for protection. All crimes perpetrated
against the rights and property of the citizen are punished in the State courts or in the Territorial courts,
and not in the Federal courts. Property, life, all your
rights are under the protection of the local law. Then,
if my horse, or your oxen, or dry goods, or property
of every kind is dependent upon the local law for
protection, not only in the States but in the Territories,
why should not negro property be subject to the same
local law? I hold that the people of the Territories
have the same right to legislate in regard to slave
property that they have in regard to any and every
other kind of property. ["Right," and applause.] The
Constitution places all kinds of property on an equal
footing. The Northern and the Southern man enter
the Territory on an exact equality, and carry their
property with them, and hold it there subject to the
local law. If that local law is for them, then they

will be protected; if it is against them, they had better
keep their property somewhere else. Why, then, should
we prohibit the settlers of the Territory from introducing or excluding slavery, either to gratify the Republicans in the North or the Southern Oppositionists
in the slave States? If we will only apply the great
principle of non-intervention by Congress and self-
government in the Territories, leaving the people to
do as they please, there will be peace and harmony
between all sections of the Union. What interest have
you in Ohio in the question of slavery in South Carolina? You say that you do not think that slavery is
necessary or beneficial. That may be true, but your
opinion might be different if your property was all
invested in a nice plantation in South Carolina, where
the white man cannot live and cultivate the soil. In
Ohio it is a question only between the white man and
the negro. [Laughter.] But if you go further South
you will find that it is a question between the negro
and the crocodile. [Renewed laughter.] The question
then may be a very different one under different cli-
mates. Our fathers, when they framed this Government
under which we live, understood this question just as
well, and even better, than we do now. They knew
when they made this Republic that a country so broad
as ours, with such a variety of climate, soil, and productions, must have a variety of interests, requiring
different laws adapted to each locality. They knew that
the laws which would suit the green hills of New
England were illy adapted to the rice plantations of
South Carolina; that the laws and regulations which
would suit the corn and wheat fields of Ohio might

not be well adapted to the sugar plantations of Louisiana; that the people in different localities, having a different climate, different interests and necessities, would want different laws adapted to each locality; and hence, when the Constitution was made, it was adopted on the theory that each State should decide the slavery question for itself, and also all the local and domestic questions. At that time the Union was composed of thirteen States, twelve of which were slave, and one was a free State. Suppose Governor Chase had lived in those days—had been a member of that Convention; and suppose he had risen in his seat and declared that there must be conformity in the local institutions of the different States; or rather, suppose that Mr. Seward had then been living, and a member of that Convention, and had announced that there must be such uniformity, and had declared that there was an irrepressible conflict between free labor and slave labor, free institutions and slave institutions, and that they could not exist together, but must become all free or all slave. What do you think would have been the result? Do you imagine that slavery would have been prohibited everywhere by the Constitution? Would the one free State of Massachusetts have outvoted the other twelve slave States, and have prohibited slavery? On the other hand, if this modern Republican doctrine of uniformity had then prevailed, would it not have fastened slavery by a Constitutional provision on every inch of American soil. ["True," and cheers.] Thus you see that if this doctrine of uniformity had then prevailed, the twelve slaveholding States would have outvoted the one free State, and have established

slavery over the whole continent by an irrepressible
Constitutional provision. The friends of freedom then
protested against uniformity, and contended that each
State should decide the question for itself, just as the
Colonies had contended before them. [Cheers.] Under
that great principle of popular sovereignty, one half
of the original slaveholding States have since abolished
slavery. Connecticut, New Hampshire, Rhode Island,
New York, New Jersey, and Pennsylvania have each
abolished slavery. This result was not accomplished by
the Wilmot Proviso, or by the Ordinance of 1787, or
by the Republican platform, or by the action of Congress, but it was abolished by the free and voluntary
action of the people in each State, acting as they pleased.
["Hear, hear."] I have often been told in Illinois by
the Republicans, and I suppose you have heard the
same here, that Illinois is a free State because of the
sagacity of our fathers in adopting the Ordinance of
1787. I have heard of people assembling in the Western
Reserve of Ohio, and celebrating with great pomp and
veneration the 13th of July because it was the day
on which the Ordinance of 1787 was passed, prohibiting
slavery northwest of the Ohio River; and the learned
speakers would tell the present generation that you
are a free State in Ohio because of that Ordinance.
I should not have the same respect for my fellow
citizens of Ohio, which I do so sincerely entertain,
if I thought that you were free merely because you
could not help it. [Great applause.] They tell you that
Ohio is not free, because she is composed of men; is
not free, because every man has a heart that loves
freedom; is not free, because she wishes and desires;

but she is free because Congress has said so fifty years ago, and would not let her be otherwise. [Cheers.] I tell the people of my State that if they were only free because Congress would not allow them to be otherwise, they do not deserve their freedom. [Great applause.] No people deserve freedom except those who cherish and love it, and will fight for it when they win it. [Cries of "That's right," and cheers.] Gentlemen of Ohio, you are a free State because you chose to be free. [Cries of "That's the doctrine."] You are a free State because you choose to make your own laws, decide your own policy at the ballot box; and you have the laws under which you are now governed be- cause you made them, and not because Congress told you that you must have them. I recognize your right to make just such local laws and establish just such domestic institutions as you choose. When I travel and stop and spend a day with you, as on this occasion, if I do not like your laws I hope I will have the good sense to keep it to myself, and mind my own business— [laughter and applause]—and if you should find any citizen of Illinois coming here, into Ohio, and telling you that your laws do not suit him, all you have to do is to tell him that you did not make them for him— [great laughter]—that you made them for yourselves, and they suit you; and if he does not like them, he can continue to live on the other side of the Wabash. So it should be everywhere throughout the country. If old Virginia, who gave you the land where you now live and where that magnificent temple of liberty has been erected [pointing to the State Capitol] and who you ought to respect, should send her citizens here to

tell you that she does not like your laws, answer that
your veneration cannot protect her in her impudence
in interfering with your rights of self-government. [Ap-
plause.] If you go over to Virginia to steal her negroes,
I trust she will catch you and put you in jail with other
thieves. [Laughter and applause.] If you do not like
old Virginia's laws, stay on this side of the Ohio River
and mind your own business. If this principle is observed, there will be peace and harmony between all
the different States of the Union; but we find some men
who have settled down here in Ohio, who have come
to the conclusion that because you have a law that
suits you here everybody else ought to have it. Suppose
you were to apply that same rule to the social circle,
what would become of your peace and harmony. Must
every lady wear the same bonnet, and every man wear
the same dress? Must we have uniformity throughout?
Because you have a good thing, do you think it is
good for everybody else? [Laughter.] Does every principle extend to every man? There is tyranny in that
family that compels every member of it to exact obedience to one man's will. There is tyranny wherever
you compel uniformity by the power of the federal
government in the local domestic institutions of a
people. [Applause.] The great principle of liberty is
to leave every man and every woman perfectly free in
their action to the full extent that is consistent with
the safety and the peace of society, and that principle
should be applied to States, Territories, and political
communities as well as to individuals. Let that principle
prevail, and there will be a happy brotherhood between
the free and slave States. Why cannot we now live in

peace with our Southern brethren as we did in times
of old, when we fought by their sides and they by ours
to establish the right of the Colonies and Territories
to govern themselves? You found there the patriot army
commanded by the illustrious Washington, and Southern men under him and surrounding him. You found
Southern and Northern men fighting in a common
cause, pouring out their blood upon the same battlefield, and exposing their lives to the same hazard in
order that they and their posterity in all time to come,
might enjoy those great principles of self-government
for which they were struggling. Why cannot we Southern and Northern men now join, and side by side as
before, in a common cause, protect the right of every
State and every Territory, every Colony and every
Province, to govern itself in respect to its own local
and domestic concerns? Why should the North be
arrayed against the South, and the South against the
North? These geographical parties are of recent origin.
They were unknown in the times of the Revolution,
when our liberties were first established. Go to one
of the Republican meetings, and you will find their
orators will deal in appeals to the Southern passions
and Southern prejudices against Northern people and
Northern institutions. What is the object of these men
now in thus fanning the flames of sectional strife at the
North and the South, dividing the people by a geographical line, and making them enemies on the right
of the line to those who are on the left? To what
patriotic object can this course be pursued that is the
object of the Republican party, except it be to fan
sectional strife and discord? Take their platform from

the begining to the end, and it has a negro under every plank. There is not a white plank in their entire platform. It is all armed against the South, and if you go South among the fire-eaters of Louisiana you will find their petitions aimed as directly against the North. A Northern man does not know the bad set of men he lives among until he goes down South and hears it, and a Southern man does not know what a bad character he is until he attends a Republican meeting and hears himself described. Now, the Democratic party desires to harmonize all conflicting interests and passions in the Republic upon that great principle which underlies all our institutions, and declares that the people in every State and every Territory shall be free to decide the slavery question, and every other question, for themselves. But the trouble is that you will find every once in a while a man—I know that there are not enough of them in the country to make mile posts along the railroad—but there is once in a while a man who will tell you that slavery exists in the Territories by virtue of the Constitution of the United States; and wherever a Northern man makes that discovery you will find that the Southerner at once seizes it and declares that if slavery does exist in the Territory by authority of the Constitution, it is then the duty of Congress to pass all laws necessary to protect the rights secured by the Constitution; and then comes the demand for the slave code in the Territories. Now, there need be no diversity of principle on this question if each man will read the Constitution of the United States, and then take an oath to support it. Just look into the Constitution, and then you will find what a slave is, who may be a slave, where they may be held, and by what authority they are held. You will find it all in one section. I have not the book with me, but I can repeat that section to you.

"No person held to service in labor in one State under the law thereof, escaping into another, shall be released by any law or regulation therein, but shall be delivered up to the party to whom said service or labor may be due."

Now, by the express provisions of that clause of the Constitution, a slave is a person held to service or labor in one State under the laws thereof—not under the Constitution of the United States—not under the laws of the United States—not by virtue of any federal authority, but in a State under the laws thereof. What becomes of this newly discovered doctrine that slavery exists everywhere by virtue of the Constitution of the United States? It is denied by the Constitution itself. Every child who has ever read the instrument knows that slavery is the creature of the local law, exists only where the local law sanctions and establishes it, and exists only in a State under the laws thereof; and inasmuch as a Territory is a State within the meaning of that clause of the Constitution, slavery may exist in a Territory the same as in a State, under the laws thereof. Hence, if the people of a Territory desire slavery, all they have to do is to pass laws sanctioning and protecting it. If they do not want slavery, all they have to do is to withhold all legislation and all protection. Thus you find that the people of the Territories, as well as of the States, have the right to regulate that question for themselves. But there will come up

a question at the opening of the next session of
Congress that will put the Republicans to the test in
the doctrine of federal intervention—and not only the
Republicans but the Southern opposition to the Democracy also. The people of New Mexico, which Territory
was organized in 1850, refused for many years to sanction or protect slavery, but about twelve months ago
the legislature passed a law establishing a slave code
for the Territory and protecting the institution in
their midst. On the other hand, in the Territory of
Kansas, which was organized in 1854, the first legislature
that assembled passed a slave code and established
slavery in the Territory, and that act remained on the
statute books until the 9th day of February, 1858,
when they passed another act in the following words:

Be it enacted, That an act entitled "An Act to punish
offences against slave property," which took effect on
the 15th of September, 1855, be and the same is hereby
repealed.

By that unfriendly legislation on the part of Kansas
in repealing all laws providing for the protection of
slave property, all laws punishing crimes against slave
property, and all laws conferring jurisdiction upon the
Courts to try men for offences against that kind of
property, slavery has been and is excluded from the
Territory; and by the slave code established in New
Mexico about the time it was repealed in Kansas,
slavery exists in the former Territory. Now, the Republican party, by its platform adopted at Philadelphia,
stands pledged to the power and duty of Congress to
prohibit slavery everywhere in the Territories, and we
may expect to see that party, at the opening of the next

session of Congress, bring in a law to repeal the slave code of New Mexico and to prohibit slavery in that Territory. If they are conscientious and sincere men they will do it, for it is the fundamental article in their creed—the cornerstone in their temple—the only Territorial plank in their platform. If they are honest men they must bring forward their bill to repeal the slave code of New Mexico; and at the same time that Mr. Seward brings in his bill to abolish slavery in that Territory, we must expect to find a Kentucky member of Congress—one of those recently elected by the Opposition upon the doctrine of Congressional intervention—bringing in a bill to establish a slave code for Kansas. Of course, the Southern Opposition, who are pledged to Congressional intervention and Congressional protection of slavery in the Territories, must bring forward their bill to establish and protect slavery in Kansas. Thus we have presented to us two cases for Congressional intervention—one from the North and the other from the South—one against slavery and the other for slavery—one to compel the people not to have slavery when they want it, and the other to compel the people to have slavery when they do not want it. Now, what is to be the position of the Democratic party when these two bills are brought up for Congressional action. I can tell you what course one man will pursue. It will be to tell the Republicans that they shall not interfere with the institutions of New Mexico, and then to say to the Southern interventionists: "Hands off—you shall not touch the domestic institutions of Kansas!" [Cries of "Right," and cheers.] We will say to the Republicans: "If the people of New Mexico

want a slave code, they have a right to it, and if they
desire slavery, let them have it until they get tired of
it, and then let them abolish it themselves. It is their
business, not ours." And then to the Southern men we
will say, "If the people of Kansas do not want slavery,
it shall not be forced on them; if they do not want a
slave code, Congress shall not force one upon them;
if they ever desire one, let them make it themselves.
It is their business, affects their rights and interests,
and let them adjust it satisfactorily to themselves."
With all due respect to this intelligent audience, permit
me to say that it is a great mistake for you to suppose
that you know better what the people of New Mexico
want than they do themselves. It is a great mistake
for Southern Oppositionists and Southern fire-eaters to
imagine that they know better what the people of
Kansas need than the people who live there. It is a
great mistake to suppose that you or they are any more
disinterested than the people of the Territories themselves. If you are capable of deciding the slavery question for yourselves in Ohio, and have brains enough
not only to decide it here but to decide it for the
people of Kansas and New Mexico, would you be any
less gratified to do so when you moved to these Territories, and became citizens of them? Who are the
people of the Territories that they are not capable of
self-government? Are they not your brothers and cous-
ins, and sons and fathers? Are they not as capable of
governing themselves there as you are of governing
yourselves here? [Cries of "Yes," and applause.] Why,
then, should you try to interfere with them? Oh, you are
afraid they will make bad laws! Well, if they do make

bad laws, perhaps you would not have much the advantage of them. Still, I will not say you have bad laws in Ohio, but I do know some States where the laws are not very good ones; but if they choose to make bad laws it is their right to do it, and let them suffer under them until they get tired of them, when they will elect members to the legislature who will repeal them. This pretence that you cannot trust the people for fear they will ruin themselves by bad laws is always the resort of tyrants the world over. Just go to Francis Joseph of Austria, and ask him why he did not allow the Italians over in Lombardy to make their own laws. He would tell you at once that if he had done so they would have ruined themselves by bad laws. So it is throughout the world. Tyrants and despots never will trust the people because they are not capable of governing themselves. They love the people so much that they will not allow them to burn their fingers and ruin themselves by bad legislation. No; this doctrine that the people of a Territory cannot govern themselves will not do. Whenever there are people enough in a Territory to entitle them to be organized into a government, they are capable of self-government. If they are not, why do you give them a government? If they are not able to make laws to govern themselves in respect to their domestic concerns, why do you give them a legislative at all? You hear gentlemen say that the first few settlers were squatters on the public domain, and ought not to be permitted to make laws for other people who have not yet gone there. Well, if they ought not to be permitted to make laws, why do you give them a government? Why do you give it to them unless they are enough to constitute a government, and are able to exercise the power after you have given it to them? This cry about squatter sovereignty has failed to frighten the children anywhere North or South. When the term was first used by Mr. Calhoun, he was alluding not to the powers of a Territorial government under the Constitution and laws of the United States, but to the right of a few squatters on the public domain, but in violation of law, to set up a government independent of the Government of the United States. For instance, a large number of people had gone to Oregon before the treaty of joint occupancy had been annulled, and before we had extended the laws of the United States over it; and finding no law to protect them, they established a government of their own, and by that government excluded slavery. The government was against the laws of the United States, was not accountable to the United States, and Mr. Calhoun pronounced it squatter sovereignty because the settlers were there in violation of law, and had a government in antagonism to that of the United States. Well, he denounced that, and since his death you will find young Calhouns, all around the country, talking about squatter sovereignty without knowing how they are applying the term. But, call it what you please, I hold that it is the inherent, inalienable right of all American citizens, when forming themselves into governments according to law, to govern themselves in respect to their local and domestic concerns; and I will apply that principle to the Territories as well as to the States. Let it only be observed, and this people can live in peace forever, and the Union can continue to exist in all time to come, divided into free and slave States, as our fathers made it. Adopt that principle, and this Government is capable of indefinite expansion. Steady growth and gradual expansion is one of the laws of our national existence. With the rapid national increase and the foreign emigration and fraternization, more territory is required for homes for our citizens. It was thought when the Revolution was fought that the few States along the Atlantic slope were all the territory that would ever be needed. The doctrine of that day was that the Ohio Valley was too far off to be united with the Atlantic States. At another period it was thought that we would never wish to go beyond the Mississippi River, and that there was more territory east of it than we would ever want; but a few years more exposed the folly of such an idea, and Mr. Jefferson acquired Louisiana, extending our domains to the Rocky Mountains, and perhaps including part of Oregon. Still there were those who thought we had territory enough and too much. In the days of John Quincy Adams, Jackson, Van Buren, Harrison, and Tyler, there was a settled policy to remove the Indians from Ohio, Indiana, Georgia, Alabama, and Mississippi, and plant them on the west side of the Mississippi, in Arkansas, Missouri, and Iowa, making a perpetual barrier from Texas to Canada, by pledging the faith of this nation that they should never be disturbed in their new settlements or included within any State or Territory so long as grass should grow and water run. The idea was to make an Indian barrier, beyond which civilization, Christianity, and democracy should never go. I had the honor to be the first to make the assault upon that policy that was to separate the Mississippi Valley from the Pacific Ocean, and I brought in the Nebraska bill as early as 1843–44 to break up that policy. I renewed it each year for ten years until I broke the barrier through, and the last finishing touch by which it was brought about was given by my friend here, Colonel Manypenny, as Commissioner of Indian Affairs, who had the glory of doing the finishing act that broke the barrier and consecrated to settlement the whole country stretching to the Pacific Ocean. Now we have reached the Pacific, we have acquired California and New Mexico, we are told that we have enough and we will never want more. That is what they told me in 1850 when they made the Clayton-Bulwer Treaty about Central America. I denounced it in the Senate because it contained a pledge that neither the United States nor Great Britain would ever colonize, annex, or exercise dominion over any part of Central America. They asked me what I wanted with Central America; I told them I did not want it then, but the time would come when our safety and destiny would compel us to take it; and I would never pledge the faith of this nation to any foreign power, that we would never do in all time to come what our interest, safety, and honor might compel us to do. I resisted the Clayton-Bulwer Treaty, therefore, because it contained a pledge that the United States would never acquire dominion over our great highway to California. Why, they said, it was so far we would never want it. I told them, yes, it was a good ways off—that it was half way to California, and on the direct route to it. Well, perhaps, the time has not yet come for us to want Central America, but the time is coming. We are bound to extend and spread until we absorb the entire continent of America, including the adjacent islands, and become one grand ocean-bound republic. [Cheers.] I do not care whether you like it or not; you cannot help it! It is the decree of Providence. This continent was set apart as an asylum for the oppressed of the whole world, and as a nursery for liberty—and here the people are collecting from all parts of the world, and taking shelter under the shadows of the great tree of Liberty. This emigration cannot be stopped, and you must have more land. A wise man always conforms his action to a policy which he cannot prevent, and hence I say, Let America have a policy in harmony with her destiny. Let us be what our numbers and what our position require us to be—not only an example to the friends of liberty, but a terror to the oppressors of man throughout the world. Let America have a firm, fixed policy abroad as well as at home; but, above all, let our policy at home be that which serves and preserves liberty—liberty at the fireside—liberty in the regulation of our local and domestic concerns. Now, my friends, why should not all conservative men—all lovers of peace and of the law— all friends of the Union—rally in support of these great principles upon which our Union was formed, and from the maintenance of which can you alone expect harmony and peace. In conclusion, permit me to return you my acknowledgments for the cordial reception and attentive audience you have given me today. I feel profoundly grateful to you, and would not be just to myself or my own feelings if I retired from the stand without making my acknowledgments to your kindness. [At the close of Mr. Douglas' remarks, he was greeted with the most enthusiastic and long-continued applause.]

SPEECH OF STEPHEN A. DOUGLAS

at Cincinnati, Ohio, September 9, 1859 [1]

Fellow Citizens of Cincinnati: There seems to be a fatality accompanying my attempts to address you on the great political topics of the day. Four years ago when I came here for the purpose of addressing you, I was attacked with a disease of the throat, which deprived me of the opportunity of being heard and confined me to my room for many months. While on my way here yesterday I had a recurrence of the same attack which rendered it impossible for me to comply with my engagement to address you last night, and I fear I will not be able to address you this evening in a way satisfactory to you or myself; but trust that if you indulge me for a few moments until we shall get fairly into the subject that my voice will return, so that I shall be able to be heard even to the extremities of this immense crowd.

I desire to say, in the first place, that it is no part of my present purpose to discuss any question appertaining to the internal polity or domestic affairs of the State of Ohio. So far as the topics that are now pending before the country affect your internal affairs, I choose to leave them to those who are directly interested in them; but there are certain great principles of universal application, affecting the people of the entire country, in which we are all alike interested, and which can be advocated in Cincinnati as well as

[1] *Cincinnati Enquirer,* September 10, 1859.

in Louisville—in the free States as well as in the slaveholding States. So long as we live under a Constitution,
which is the paramount law of the entire Republic,
any political creed is radically wrong which cannot
be proclaimed in the same form wherever the American
flag waves or the Constitution rules. [Cheers.] You will
permit me to remark, also, that the Democratic party
is the only political organization in this country which
can preserve the peace, the harmony, and the fraternity
of this glorious Union. [Renewed cheering.] There ever
has been—there ever will be—two parties in this country: the one is founded on the great fundamental principle of self-government, which underlies all our institutions; the other is the antagonism of the Democratic
party.

The history of the Democratic party is the history of
this Republic; the record of the Democratic achieve-
ments contains a list of all those glorious measures
which have characterized the unparalleled growth and
development of this Republic. The Opposition party
to the Democracy at some periods of our history has
been known by one name, at another by another, but
still its cardinal features are opposition to the Democratic organization and principles. In the Northern
States, at this time, this Opposition party is known as
the Republican party; in the Southern States it does
not assume that name, but sympathizes with all the
Republicans in all their implacable hostilities to the
Democratic party. The great question which separates
the Democratic party from the Opposition party at the
present time involves the slavery question, the Opposition party contending that the slavery question is a

federal question to be determined and controlled by federal authority, and the Democratic party holding that the slavery question is a local question, a State question, depending on local authority and to be determined by the people interested in it in the several States and Territories of this Union.

According to the platform of the Republican party, adopted at Philadelphia in 1856, it is affirmed that Congress has the power and duty to prohibit slavery in all the Territories of the United States, and they assert the sovereign power of Congress over the Territories for their government. This doctrine of the sovereign power of the general government over the Territories or Colonies is not new, nor is it advanced by the Republicans of the present day for the first time. The same doctrine was asserted by the King and Parliament of Great Britain over the American Colonies before the Revolution. You will all recollect that the great Webster said, and many others have repeated the remark, that the American Revolution was fought against a pre-amble—that preamble to an act of Parliament declaring that the British Parliament had the power and the right to bind the American Colonies in all cases whatever. To that preamble the Colonies replied, denying the right of Parliament to interfere with their local and domestic concerns. When the American Colonies assembled at Philadelphia, in 1774, for the first time, they proceeded to assert a Bill of Rights for the Colonies. In that Bill of Rights, they acknowledged and conceded to Parliament the right to pass all laws regulating commerce and touching those matters which were Imperial and not Colonial. But on the other hand they

asserted that these Colonies possessed the sole and exclusive power of legislation in their respective Provincial legislatures in all cases of taxation and internal
polity. Thus, you will find the Tories of the Revolution
asserted the very doctrine at that day contended for by
the Republicans of this day: that Congress, or Parliament, have sovereign power over the Colonies or
Territories for their government. Our fathers of the
Revolution resisted that claim of Parliamentary sovereignty over the Colonies with blood, and with their
lives, during the Revolutionary War; and the Democratic party of this day are prepared to resist, by all
Constitutional means, this claim of the Republican
party to exercise sovereign power over the Colonies or
Territories of the United States. [Cheers.]

If any person will take the trouble to trace the history
of this question, he will find that the Democratic party
today stands precisely where the Whigs of the Revolution stood, and that the opponents of the Democracy
advocate the same principles that were contended for
by the British Parliament and the Tories of the Revolution. I do not use these terms in any offensive sense.
I do not impeach the patriotism, nor impugn the
motives of those who advocate this doctrine of the right
of Congress to bind the Territories in all cases whatever. I simply assert that their claim of sovereignty
over the Territories is the precise claim against which
all the battles of the Revolution were fought, when
that claim was urged by the British Parliament over the
American Colonies. The Republicans declare in their
platform that in the exercise of this sovereign power
over the Territories, it is the duty of Congress to

prohibit slavery, wherever it may be found, in all the Territories of the United States. The Southern Opposition party on the other hand assert the sovereign power of Congress over the slavery question, and demand that it shall be exercised for the protection and maintenance of slavery in all the Territories of the United States.

Thus you find that the Southern Opposition party and the Northern Republican party advocate the same principle—that of Congressional intervention on the subject of slavery—and differ only as to the application of that principle. The Northern interventionists demand that the power of the federal government shall be exercised to destroy and prohibit slavery everywhere in the Territories; the Southern interventionists demand that the power of the federal government shall be exerted to protect and maintain slavery in the Territories. On the other hand, the Democratic party stand firmly by the principle of non-intervention by Congress with slavery anywhere, and popular sovereignty in the States and Territories alike. [Tremendous cheering.] The Democratic principle on this subject was never more clearly defined than in the letter of Mr. Buchanan accepting the Cincinnati nomination in 1856. [Continued cheering.] In that letter of acceptance, as you will find it represented in that banner over your heads [pointing to a large banner suspended across the street], Mr. Buchanan declared that the principles of the Nebraska bill were as ancient as free government itself, and asserted that the people of a Territory, like those of a State, should decide for themselves whether slavery should or not exist within their limits. I stand here tonight defending that great principle of popular sovereignty and self-government in the precise language of James Buchanan in his letter of acceptance. [Applause.]

The Democratic party are a unit in the assertion of the principles of the Cincinnati platform. Let us stand by that platform as it reads and as it was expounded in the canvass of 1856, and explained by Mr. Buchanan in his letter of acceptance. The Cincinnati platform is as good a platform as any Democrat has a right to demand. Let us stand firmly upon it as it exists, without the addition of a single plank or the removal of a single pillar. [Applause.] Standing upon that platform the Democratic party asserts that the people of a Territory, like those of a State, have a right to decide for themselves whether slavery shall or shall not exist within their limits. The enemies of the Democratic party, North and South, deny this doctrine of non-intervention and popular sovereignty. The Southern interventionists demand intervention by Congress for the protection and maintenance of slavery; the interventionists of the North demand the interference of Congress for the destruction and prohibition of slavery. The Democracy everywhere deny the right of Congress to interfere, one way or the other, for or against slavery; but assert that the people themselves shall decide whether they will or will not have slavery within their limits.

These different positions of the Democratic party and our opponents are not merely idle, speculative, or theoretical questions. They are practical issues presented to the people this day for settlement. Already has New Mexico on the one hand, and Kansas on the

other, presented a case for Congressional intervention.
You will remember that several years after the passage
of the organization of the Territory of New Mexico,
the legislature refused to pass a slave code for the protection of slave property in the Territory. But during
the last year the Territorial legislature of New Mexico
passed a slave code protecting and maintaining slavery
in the Territory as a domestic institution, and punishing all offenses against slave property. The Republican
party stands pledged by their platform to repeal the
slave code which the people of New Mexico have
adopted, and to abolish slavery where the people have
declared that they want it. On the other hand, the
people of Kansas Territory, through their first legislature, passed a law protecting and maintaining slavery
in that Territory; but on the 9th of February, 1858,
the Territorial legislature of Kansas repealed their slave
code, abolished all the remedies for the protection of
slave property, and withdrew from the Courts any jurisdiction over the subject. By this unfriendly legislation
on the part of Kansas, slavery today is excluded from
that Territory. Now the Southern Opposition to the
Democratic party tell you that Congress must interfere,
and maintain and protect slavery in Kansas against the
wishes of the people and in defiance of the local law,
while the Northern Opposition, called the Republican
party, demand that Congress shall deprive the people
of New Mexico of slavery, and abolish the slave code
against the wishes of the people and in violation of
the local law. To both of these doctrines the Democratic
party maintains a strong, inflexible, and irresistible opposition. [Cheers.] We assert that if the people of New

Mexico want slavery they have a right to it. [Cheers.] We assert that if they want a slave code they have a right to pass it. We assert that they, having passed such a code through their legislature, it must and shall stand the law of the land until they repeal it themselves; and in reference to Kansas, the Democratic party also assert that if the people of Kansas do not want slavery it shall not be forced on them. We assert that if Kansas does not want a slave code, Congress shall never compel her to have it [cheers]; that if the people of Kansas prefer free institutions, they have a right to them; and that the Southern Opposition, or the Northern Opposition, or any other Opposition, shall not overrule the wishes of the people. [Applause.]

Now, if the Opposition to the Democratic party, either North or South, are sincere in their professions, they are compelled at the next session of Congress to bring forward a law to carry out their doctrines in the Territories. If Mr. Seward be an honest man, he must bring in a bill to abolish slavery and repeal the slave code of New Mexico. If the Southern Opposition members, elected in Kentucky and other Southern States, be honest men when they assert that it is the duty of Congress to protect slavery in the Territories against the wishes of the people, then they are bound to bring in laws to establish and maintain slavery in Kansas, in opposition to the wishes of the people. Hence I say the question of intervention or non-intervention of Congress with the domestic concerns of the Territories can be no longer postponed. That issue must be met. Either the doctrine of non-intervention and popular sovereignty must be acquiesced in and carried out in good faith, or else Congress must interfere for slavery or against slavery, in opposition to the wishes of the people in each locality. Now let me ask you how you can ever have peace on the slavery question so long as Congress is allowed to interfere with it. Any man who advocates Congressional intervention is an enemy to the peace and harmony of the States of this Union.

There can be no peace on the slavery question; there can be no truce in the sectional strife; there can be no fraternity between the Northern and Southern States so long as Congress is permitted to interfere with the local and domestic institutions of any Territories of this Union. That question was decided distinctly in 1850, when the Compromise Measures were passed. You all recollect that during that struggle, there was a Southern party demanding Congressional intervention to maintain slavery in opposition to the wishes of the people, and, on the other hand, there was an ultra Northern antislavery party demanding Congressional intervention to abolish and prohibit slavery, regardless of the wishes of the people or the local law. These two ultra parties, these two interventionists, the one Southern and the other Northern, disturbed the harmony of the country, and periled the existence of the Union.

In that great struggle, the immortal Clay, who had performed his mission on earth, and retired to the shades of Ashland to prepare for a better and a happier world, soon, in his retirement, heard the rumbling, harsh, discordant notes of sectional strife and sectional controversy, and came forth from his home to resume his seat in the Senate—that great theater of his great deeds—to see if he, by his experience, by his wisdom, and by the renown of his famous name, could not do something to calm the troubled waters, and restore peace and fraternity to a divided and distracted country. [Cries of "Glorious" and "Hear, hear."]

From the moment that Henry Clay made his appearance in the Senate, all party strife was hushed; all partisan controversy ceased; the voice of discord was no longer heard; and Clay was recognized and proclaimed the leader of all the Union men North and South, Whigs and Democrats. For the period of six months we assembled in caucus every day, with Clay in the chair, Cass upon his right and Webster upon his left hand, and the Whigs and Democrats ranged on either side, promiscuously supporting and sustaining Clay in his efforts to devise a plan to restore peace and harmony to the country. [Cheers.]

You all know the result of these deliberations—the Compromise Measures of 1850 were adopted, peace was restored, and the country was again reunited. Now, let me ask you upon what principle does that Compromise rest. Examine the bills and search the records, and you will find that the great principle which underlies those measures is the right of the people of each State, and each Territory while a Territory, to decide the slavery question for themselves. [Three cheers.] Mr. Seward, Governor Chase, Mr. Sumner, and the leaders of the Republican party united with the Southern fire-eaters in resisting the Compromise Measures of 1850 because they asserted the doctrine of non-intervention and popular sovereignty.

We passed those measures over their heads. The Union men, Whigs and Democrats, Clay, Webster, and

Cass, supported and sustained by the younger men of the two parties, passed the Compromise Measures, and adopted the principle of non-intervention and popular sovereignty over the heads of Northern abolitionists and Southern disunionists. [Cheers.] I stand here to-night to vindicate and maintain that same principle of non-intervention and popular sovereignty against Northern abolitionists and Southern interventionists. [Three cheers for Douglas.] I care not where the interventionist lives, by what name he calls himself, or on which side he intervenes, he is an enemy of Democratic principles if he is intervening at all against the peace of the country. [Cheers.]

This great principle must be met and must be decided in the Presidential election of 1860. [Cries of "You are our choice," "Hurrah for Douglas," "He's the man," etc.]

Mr. Seward, who is the most eminent and authoritative expounder of Republican principles, according to the modern designation of the party, tells you there is an "irrepressible conflict" between freedom and slavery, free labor and slave labor, free States and slave States, which must continue to rage until the States all become free or all become slave. [A voice, "The star-spangled banner."] Mr. Seward is undoubtedly a man of eminent ability—he is the most authoritative expounder of Republican doctrines; but when he uttered that sentiment he ought to have felt bound by a sense of justice and courtesy to have acknowledged that he borrowed the sentiment from an eminent leader of his own party. [Laughter.] Three months previous to Mr. Seward's Rochester speech, Mr. Abraham Lincoln, of Illinois, in making a speech accepting a nomination of the Republican party of his State, had announced the same principle in more explicit and emphatic language. He told the people of Illinois that "agitation would not cease until a crisis should be met and passed"; that "a house divided against itself could not stand"; that "this Union, separated into free and slave States, could not endure permanently, and that the contest must go on until the States should become all free or all slave— all the one thing or all the other."

Did you ever hear of a Republican that dissented from the position of Mr. Lincoln in that canvass in Illinois? [A voice, "Never."] Does not the Republican party throughout the land acquiesce in and endorse the doctrine of Mr. Seward in his Rochester speech, or the similar sentiments of Governor Chase, in Ohio? [A voice, "We are satisfied."] The doctrine of the leader of the Republican party is that the States must become all free or all slave; that they can not endure part free and part slave; that the contest must continue and increase in fury until the one class of States has been annihilated by the complete triumph of the other. Such is the real purpose of the Republican party. Now, when do you expect to have peace on the slavery question? When do you expect to have harmony between Cincinnati and Covington, between Ohio and Kentucky, if you wait until the States become all free or all slave? [A voice, "When they change their politics."] A Republican in the crowd says he expects that harmony when freedom triumphs. There you find an endorsement of the position of Seward and Lincoln, that the States must be all free in order to have harmony. [A voice, "Hit him again."]

Let us examine for a moment this doctrine of uniformity contended for by the Republicans on the slavery question. Is that doctrine consistent with the genius and principles of our federal Constitution?

I assert that the framers of the Constitution neither contemplated nor desired uniformity in respect to the local and domestic institutions of the several States. They knew that in a country as broad as this, with such variety of climate, of soil, and of interest, there must be necessarily a corresponding variety in the local laws and domestic institutions, adapted to the wants and interests of each locality. [Cries of "Hear, hear" and "That is it."] They knew that the laws and institutions which were well adapted to the granite hills of New Hampshire were unsuited to the tobacco plantations of Virginia; they knew that the laws and institutions which were adapted to the wheat fields and corn fields of Ohio, were not well adapted to the sugar plantations of Louisiana; they knew that the laws and institutions which would suit the prairies of Illinois would be unsuited to the gulches and placers and gold mines of California.

Knowing these facts, they framed a system of government composed of independent States, each with a legislature of its own, with sovereign power to make all laws and all institutions affecting their internal policy to suit themselves, without the intervention of Congress or any other power on Earth. [A voice on the skirts of the crowd—"Hurrah!"]

But let us suppose for a moment that this new doctrine of uniformity in the domestic institutions had prevailed when the Constitution had been framed; what could have been the result? Bear in mind that the

Union was then composed of thirteen States, twelve of which were slaveholding States, and one only was a free State. Suppose Mr. Seward or Mr. Lincoln had been a member of the Convention which had framed the Constitution, and had risen and fixing his eye upon the immortal Washington, who presided over that august body, had said, "A house divided against itself can not stand; this Union composed of free and slave States can not endure; there is an irrepressible conflict between freedom and slavery, free States and slave States, which must endure until slavery shall be abolished everywhere, or established everywhere, throughout the Republic."

Suppose they had succeeded in impressing this new, modern Republican doctrine on the Convention that framed the Constitution; do you think that slavery would have been abolished in all the States? Do you think that the one free State would have outvoted the twelve slaveholding States in that Convention, and abolished slavery everywhere? Or would the twelve slave States have outvoted the one free State, and finally established slavery on every inch of the American Republic by an irrepealable Constitutional provision? [Applause.]

Thus, you see, if this modern doctrine of uniformity on the slavery question had prevailed when the Government was founded, we would have been a united slaveholding nation, with slavery fastened on the people of Ohio today, beyond the power of resistance. [Voices, "That is so," "That is the truth."] At that day the friends of freedom and the enemies of slavery only asked that Congress should not interfere; that the fed-

eral government should not wield its power either for
or against; but that each State should be left free to
decide for itself.

The Convention acted upon the principle asserted
in that moral triumph of the day, that error could be
tolerated as long as freedom of opinion was preserved
to combat it. They were willing to leave each State
as they found it, free or slave, with the right to continue
slavery as they pleased. Our system of government was
established on that principle, the principle which they
had inherited from the Colonies, which they had
achieved by the blood of the Revolution. The principle
was not new to the framers of the Constitution. They
knew that the first serious point of dispute between the
American Colonies and the British Government had
arisen on the slavery question; they knew that the
American Colonies, before the Revolution, always
claimed the right to decide the slavery question to suit
themselves as a local, domestic institution affecting their
internal polity. They knew that this Government had
denied that right to the Colonies, and, in lieu of that
right, reasserted the doctrine that Parliament possessed
sovereign power over the Colonies, and could bind
them in all cases whatsoever, including the slavery
question; the same as the modern Republican party and
the interventionists, North and South, claim that Congress possesses the sovereign power over the Territories,
and hence may intervene, in violation of the wishes of
the people and the sanctity of the local law, to overrule local legislation and control the domestic institutions.

Our fathers, before the Revolution, claimed that it

was the birthright of Englishmen—the inalienable right —when formed into communities, to decide all local questions to suit themselves, and the battles of the Revolution were fought in defense of that principle.

Now, let me ask of you if it was the birthright of all Englishmen before the Revolution to decide these local questions to suit themselves, did it not become the birthright of all Americans after the Revolution, by virtue of it, to settle all such questions to suit themselves? [A voice, "That is so!"] In other words, are not the people of American Territories, being American citizens—our brethren and kindred—entitled to as many rights of self-government as British subjects were before the Revolution? [A voice, "They ought to be."]

The Democratic party only claim for the Territories those identical rights which our fathers claimed and maintained at the point of the bayonet for the American Colonies. You must bear in mind that our fathers were not contending for the rights of the sovereign States; they were struggling for the rights of Colonies— of Provinces—of Territories—their exclusive right to govern themselves in respect to their local and internal polity; and because Great Britain would not permit them to exercise their right they then struck for independence rather than give up the inestimable privileges of self-government. [A voice, "That was all right."]

I stand tonight, as I have stood for ten years, vindicating this great and inestimable right of local self-government in all political communities—States as well as Territories. [A voice, "We'll make you President"; another, "You have got your baggage checked and a through ticket."] That is the mission of the Democratic party to maintain this inestimable right. It was once the joint duty of the Whig and Democratic parties, according to their respective pledges, to maintain that principle independent of party creeds. In 1850 that doctrine was incorporated into the Territorial policy by the joint action of the two great parties.

At that day it was unfair and unjust to claim the doctrine as peculiarly Democratic or peculiarly Whig to the exclusion of the other party, for it was the joint work and common property of both parties; accordingly in 1852, when the Whig party assembled in National Convention at Baltimore and nominated General Scott as its candidate for the Presidency, they incorporated into the platform a resolution declaring the purpose and pledge of the Whig party in all time to come to adhere to the principles of the Compromise Measures of 1850 as the rule of action in the organization of Territories and the admission of new States. When the Democratic party assembled in National Convention at the same place one month afterward and nominated General Pierce for the Presidency, we asserted the same principle and gave the same pledge. Thus the two great parties—the Whig and Democratic—in 1852 stood pledged to stick to doctrines of non-intervention and popular sovereignty.

When, at a subsequent term, Mr. Seward and Governor Chase and Mr. Sumner and others concluded to strangle the old Whig party and abolitionize its Northern forces, they found it necessary to abolish the party, to dissolve its organization, and change its name before they could repudiate the doctrine of non-intervention and popular sovereignty. They appealed to all the old

Whigs of the country to remain steadfast in their hatred
to Democracy and their hostility to the Democratic
organization, while they tied cords around their hands
and feet, blindfolded them, and led them into the
abolition camp for Father Giddings to christen them
in the abolition faith. [Laughter—a voice, "Hit him
again, he has no friends here!"] Even to this day whenever an old line Whig who has stood by his faith and
by his integrity refuses to join the abolitionists, or
to be enrolled in the Republican ranks, he is called a
deserter. Deserter from what? Did he ever belong to a
sectional party? [A voice, "No, sir: Was a Whig ever an
abolitionist?"]

But yet every old Whig who stands today where Clay
stood in 1850, and at the time of his death, asserting
the doctrine of non-intervention and popular sovereignty and acting with those who stand firm by
that doctrine, is abused by the Republican party as
a turncoat and a traitor. To all men who make that
charge against the old Whigs, I will remind them of
the last speech of Henry Clay before the legislature of
Kentucky, in which he told them that if the day ever
came, as he apprehended it must soon, when the Whig
party would be reduced to a miserable abolition faction,
that he would join the Democracy and uphold the
Constitution. [Applause.] Clay, to the last, stood forth
as the embodiment of Union principles, Union measures, conservative views, which would keep united, as
bands of brothers, all the States of this Union, and make
the Republic perpetual.

The Whig party was pre-eminently a conservative
party. Since that Whig party has been dissolved, and

the sectional men that belonged to it have gone over to the Opposition and become the interventionists either in the North or South, there was nothing left for the conservative Whigs except to join the Democracy, and by our joint efforts, if possible, maintain the peace of the country and the perpetuity of the Union.

I assert to you again, peace and fraternity cannot be maintained between the different sections of the Union except on the great principles of non-intervention and popular sovereignty. Hence, let us unite as one man in favor of these doctrines. [A voice, "Good boy!"] Let not any personal jealousy, nor personal rivalry, nor personal hatred, disturb the harmony of the only party that can preserve the Union. [Applause.]

In regard to former disputes, and the animosities growing out of them, "Let the dead bury the dead." [Applause.] Remember those disputes only for the purpose of profiting by them and avoiding the evils which produced them. While I would make any sacrifice, personal to myself, to preserve the unity and harmony of the Democratic party in its time-honored principles, never, never would I yield one iota, one jot, or one tittle of those principles to gain the Presidency. [Applause.] The Democratic party has a higher duty, a nobler province, and a more honorable aim than merely to carry an election, and get possession of the Government.

The mission of the Democratic party is to maintain inviolate those great principles of State equality and popular sovereignty and local self-government on which our entire political system rests. We should remember that the great characteristic feature of a free government

is obedience to law. There can be no liberty without
law and there can be no law unless there is implicit
obedience to the constituted authorities within their
legitimate spheres. [Applause.]

The Constitution of the United States has declared
that that instrument and all laws passed in pursuance
of it are the supreme law of the land, anything in the
constitution and law of any State to the contrary notwithstanding; and that all State judges are bound
thereby [a voice, "Now for Swan"; another voice, "Give
us a little talk about Swan"]; and whenever the people of Ohio, or any portion of them, elect a judge of
the supreme court of this State, before he can enter
upon the discharge of the functions of his office, he
is required to place his hand upon the holy evangelists
and appeal to the everliving God for the sincerity of
his vow, that he will support and maintain the Constitution of the United States, anything in the constitution and laws of the State of Ohio to the contrary
notwithstanding. [Applause.]

Yet I have heard that of a political party who desire
a man for judge who [a voice, "Now we get it!"] would
stand pledged to violate the very oath which he was
compelled to take as a condition to taking office, before
he should be qualified to decide upon your rights. [A
voice, "Take his scalp off."] Let me say to you that
obedience to law, obedience to the constituted authorities, within the sphere of their local and Constitutional
duties, is the first and highest duty of an American
citizen.

If a law be an unwise one, or unjust, submit to it
until the next election, when it is your duty to elect

men who will repeal it. If the law be repugnant to the Constitution of your country, it is null and void, and that Constitution has created a Supreme Court as the proper and only tribunal to ascertain that fact, and you and I and every other citizen is bound by their decision. The Democratic party therefore stand by the Constitution as our fathers made it; by the laws as they are recorded on the statute book; by the decisions of the courts, until they are reversed; and by the constituted authorities, against mob law and violence. [A voice, "That is so, by George, whether it is Know-Nothingism or anything else."]

Now, my friends, what safety or security is there for a citizen who is not willing to abide by the law and the constituted authorities. The only alternative is mob law and violence. You have had a specimen of that upon the Fugitive Slave Law. A political party has arisen which declares that their consciences will not permit them to obey and execute any law which they disapprove of. Did you ever find a lawbreaker who approved the law that imposed penalty upon him? Whenever you allow a man to interpose his conscience against the law of the land, your law is subverted and all constitutional authority is destroyed.

Then in conclusion, I appeal to you, as American citizens, as lovers of liberty, as members of the only national party which can preserve the Union, to stand by the Constitution, the law, and the constituted authority.

My friends, I owe an apology to you for inflicting upon you so long a speech under circumstances that rendered it impossible for me to do justice to myself, or to the subject, or to you.

The patience and marked respect with which you have listened to me only increase my obligation. Never has a public man had so many opportunities to feel grateful to an enlightened people as I have since I left Washington on my road home to Illinois. Wherever I have been, I have been received with open arms, and apparently with warm congratulations. [A voice, "You deserved it."] I have not vanity enough, nor will I do you the injustice, to suppose that all of these testimonials are intended as personal compliments to myself. I have reason to know (and I feel proud in that knowledge, and I thank God that is so) that you intended these demonstrations as a mark and an emphatic approval and endorsement of your devotion [a voice, "To S. A. Douglas—to yourself"]—No, sir, to that great principle which declares, in the language of Mr. Buchanan, that "the people of a Territory, like those of a State, shall decide for themselves whether slavery shall or shall not exist within their limits."

OBSERVATIONS ON SENATOR DOUGLAS'
VIEWS OF POPULAR SOVEREIGNTY

as Expressed in Harper's Magazine for September, 1859 [1]

Everyone knows that Mr. Douglas, the Senator from Illinois, has written and printed an elaborate essay, comprising thirty-eight columns of *Harper's Magazine,* in which he has undertaken to point out the "dividing line between federal and local authority." Very many persons have glanced over its paragraphs to catch the leading ideas without loss of time, and some few have probably read it with care.

Those who dissent from the doctrines of this paper owe to its author, if not to his arguments, a most respectful answer. Mr. Douglas is not the man to be treated with a disdainful silence. His ability is a fact unquestioned; his public career, in the face of many disadvantages, has been uncommonly successful; and he has been for many years a working, struggling candidate for the Presidency. He is, moreover, the coryphaeus of his political sect—the founder of a new school—and his disciples naturally believe in the infallible verity of his words as a part of their faith.

The style of the article is, in some respects, highly commendable. It is entirely free from the vulgar claptrap of the stump; has no vain adornment of classical scholarship; it shows no sign of the eloquent Senator;

[1] Washington *Constitution,* September 10, 1859. This article was first published anonymously, although it soon became known that it had been written by Attorney-General Jeremiah Black.

it is even without the logic of the great debater. Many portions of it are very obscure. It seems to be an unsuccessful effort at legal precision, like the writing of a judge, who is trying in vain to give good reasons for a wrong decision on a question of law which he has not quite mastered.

With the help of Messrs. Seward and Lincoln, he has defined accurately enough the platform of the so-called Republican party; and he does not attempt to conceal his conviction that their doctrines are, in the last degree, dangerous. They are, most assuredly, full of evil and saturated with mischief. The "irrepressible conflict" which they speak of with so much pleasure between the "opposing and enduring forces" of the Northern and Southern States will be fatal, not merely to the peace of the country, but to the existence of the Government itself. Mr. Douglas knows this, and he knows, also, that the Democratic party is the only power which is, or can be, organized to resist the Republican forces or oppose their hostile march upon the capital. He who divides and weakens the friends of the country at such a crisis in her fortunes assumes a very grave responsibility.

Mr. Douglas separates the Democratic party into three classes, and describes them as follows:

First.—Those who believe that the Constitution of the United States neither establishes nor prohibits slavery in the States or Territories beyond the power of the people legally to control it, but "leaves the people thereof perfectly free to form and regulate their domestic institutions in their own way, subject only to the Constitution of the United States."

Second.—Those who believe that the Constitution establishes slavery in the Territories, and withholds from Congress and the Territorial Legislature the power to control it; and who insist that, in the event the Territorial Legislature fails to enact the requisite laws for its protection, it becomes the imperative duty of Congress to interpose its authority and furnish such protection.

Third.—Those who, while professing to believe that the Constitution establishes slavery in the Territories beyond the power of Congress or the Territorial Legislature to control it, at the same time protest against the duty of Congress to interfere for its protection; but insist that it is the duty of the Judiciary to protect and maintain slavery in the Territories without any law upon the subject.

We give Mr. Douglas the full benefit of his own statement. This is his mode of expressing those differences, which, he says, disturb the harmony, and threaten the integrity, of the American democracy. These passages should, therefore, be most carefully considered.

The first class is the one to which he himself belongs, and to both the others he is equally opposed. He has no right to come between the second and third class. If the difference which he speaks of does exist among his opponents, it is their business, not his, to settle it or fight it out. We shall, therefore, confine ourselves to the dispute between Mr. Douglas and his followers on the one hand, and the rest of the Democratic party on the other, presuming that he will be willing to observe the principle of non-intervention in all matters with which he has no concern.

We will invert the order in which he has discussed the subject, and endeavor to show—

1. That he has not correctly stated the doctrine held by his opponents; and,

2. That his own opinions, as given by himself, are altogether unsound.

I. He says that a certain portion of the Democratic party believe, or profess to believe, that *the Constitution establishes slavery* in the Territories, and insist that it is the duty of the Judiciary to maintain it there *without any law* on the subject. We do not charge him with any intention to be unfair; but we assert that he has in fact done wrong to, probably, nineteen-twentieths of the party by attempting to put them on grounds which they never chose for themselves.

The Constitution certainly does not *establish* slavery in the Territories, nor anywhere else. Nobody in this country ever thought or said so. But the Constitution regards as sacred and inviolable all the rights which a citizen may legally acquire in a State. If a man acquires property of any kind in a State, and goes with it into a Territory, he is not for that reason to be stripped of it. Our simple and plain proposition is, that the legal owner of a slave or other chattel may go with it into a federal Territory without forfeiting his title.

Who denies the truth of this, and upon what ground can it be controverted? The reasons which support it are very obvious and very conclusive. As a jurist and a statesman, Mr. Douglas ought to be familiar with them, and there was a time when he was supposed to understand them very well. We will briefly give him a few of them.

1. It is an axiomatic principle of public law that a right of property, a private relation, condition, or *status*, lawfully existing in one State or country, is not changed by the mere removal of the parties to another country, unless the law of that other country be in direct conflict with it. For instance: A marriage legally solemnized in France is binding in America; children born in Germany are legitimate here if they are legitimate there; and a merchant who buys goods in New York according to the laws of that State may carry them to Illinois and hold them there under his contract. It is precisely so with the *status* of a negro carried from one part of the United States to another; the question of his freedom or servitude depends on the law of the place where he came from, and depends on that alone, if there be no conflicting law at the place to which he goes or is taken. The federal Constitution, therefore, recognizes slavery as a legal condition wherever the local governments have chosen to let it stand unabolished, and regards it as illegal wherever the laws of the place have forbidden it. A slave being property in Virginia, remains property; and his master has all the rights of a Virginia master wherever he may go, so that he go not to any place where the local law comes in conflict with his right. It will not be pretended that the Constitution itself furnishes to the Territories a conflicting law. It contains no provision that can be tortured into any semblance of a prohibition.

2. The dispute on the question whether slavery or freedom is local or general is a mere war of words. The black race in this country is neither bond nor free by virtue of any general law. That portion of it which

is free is free by virtue of some local regulation, and the slave owes service for a similar reason. The Constitution and laws of the United States simply declare that everything done in the premises by the State government is right, and they shall be protected in carrying it out. But free negroes and slaves may both find themselves outside of any State jurisdiction, and in a Territory where no regulation has yet been made on the subject. There the Constitution is equally impartial. It neither frees the slave nor enslaves the freeman. It requires both to remain *in statu quo* until the *status* already impressed upon them by the law of their previous domicile shall be changed by some competent local authority. What is competent local authority in a Territory will be elsewhere considered.

3. The federal Constitution carefully guards the rights of private property against the federal government itself, by declaring that it shall not be taken for public use without compensation, nor without due process of law. Slaves are private property, and every man who has taken an oath of fidelity to the Constitution is religiously, morally, and politically bound to regard them as such. Does anybody suppose that a Constitution which acknowledges the sacredness of private property so fully would wantonly destroy that right, not by any words that are found in it, but by mere implication from its general principles? It might as well be asserted that the general principles of the Constitution gave Lane and Montgomery a license to steal horses in the valley of the Osage.

4. The Supreme Court of the United States has decided the question. After solemn argument and careful consideration, that august tribunal has announced

its opinion to be that a slaveholder, by going into a federal Territory, does not lose the title he had to his negro in the State from which he came. In former times, a question of Constitutional law once decided by the Supreme Court was regarded as settled by all, except that little band of ribald infidels, who meet periodically at Boston to blaspheme the religion and plot rebellion against the laws of the country. The leaders of the so-called Republican party have lately been treading close on the heels of their abolition brethren; but it is devoutly to be hoped that Mr. Douglas has no intention to follow their example. In case he is elected President, he must see the laws faithfully executed. Does he think he can keep that oath by fighting the Judiciary?

5. The legislative history of the country shows that all the great statesmen of former times entertained the same opinion, and held it so firmly that they did not even think of any other. It was universally taken for granted that a slave remained a slave, and a free man a freeman, in the new Territories, until a change was made in their condition by some positive enactment. Nobody believed that a slave might not have been taken to and kept in the Northwest Territory if the Ordinance of 1787 or some other regulation had not been made to prohibit it. The Missouri restriction of 1820 was imposed solely because it was understood (probably by every member of that Congress) that, in the absence of a restriction, slave property would be as lawful in the eye of the Constitution above 36° 30′ as below; and all agreed that the mere absence of a restriction did, in fact, make it lawful below the Compromise line.

6. It is right to learn wisdom from our enemies.

The Republicans do not point to any express provision of the Constitution, nor to any general principle embraced in it, nor to any established rule of law which sustains their views. The ablest men among them are driven by stress of necessity to hunt for arguments in a code unrevealed, unwritten, and undefined, which they put above the Constitution or the Bible, and call it "higher law." The ultra abolitionists of New England do not deny that the Constitution is rightly interpreted by the Democrats as not interfering against slavery in the Territories; but they disdain to obey what they pronounce to be "an agreement with death and a covenant with hell."

7. What did Mr. Douglas mean when he proposed and voted for the Kansas-Nebraska Bill repealing the Missouri restriction? Did he intend to tell Southern men that, notwithstanding the repeal of the prohibition, they were excluded from those Territories as much as ever? Or did he not regard the right of a master to his slave perfectly good whenever he got rid of the prohibition? Did he, or anybody else at that time, dream that it was necessary to make a positive law in favor of the slaveholder before he could go there with safety? To ask these questions is to answer them. The Kansas-Nebraska Bill was not meant as a delusion or a snare. It was well understood that the repeal alone of the restriction against slavery would throw the country open to everything which the Constitution recognized as property.

We have thus given what we believe to be the opinions held by the great body of the Democratic party—namely, that the federal Constitution does not estab-

lish slavery anywhere in the Union; that it permits a
black man to be either held in servitude or made free
as the local law shall decide; and that in a Territory
where no local law on the subject has been enacted,
it keeps both the slave and the free negro in the *status*
already impressed upon them, until it shall be changed
by competent local authority. We have seen that this
is sustained by the reason of the thing, by a great principle of public law, by the words of the Constitution,
by a solemn decision of the Supreme Court, by the
whole course of our legislation, by the concession of
our political opponents, and, finally, by the most important act in the public life of Mr. Douglas himself.

Mr. Douglas imputes another absurdity to his opponents when he charges them with insisting "that it is
the duty of the Judiciary to protect and maintain
slavery in the Territories *without any law upon the
subject.*" The judge who acts without law acts against
law; and surely no sentiment so atrocious as this was
ever entertained by any portion of the Democratic
party. The right of a master to the services of his slave
in a Territory is not against law, nor without law, but
in full accordance with law. If the law be against it
we are all against it. Has not the emigrant to Nebraska
a legal right to the ox team which he bought in Ohio
to haul him over the plains? Is not his title as good
to it in the Territory as it was in the State where
he got it? And what should be said of a judge who tells
him that he is not protected, or that he is maintained,
in the possession of his property "without any law upon
the subject?"

II. We had a right to expect from Mr. Douglas at

least a clear and intelligible definition of his own doctrine. We are disappointed. It is hardly possible to conceive anything more difficult to comprehend. We will transcribe it again, and do what can be done to analyze it.

Those who believe that the Constitution of the United States neither establishes nor prohibits slavery in the States or Territories beyond the power of the people legally to control it, but "leaves the people thereof perfectly free to form and regulate their domestic institutions in their own way, subject only to the Constitution of the United States."

The Constitution neither establishes nor prohibits slavery in the States or Territories. If it be meant by this that the Constitution does not, *proprio vigore,* either emancipate any man's slave or create the condition of slavery and impose it on free negroes, but leaves the question of every black man's *status,* in the Territories as well as in the States, to be determined by the local law, then we admit it, for it is the very same proposition which we have been trying to prove. But if, on the contrary, it is to be understood as an assertion that the Constitution does not permit a master to keep his slave, or a free negro to have his liberty, in all parts of the Union where the local law does not interfere to prevent it, then the error is not only a very grave one, but it is also absurd and self-contradictory.

The Constitution neither establishes nor prohibits slavery in the States or Territories beyond the power of the people legally to control it. This is sailing to Point-No-Point again. Of course a subject which is *legally* controlled cannot be beyond the power that controls it. But the question is, what constitutes legal control, and when are the people of a State or Territory in a condition to exercise it.

The Constitution of the United States . . . leaves the people perfectly free *. . . , and subject only to the Constitution of the United States.* This carries us round a full circle, and drops us precisely at the place of beginning. That the Constitution leaves everybody subject to the Constitution, is most true. We are far from denying it. We never heard it doubted, and expect we never will. But the statement of it proves nothing, defines nothing, and explains nothing. It merely darkens the subject, as words without meaning always do.

But notwithstanding all this circuity of expression and consequent opaqueness of meaning in the magazine article of Mr. Douglas, we think we can guess what his opinions are or will be when he comes to reconsider the subject. He will admit (at least he will not undertake to deny) that the *status* of a negro, whether of servitude or freedom, accompanies him wherever he goes, and adheres to him in every part of the Union until he meets some local law which changes it.

It will also be agreed that the people of a State, through their legislature, and the people of a Territory, in the constitution which they may frame preparatory to their admission as a State, can regulate and control the condition of the subject black race within their respective jurisdictions, so as to make them bond or free.

But we here come to the point at which opinions diverge. Some insist that no citizen can be deprived of his property in slaves, or in anything else, *except* by the provisions of a State constitution or by the act of a State legislature; while others contend that an unlimited control over private rights may be exercised by a Territorial legislature as soon as the earliest settlements are made.

So strong are the sentiments of Mr. Douglas in favor of the latter doctrine that if it be not established he threatens us with Mr. Seward's "irrepressible conflict," which shall end only with the universal abolition or the universal dominion of slavery. On the other hand, the President, the Judges of the Supreme Court, nearly all the Democratic members of Congress, the whole of the party South, and a very large majority North are penetrated with a conviction that no such power is vested in a Territorial legislature, and that those who desire to confiscate private property of any kind must wait until they get a constitutional convention or the machinery of a State government into their hands. We venture to give the following reasons for believing that Mr. Douglas is in error.

The Supreme Court has decided that a Territorial legislature has not the power which he claims for it. That alone ought to be sufficient. There can be no law, order, or security for any man's rights unless the Judicial authority of the country be upheld. Mr. Douglas may do what he pleases with political conventions and party platforms, but we trust he will give to the Supreme Court at least that decent respect which none but the most ultra Republicans have yet withheld.

The right of property is sacred, and the first object of all human government is to make it secure. Life is

always unsafe where property is not fully protected.
This is the experience of every people on earth, ancient
and modern. To secure private property was a principal
object of Magna Charta. Charles I afterwards attempted
to violate it, but the people rose upon him, dragged him
to the block, and severed his head from his body. At a
still later period another monarch for a kindred offence
was driven out of the country, and died a fugitive and
an outcast. Our own Revolution was provoked by that
slight invasion upon the right of property which consisted in the exaction of a trifling tax. There is no
government in the world, however absolute, which
would not be disgraced and endangered by wantonly
sacrificing private property even to a small extent. For
centuries past such outrages have ceased to be committed in times of peace among civilized nations.

Slaves are regarded as property in the Southern States.
The people of that section buy and sell, and carry on
all their business, provide for their families, and make
their wills and divide their inheritances on that assumption. It is manifest to all who know them that no
doubts ever cross their minds about the rightfulness of
holding such property. They believe they have a direct
warrant for it, not only in the examples of the best
men that ever lived, but in the precepts of Divine
revelation itself; and they are thoroughly satisfied that
the relation of master and slave is the only one which
can possibly exist there between the white and the
black races without ruining both. The people of the
North may differ from their fellow citizens of the South
on the whole subject, but knowing, as we all do, that
these sentiments are sincerely and honestly entertained,

we cannot wonder that they feel the most unspeakable indignation when any attempt is made to interfere with their rights. This sentiment results naturally and necessarily from their education and habits of thinking. They cannot help it, any more than an honest man in the North can avoid abhorring a thief or housebreaker.

The jurists, legislators, and people of the Northern States have always sacredly respected the right of property in slaves held by their own citizens within their own jurisdiction. It is a remarkable fact, very well worth noticing, that no Northern State ever passed any law to take a negro from his master. All laws for the abolition of slavery have operated only on the unborn descendants of the negro race, and the vested rights of masters have not been disturbed in the North more than in the South.

In every nation under Heaven, civilized, semibarbarous, or savage, where slavery has existed in any form at all analogous to ours, the rights of the masters to the control of their slaves as property have been respected; and on no occasion has any government struck at those rights, except as it would strike at other property. Even the British Parliament, when it emancipated the West India slaves, though it was legislating for a people three thousand miles away and not represented, never denied either the legal or the natural right of the slaveowner. Slaves were admitted to be property, and the Government acknowledged it by paying their masters one hundred millions of dollars for the privilege of setting them free.

Here, then, is a species of property which is of

transcendent importance to the material interests of the South—which the people of that region think it right and meritorious in the eyes of God and good men to hold—which is sanctioned by the general sense of all mankind among whom it has existed—which was legal only a short time ago in all the States of the Union, and was then treated as sacred by every one of them—which is guaranteed to the owner as much as any other property is guaranteed by the Constitution; and Mr. Douglas thinks that a Territorial legislature is competent to take it away. We say, No; the supreme legislative power of a sovereign State alone can deprive a man of his property.

This proposition is so plain, so well established, and so universally acknowledged, that any argument in its favor would be a mere waste of words. Mr. Douglas does not deny it, and it did not require the thousandth part of his sagacity to see that it was undeniable. He claims for the Territorial government the right of confiscating private property on the ground that *those governments* ARE *sovereign*—have an uncontrollable and independent power over all their internal affairs. That is the point which he thinks is to split the Democracy and impale the nation. But it is so entirely erroneous, that it must vanish into thin air as soon as it comes to be examined.

A Territorial government is merely provisional and temporary. It is created by Congress for the necessary preservation of order and the purposes of police. The powers conferred upon it are expressed in the organic act, which is the charter of its existence, and which may be changed or repealed at the pleasure of Congress.

In most of those acts the power has been expressly
reserved to Congress of revising the Territorial laws,
and the power to repeal them exists without such
reservation. This was asserted in the case of Kansas by
the most distinguished Senators in the Congress of 1856.
The President appoints the Governor, judges, and all
other officers whose appointment is not otherwise provided for, directly or indirectly, by Congress. Even the
expenses of the Territorial government are paid out
of the federal Treasury. The truth is, they have no
attribute of sovereignty about them. The essence of
sovereignty consists in having no superior. But a Territorial government has a superior in the United States
Government, upon whose pleasure it is dependent for
its very existence—in whom it lives, and moves, and has
its being—who has made and can unmake it with a
breath.

Where does this sovereign authority to deprive men
of their property come from? This transcendent power,
which even despots are cautious about using, and which
a constitutional monarch never exercises—how does it
get into a Territorial legislature? Surely it does not
drop from the clouds; it will not be contended that
it accompanies the settlers, or exists in the Territory
before its organization. Indeed, it is not to the people,
but to the government of a Territory, that Mr. Douglas
says it belongs. Then Congress must give the power at
the same time that it gives the Territorial government.
But not a word of the kind is to be found in any organic
act that ever was framed. It is thus that Mr. Douglas'
argument runs itself out into nothing.

But if Congress *would* pass a statute expressly to give

this sort of power to the Territorial governments, they still would not have it; for the federal government itself does not possess any control over men's property in the Territories. That such power does not exist in the federal government needs no proof: Mr. Douglas admits it fully and freely. It is, besides, established by the solemn decision of Congress, by the assent of the Executive, and by the direct ratification of the people acting in their primary capacity at the polls. In addition to all this, the Supreme Court have deliberately adjudged it to be an unalterable and undeniable rule of Constitutional law.

This acknowledgment that Congress has no power, authority, or jurisdiction over the subject literally *obliges* Mr. Douglas to give up his doctrine, or else to maintain it by asserting that a power which the federal government *does not possess* may be *given by Congress to the Territorial government*. The right to abolish African slavery in a Territory is not granted by the Constitution to Congress; it is withheld, and therefore the same as if expressly prohibited. Yet Mr. Douglas declares that Congress may give it to the Territories. Nay; he goes further, and says that the *want* of the power in Congress is the *very reason* why it can delegate it—the general rule, in his opinion, being that Congress cannot delegate the powers it possesses, but may delegate such, "and only such, as Congress cannot exercise under the Constitution"! By turning to pages 520 and 521 [pages 64-65 in this book] the reader will see that this astounding proposition is actually made, not in jest or irony, but solemnly, seriously, and, no doubt, in perfect good faith. On this principle, as

Congress cannot exercise the power to make an *ex post facto* law, or a law impairing the obligation of contracts, *therefore* it may authorize such laws to be made by the town councils of Washington city or the levy court of the District. If Congress passes an act to hang a man without trial, it is void, and the judges will not allow it to be executed; but the power to do this prohibited thing can be Constitutionally given by Congress to a Territorial legislature!

We admit that there are certain powers bestowed upon the general Government which are in their nature judicial or executive. With them Congress can do nothing, except to see that they are executed by the proper kind of officers. It is also true that Congress has certain legislative powers which cannot be delegated. But Mr. Douglas should have known that he was not talking about powers which belonged to either of these classes, but about a legislative jurisdiction totally forbidden to the federal government, and incapable of being delegated for the simple reason that it does not Constitutionally exist.

Will anybody say that such a power ought, as a matter of policy or for reasons of public safety, to be held by the provisional governments of the Territories? Undoubtedly no true patriot, nor no friend of justice and order, can deliberately reflect on the probable consequences without deprecating them.

This power over property is the one which in all governments has been most carefully guarded because the temptation to abuse it is always greater than any other. It is there that the subjects of a limited monarchy watch their king with the greatest jealousy. No republic has ever failed to impose strict limitations upon it. All free people know that, if they would remain free, they must compel the government to keep its hands off their private property; and this can be done only by tying them up with careful restrictions. Accordingly, our federal Constitution declares that "no person shall be deprived of his property except by due process of law," and that "private property shall not be taken for public use without just compensation." It is universally agreed that this applies only to the exercise of the power by the Government of the United States. We are also protected against the State governments by a similar provision in the State constitutions. Legislative robbery is therefore a crime which cannot be committed either by Congress or by any State legislature, unless it be done in flat rebellion to the fundamental law of the land. But if the Territorial governments have this power, then they have it without any limitation whatsoever and in all the fullness of absolute despotism. They are omnipotent in regard to all their internal affairs, for they are *sovereigns, without a constitution to hold them in check*. And this omnipotent sovereignty is to be wielded by a few men suddenly drawn together from all parts of America and Europe, unacquainted with one another, and ignorant of their relative rights. But if Mr. Douglas is right, those governments have all the absolute power of the Russian autocrat. They may take every kind of property in mere caprice, or for any purpose of lucre or malice, without process of law and without providing for compensation. The legislature of Kansas, sitting at Lecompton or Lawrence, may order the miners to give up every ounce of gold that has been dug at Pike's Peak. If the authorities of Utah should license a band of marauders to despoil the emigrants crossing the territory, their sovereign right to do so cannot be questioned. A new Territory may be organized, which Southern men think should be devoted to the culture of cotton, while the people of the North are equally certain that grazing alone is the proper business to be carried on there. If one party, by accident, by force, or by fraud, has a majority in the legislature, the negroes are taken from the planters; and if the other set gains a political victory, it is followed by a statute to plunder the graziers of their cattle. Such things cannot be done by the federal government, nor by the governments of the States; but, if Mr. Douglas is not mistaken, they can be done by the Territorial governments. Is it not every way better to wait until the new inhabitants know themselves and one another; until the policy of the Territory is settled by some experience; and above all, until the great powers of a sovereign State are regularly conferred upon them and properly limited, so as to prevent the gross abuses which always accompany unrestricted power in human hands?

There is another consideration which Mr. Douglas should have been the last man to overlook. The present Administration of the federal government, and the whole Democratic party throughout the country, including Mr. Douglas, thought that in the case of Kansas the question of retaining or abolishing slavery should not be determined by any representative body without giving to the whole mass of the people an opportunity of voting on it. Mr. Douglas carried it further, and warmly opposed the constitution, denying even its validity because other and undisputed parts of it had not also been submitted to a popular vote. Now he is willing that the whole slavery dispute in any Territory, and all questions that can arise concerning the rights of the people to that or other property, shall be decided at once by a Territorial legislature without any submission at all. Popular sovereignty in the last Congress meant the freedom of the people from all the restraints of law and order; now it means a government which shall rule them with a rod of iron. It swings like a pendulum from one side clear over to the other.

Mr. Douglas' opinions on this subject of sovereign Territorial governments are very singular; but the reasons he has produced to support them are infinitely more curious still. For instance, he shows that Jefferson once introduced into the old Congress of the Confederation a *plan* for the government of the Territories, calling them by the name of "new States," but not making them anything like sovereign or independent States; and though this was a mere experimental *project,* which was rejected by Congress, and never afterwards referred to by Jefferson himself, yet Mr. Douglas argues upon it as if it had somehow become a part of our fundamental law.

Again: He says that the States gave to the federal government the same powers which as Colonies they had been willing to concede to the British Government, and kept those which as Colonies they had claimed for themselves. If he will read a common school history of the Revolution, and then look at Art. I, Sec. 8, of the Constitution, he will find the two following facts fully established: 1. That the federal government has "power to lay and collect taxes, duties, imposts, and excises"; and, 2. That the Colonies, before the Revolution, utterly refused to be taxed by Great Britain, and, so far from conceding the power, fought against it for seven long years.

There is another thing in the article which, if it had not come from a distinguished Senator, and a very upright gentleman, would have been open to some imputation of unfairness. He quotes the President's message, and begins in the middle of a sentence. He professes to give the very words, and makes Mr. Buchanan say: "That slavery exists in Kansas by virtue of the Constitution of the United States." What Mr. Buchanan did say was a very different thing. It was this: "It has been solemnly adjudged by the highest judicial tribunal known to our laws, that slavery exists in Kansas by virtue of the Constitution of the United States." Everybody knows that by treating the Bible in that way you can prove the non-existence of God.

The *argumentum ad hominem* is not fair, and we do not mean to use it. Mr. Douglas has a right to change his opinions whenever he pleases. But we quote him as we would any other authority equally high in favor of truth. We can prove by himself that every proposition he lays down in *Harper's Magazine* is founded in error. Never before has any public man in America so completely revolutionized his political opinions in the course of eighteen months. We do not deny that the change is heartfelt and conscientious. We only insist that he formerly stated his propositions much more clearly, and sustained them with far greater ability and better reasons, than he does now.

When he took a tour to the South, at the beginning of last winter, he made a speech at New Orleans in which he announced to the people there that he and his friends in Illinois *accepted the Dred Scott decision,* regarded *slaves* as *property,* and fully admitted the right of a Southern man to go into any *federal Territory* with his slave, and to hold him there *as other property is held.*

In 1849 he voted in the Senate for what was called Walker's amendment, by which it was proposed to put all the internal affairs of California and New Mexico under the domination of the *President,* giving him almost unlimited power, *legislative, judicial, and executive,* over the *internal affairs* of those Territories. (See the *Congressional Globe,* 30th Congress.) Undoubtedly this was a strange way of treating sovereignties. If Mr. Douglas is right now, he was guilty then of most atrocious usurpation.

Utah is as much a sovereign State as any other Territory and as perfectly entitled to enjoy the right of self-government. On the 12th of June, 1857, Mr. Douglas made a speech about Utah at Springfield, Illinois, in which he expressed his opinion strongly in favor of *the absolute and unconditional repeal* of the organic act, *blotting the Territorial government out of existence,* and putting the people under the sole and exclusive jurisdiction of the United States, *like a fort, arsenal, dockyard, or magazine.* He does not seem to have had the least idea then that he was proposing to extinguish a sovereignty, or to trample upon the sacred rights of an independent people.

The report which he made to the Senate in 1856, on the Topeka constitution, enunciates a very different doctrine from that of the magazine article. It is true that the language is a little cloudy, but no one can understand the following sentences to signify that the Territorial governments have sovereign power to take away the property of the inhabitants:

The sovereignty of a Territory remains in *abeyance, suspended* in the United States, *in trust for the people until they shall be admitted into the Union as a State. In the meantime* they are admitted to enjoy and exercise all the rights and privileges of self-government *in subordination to the Constitution* of the United States, and IN OBEDIENCE TO THE ORGANIC LAW, passed by Congress in pursuance of that instrument. These rights and privileges are *all* derived from the Constitution *through the act of Congress,* and must be exercised and enjoyed in subjection to all the limitations and restrictions which that Constitution imposes.

The letter he addressed to a Philadelphia meeting, in February, 1858, is more explicit, and, barring some anomalous ideas concerning the *abeyance* of the power and the *suspension* of it *in trust,* it is clear enough:

Under our Territorial system, it requires sovereign power to ordain and establish constitutions and governments. While a Territory may and should enjoy all the rights of self-government, *in obedience to its organic law,* it is NOT A SOVEREIGN POWER. The *sovereignty* of a Territory *remains in abeyance, suspended* in the United States, *in trust for the people when they become a State,* and *cannot be withdrawn from the hands of the trustee and vested in the people of a Territory without the consent of Congress.*

The report which he made in the same month from

the Senate Committee on Territories is equally distinct,
and rather more emphatic against his new doctrine:

> This committee in their reports have always held that *a
> Territory is not a sovereign power;* that the sovereignty of
> a Territory is in abeyance, suspended in the United States,
> in trust for the people when they become a State; that the
> United States, as trustees, cannot be divested of the sov-
> ereignty, nor the Territory be invested with the right to
> assume and exercise it, without the consent of Congress.
> If the proposition be true that sovereign power alone can
> *institute governments,* and that the sovereignty of a Ter-
> ritory is in abeyance, suspended in the United States, in
> trust for the people when they become a State, and that the
> sovereignty cannot be divested from the hands of the trus-
> tee without the assent of Congress, it follows, as an in-
> evitable consequence, that the Kansas legislature did not
> and could not confer upon the Lecompton convention the
> sovereign power of ordaining a constitution for the people
> of Kansas, in place of the organic act passed by Congress.

The days are past and gone when Mr. Douglas led
the fiery assaults of the opposition in the Lecompton
controversy. Then it was his object to prove that a
Territorial legislature, so far from being omnipotent,
was powerless even to authorize an election of delegates
to consider about their own affairs. It was asserted that
a convention chosen under a Territorial law could make
and ordain no constitution which would be legally
binding. Then a Territorial government was to be
despised and spit upon, even when it invited the people
to come forward and vote on a question of the most
vital importance to their own interests. But now all
things have become new. The Lecompton dispute has
"gone glimmering down the dream of things that were,"

and Mr. Douglas produces another issue, brand new from the mint. The old opinions are not worth a rush to his present position: it must be sustained by opposite principles and reasoning totally different. The legislature of Kansas was not sovereign when it authorized a convention of the people to assemble and decide what sort of a constitution they would have, but when it strikes at their rights of property, it becomes not only a sovereign but a sovereign without limitation of power. We have no idea that Mr. Douglas is not perfectly sincere, as he was also when he took the other side. The impulses engendered by the heat of controversy have driven him at different times in opposite directions. We do not charge it against him as a crime, but it is true that these views of his, inconsistent as they are with one another, always *happen* to accord with the interests of the Opposition, always give to the enemies of the Constitution a certain amount of "aid and comfort," and always add a little to the rancorous and malignant hatred with which the abolitionists regard the Government of their own country.

Yes, the Lecompton issue which Mr. Douglas made upon the Administration two years ago is done, and the principles on which we were then opposed are abandoned. We are no longer required to fight for the lawfulness of a Territorial election held under Territorial authority. But another issue is thrust upon us to "disturb the harmony and threaten the integrity" of the party. A few words more (perhaps of tedious repetition) by way of showing what that new issue is, or probably will be, and we are done.

We insist that an emigrant going into a federal Terri-

tory retains his title to the property which he took with
him until there is some prohibition enacted by lawful
authority. Mr. Douglas cannot deny this in the face of
his New Orleans speech and the overwhelming reasons
which support it.

It is an agreed point among all Democrats that Congress cannot interfere with the rights of property in the
Territories.

It is also acknowledged that the people of a new
State, either in their constitution or in an act of their
legislature, may make the negroes within it free or
hold them in a state of servitude.

But we believe more. We believe—in submitting to
the law as decided by the Supreme Court, which declares that a Territorial legislature cannot, any more
than Congress, interfere with the rights of property in
a Territory—that the settlers of a Territory are bound
to wait until the sovereign power is conferred upon
them, with proper limitations, before they attempt to
exercise the most dangerous of all its functions. Mr.
Douglas denies this, and there is the new issue.

Why should such an issue be made at such a time?
What is there now to excuse any friend of peace for
attempting to stir up the bitter waters of strife? There
is no actual difficulty about this subject in any Territory. There is no question upon it pending before
Congress or the country. We are called upon to make
a contest, at once unnecessary and hopeless, with the
judicial authority of the nation. We object to it. We
will not obey Mr. Douglas when he commands us to
assault the Supreme Court of the United States. We
believe the Court to be right, and Mr. Douglas wrong.

SPEECH OF STEPHEN A. DOUGLAS

at Wooster, Ohio, September 16, 1859 [1]

Ladies and Gentlemen: I regret, as much as any of you possibly can, the delay in the arrival of the cars. The only excuse I can make for putting you to this inconvenience in waiting is that the Democratic party is not responsible for the delay. [Laughter.] Nor can it be charged to the account of popular sovereignty. [Renewed laughter.] I must say, however, in justice to the Pittsburgh & Fort Wayne Railroad, that it is one of the best in the country; and the only reason why we could not arrive earlier is that the great National Fair had collected more people in Chicago yesterday than could sleep in the streets last night, and the railroad had to bring them out of town.

When I was received at the cars today and during my passage up the streets through your beautiful town I was reminded of the scenes that I witnessed in my own beloved Illinois last year. I almost fancied that you were Illinoisians, right from the heart of Egypt. ["Good! Good!" and much applause.] For such a reception no man has ever received or can receive except from the genuine Democracy of the Northwest. I rejoice, therefore, that I have the opportunity of addressing you upon those great fundamental principles which bind all Democrats together, no matter what may be their locality.

It is not my purpose to discuss any question per-

[1] *Ohio Statesman* (Columbus), September 20, 1859.

taining to your internal policy or domestic concerns. Those questions are matters for you to determine for yourselves, without the interference of anybody outside of the limits of your own State. I might say that I have rather a debt of gratitude which I ought to pay to this State—one of long standing—which has been accumulating interest. Your fellow citizens, Father Giddings and Mr. Chase, have canvassed Illinois several times for my benefit, and I do not know that there is any harm in my saying a word in Ohio for their benefit. [Laughter and applause.]

However, my object is not to deal with individuals but with those principles that separate the Democracy from their opponents. I am one of those who believe that the Democratic party, under the Democratic organization, with the time-honored principles of the party emblazoned on their banner, is the only political organization that can preserve the peace, harmony, and unity of this great confederacy. If we have any disputes or misunderstandings in respect to the principles or policy of the party, let us settle them ourselves, inside of our own organization, and in conformity with our own usages. ["Hear, hear," and loud cheering.]

The principal question which divides the Democratic party from their opponents, North and South, is akin to all the measures that have separated the Democracy from their opponents in all time. So far as the slavery question is involved in the contest, it is simply a proposition of whether slavery is a federal or a local question. The Democratic party stand upon the issue that slavery is a local question, existing in the several States under the laws thereof, by State authority and not by virtue of the Constitution of the United States. If slavery be a local question affecting the internal polity and domestic affairs of the people, then it must be regulated and controlled by local authority. If, on the contrary, it be a federal question, deriving its validity from federal authority, existing by virtue of the Constitution of the United States, then it must be regulated and controlled by federal authority.

The first question to which I wish to call your attention is whether it be a federal or a local institution. To determine that question it is only necessary for you to read the Constitution of the United States and then administer to every man who denies that Democratic doctrine an oath to support the Constitution. The Constitution of the United States recognizes the title in slaves as property, and then provides who may be slaves, where they may be held, by virtue of what authority slavery may exist, and in what contingency a fugitive slave shall be returned to his owner. You find these all in the same clause of the Constitution. If any gentleman has a copy of that instrument here I will read it, and if not I will repeat it to you from memory. It is in these words: "No person held to service or labor in one State, under the laws thereof, escaping into another, shall in consequence of any law or regulation therein be discharged, but shall be delivered up to the party to whom such service or labor may be due." There you find the definition of slavery—a slave is a person held to service or labor in one state under the laws *thereof,* not under the laws of the United States, not by virtue of the Constitution of the United States, not in consequence of any federal authority, but in a State, *under the laws thereof.* Thus you find the Constitution recognizes slavery as a local and domestic institution confined to the State whose laws sanction it, and existing by virtue of State authority, and by virtue of no other authority under heaven. If slavery be a local and State institution, then it must be managed and controlled by local and State authority. You in Ohio have decided that question for yourselves, as you had a right to do under the Constitution. You have decided that in this State, with your climate, your productions, and under your circumstances, it is not good for you to have slavery. You had a right to make that decision. No man on earth has a right to question it. It was your business—it affected your own domestic concerns and internal polity. But when you have decided this question to suit yourselves your power ceases. You have no more right to interfere with slavery in Virginia than Virginia has to interfere with your domestic concerns. If the people of Virginia should get up Emigrant Aid Societies or in any other manner interfere with your domestic concerns with a view of compelling you to adopt slavery, would you not tell Virginia that they had better go back across the Ohio River. Then if your abolitionists should cross the Ohio River to interfere with the domestic affairs of Virginia, either to steal their slaves or any other property, I trust that they will teach them that they had better return to Ohio. [Cheers.]

Thus you find that the very essence of the Democratic creed upon this slavery question and upon all other local and domestic questions is that every distinct political community shall manage its own affairs, regulate them to suit itself, mind its own business, and let its neighbors alone. If you will all act upon that principle there can be peace between all the States and Territories of this Union. But we are all told by the abolitionists or Republicans that slavery is such a monstrous evil that they cannot permit the people of a Territory to manage their own concerns; they must manage them for them. Governor Chase and Father Giddings, when they come to Illinois, tell our people that the people of the Territories cannot be trusted in the management of their own concerns, and that they will ruin themselves by bad laws if you permit them to make just such laws as they please in respect to the negro. They have no objection to letting them govern themselves in respect to white men; they can trust the people of a Territory to make the laws relating to husband and wife, parent and child, and guardian and ward, and all other things that affect white men, but they cannot trust them when they come to make laws concerning the negro. ["True," and laughter.]

They seem to think that it requires a higher degree of intelligence and civilization to legislate for the negro than it does for the white man, and hence they will not permit the Territorial legislature to pass laws determining the relation between the white man and the negro in the several Territories of the United States. Where do they derive the authority of the federal government to interfere with the local and domestic concerns of the people, either in the States or the Territories? They cannot find any such authority in the Constitution of the United States; and trace back the history of the States to a period anterior to the Revolution when they were Colonies, and see if you find any

sanction for this interference on the part of the federal
government with the local and domestic concerns of
the people. Bear in mind that the first serious controversy that ever arose on the American continent
between the American Colonies and the British Government was in regard to the right of the legislature of
Virginia, then a Colony, to regulate the slavery question
to suit themselves. Believing they had more slaves than
was consistent with their interest or safety, and taking
into view the sparse, white settlements surrounded by
hostile Indian tribes, they passed a law to check and
restrain the further introduction of slaves into that
Colony. No sooner had that law been passed by Virginia
than the British merchants who were engaged in the
African slave trade petitioned the King to annul it,
and to protect them in their rights to emigrate into the
Colonies, which were the common property of the
empire, acquired by the common blood and the common treasure, and to hold their slaves, in defiance of
the local law. The King of England, being a good Republican in the modern sense of the term [laughter],
granted the prayer of the petitioners, annulled the act
of the Virginia legislature, and declared that the Colonies were the common property of the empire, acquired by the common blood and treasure, and therefore that every Englishman had a right to go into
those Colonies and carry his slaves with him, and that
a mere provincial legislature had no right to exclude
him or discriminate between them. What did old
Virginia say to that doctrine then? She said that the
people of a Colony were not property at all—she denied
that a political community, called a Colony, was prop-

erty in any sense of the term, and claimed that the Colonists were Englishmen, endowed with all the rights of Englishmen, and as such it was their birthright to make all laws governing themselves in respect to their internal concerns when they were organized into political communities. The battles of the Revolution were all fought in vindication of that great political right—the right of the Colonies, the right of Provinces, the right of dependent Territories to make their own laws and govern themselves in respect to their own internal concerns. Our fathers did not claim that the Colonies were sovereign States. They did not claim the right to exercise independent and sovereign power; but they did claim that, although Colonies or Territories, they were entitled to the exclusive right of legislation respecting their internal concerns and domestic policy, slavery included. And because Great Britain would not grant that privilege they resisted her authority, established their independence—and thereby secured to themselves and their posterity the exclusive right, in all time to come, of governing themselves.

The question which I now propound to the American people is whether the American Territories, under the Constitution of the United States, are not entitled to the same rights and privileges which our fathers claimed for the British Colonies under the British Constitution. We, the advocates of popular sovereignty, claim no more for the American Territories than our fathers fought for as Colonies. If we are not right in the assertion of this doctrine of popular sovereignty in the Territories, then the Tories of the Revolution were right in resisting the claims of our fathers. [Cheers,

and a voice, "Have you the documents here for that?"]
Yes, sir, I have the documents in the head and heart of
every American citizen [immense applause], and these
small school boys standing around here will learn every
fact I have stated in the simplest history of the United
States that may be placed in their hands. What man is
there who can read and write who does not know that
the American Colonies resisted the authority of the
British Government merely because it would not concede to them the right to govern themselves in respect
to their local and domestic concerns?

I have already remarked that the Republican party,
so far as the question of slavery is concerned, in denying the right of the people of a Territory to manage
their own domestic affairs, claim the power of Congress
to occupy the identical position that George III and
the Tories of the Revolution occupied towards the
American Colonies. I do not say it in an offensive
sense—I am not questioning their motives or their sincerity—I only take that parallel in history in order to
illustrate their doctrine in a light that every man,
woman, and child will comprehend. I happened to take
up a newspaper this morning in the cars, in which I
found the resolutions of the late Republican Convention in the State of New York. They affirm the same
doctrine. Remember that the Republican National
Convention at Philadelphia in 1856 declared that Congress possessed sovereign power over the Territories of
the United States for their government, and that in
the exercise of that power it was their right and duty
to prohibit slavery. That is the precise doctrine that
the British Parliament asserted in the preamble to the

repeal of the Stamp Act. In that preamble they declared that the Parliament of Great Britain had the right to bind the American Colonies in all cases whatsoever. The Republicans of this day declare that Congress has the right to exercise sovereign power over the people of the Territories in all cases whatsoever. Are not the positions identical? Can you tell the difference between a modern Republican and one of the Ministers of George III in the year 1776? But upon what ground is it that the Republicans claim the right of Congress to exercise sovereign power over the people of the Territories? I find it in the following resolution adopted at the New York Republican State Convention in Syracuse a few days since:

Resolved, That the Territories of the United States are the property of the people of the United States, that the Constitution has conferred upon Congress the power to make all needful rules and regulations respecting said Territories, and that it is the right and duty of Congress, as the guardian of their welfare, to preserve them free forever from all political and social nuisances, and particularly from the infamous and debasing institution of domestic slavery.

You find that in this resolution the Republicans base their right to exercise sovereign power over the Territories on the assumption that the Territories are the property of the people of the States. What are the Territories? What are they composed of? They are political communities of American citizens living on their own land, which they have bought from the federal government, and governing themselves under the principles

of the Kansas-Nebraska Bill. A Territory is a political
community with its executive, legislative, and judicial
departments, occupying a country subdivided into counties and townships, with all other organizations necessary for sustaining such a political community; and we
are told by the Republican party that a Territory thus
organized is the property of the people of the United
States. How long will it take the Republicans of the
present day to unlearn the doctrines of the British
Government and to adopt those of the American States?
[Applause.] They think the Territories are property
just because the King of Great Britain thought the
Colonies were property, but George Washington taught
George III that he was slightly mistaken on that point.
["Hear, hear," and cheers.] The Tories of the Revolution found that if the Colonies were property, that they
were pretty good fighting property at least. [Great applause.] It was that very odious designation to which
our fathers took exception. It was that claim that the
Colonists had no rights to which our fathers took exception. Our fathers said, although we are Colonists,
although we are Provinces, although we are Territories,
yet we have political and personal rights, and among
them we have the inalienable right to govern ourselves
in respect to our local and domestic concerns whenever
we are formed into political communities, no matter
whether you call them States, Territories, Provinces, or
Colonies. That is all we claim now. The Democratic
party claims for the people of the Territories no more
than that.

 We do not claim that the Territory is sovereign, we
do not claim that it is independent of the federal

government, any more than the Colonies were sovereign and independent of the British Government, but we do claim that they have the inalienable right of self-government in respect to their local and domestic concerns as our fathers claimed the same right for the American Colonies previous to the Revolution.

But a Republican will tell you that the Territories are property because the United States owns the land. That happens to be a mistake also. The United States is a landowner in the Territory of Nebraska the same as they are in the State of Ohio, and no more. The United States once owned all the land in the State of Ohio, the same as the United States once owned all the land in the Territory of Nebraska; but under our laws the moment a settler went into the Territory of Nebraska and occupied the land, he became entitled to a pre-emption right, and at the proper time proved it up, paid for his land, and became the owner of it. Hence, land which the United States does own in the Territories is that which is vacant, and has no settlers upon it; and the land upon which the people live is owned by themselves, and to which the United States has no title. [Laughter and cheers.] Just as it is in the State of Illinois today. The United States owns perhaps 100,000 acres of land in the State of Illinois, but there are no people living on it. Does that fact give the United States the right to govern Illinois? [Applause.] Does the fact of ownership of a small amount of land in our State make the State of Illinois property? Are we the property of the United States merely because the United States own a little land in the State? The United States this day own three-fourths of all the land in the State of Minnesota, but is Minnesota the property of the United States for that reason?

According to the Republican platform she would be the property, merely because the United States is a landholder within her limits. [Laughter and applause.] According to that rule Ohio is property, Indiana is property, Illinois is property, Michigan is property, Wisconsin is property, Iowa is property, Minnesota is property, Missouri is property, Arkansas is property, and Louisiana, Mississippi, Alabama, Florida, California, and Oregon are property, for the United States owns a portion of the public domain in each one of them. Does that fact make them property, or does it give the United States any right to interfere with their domestic affairs and internal concerns? If it does not, how can it give them any right to it in a Territory? The unappropriated land in a Territory belongs to the United States. The lands which have been occupied and settled under our laws belong to the settlers; and what right has the United States to govern the settler merely because it once owned the land on which he lives? And yet this heresy about the United States owning the Territories as common property has given rise to one half of the political differences that have grown out of this Territorial question. Whenever you find a man talking about the Territories being the common property of the United States, acquired by the blood and common treasure, you may know he has been reading with affectionate attention the doctrines of the Tories of the Revolution. [Cheers.]

The question then arises, What right has the United States to interfere with the local and domestic affairs

of the people of the Territories? The Constitution has
given no such right—it has conferred no such authority.
The most that can be claimed for Congress is the right
to institute governments for the Territories, as the
British Parliament instituted governments for the Colonies, leaving the Territories free to govern themselves,
the same as the Colonies were free to govern themselves.
That is the doctrine of the Democratic party, and hence
the Democracy of this country for years have stood upon
the platform which declares non-intervention by Congress and popular sovereignty in the Territories as a
cardinal article in our political faith. The Compromise
Measures of 1850 rested on that principle. You all know
that those measures, which were adopted by Whigs
and Democrats alike as an article of our political faith
in common, asserted the right of the people of a Territory to govern themselves, without excepting the slavery
question. The Kansas-Nebraska Bill was introduced and
passed for the purpose of carrying out that same principle; I am the author of that bill, and I have been
pretty genteelly abused for being the author of it. I
have seen the time when I could travel from Boston to
Chicago by the light of my own effigy [laughter and
cheers], and all along the Western Reserve of Ohio
I could find my effigy upon every tree we passed. [Re-
newed laughter.] And for what was all this abuse heaped
upon my devoted head?—simply because I had introduced into Congress, and helped to pass a bill declaring
that it was the true intent and meaning of the act not
to legislate slavery into any State or Territory nor to
exclude it therefrom, but to leave the people thereof
perfectly free to form and regulate their domestic in-

stitutions in their own way, subject only to the Constitution of the United States. [Cheers.] The Republicans endeavored to make the people believe that the
object of the Kansas and Nebraska Bill was to open
all that country to slavery, and to establish slavery in
it. But it was only necessary to read the law in which
the object was clearly defined to discover that the repeal of the Missouri Compromise was in order to leave
the people of every State and every Territory perfectly
free to form and regulate their own domestic institutions, slavery included, just as they pleased to. I hold
now that if you, the people of Ohio, want slavery, you
have a right to it. If you do not want it, no power on
earth has a right to force it on you. If the people of
Kansas want slavery, it is their political right. If they
do not want it, no power in Christendom shall ever
force it upon them if I by any effort of mine can defeat
it. [Great cheers.]

It is no answer to this argument to say that slavery
is an evil or a crime, and therefore the people should
not be permitted to ruin themselves for inflicting such
a curse upon them. It is the right of every people to
judge for themselves whether it be an evil or not. It is
their right to judge whether it be a crime. It is the
right of every community to judge for themselves the
character and nature of every institution it is proposed
to adopt. Virginia has judged that question for herself,
and decided in favor of slavery. You have judged it
for yourselves and decided it against slavery. You each
have the right to arrive at the conclusion to which
you have come, and neither has any right to interfere
with the other. So it is with the Territories. The mo-

ment you organize them into distinct political communities, governments composed of executive, legislative, and judicial departments, you invest them with the absolute right of deciding all local and domestic questions to suit themselves. But the enemies of the Democratic party are in the habit of saying that the few first settlers were squatters on the public domain, ought not to be permitted to make laws binding the people who are to come after them. Now, I admit that they ought not to be permitted to decide that or any other question until they have people enough to constitute a community capable of self-government. How many does it require? That is a question for Congress to determine, and Congress has no right to organize a Territory at all until there are people enough in it to govern themselves. Congress has no right to give them a legislature until they are capable of legislating. Hence the objection to a few people deciding the question for themselves is an objection to the organization of a Territory at all and not to the extent of the power of the Territorial legislature shall exercise when organized. If there are not enough people in Arizona to govern themselves in respect to their local and domestic concerns, then vote against a Territorial organization there. If they are not capable of self-government do not give them a legislature; for when you organize them into a government and give them a legislature, you admit by that act that they have people enough to constitute a government, that they are capable of legislating for themselves upon all rightful subjects of legislation, and hence you are estopped from urging objection. I think we have been in the habit of often organizing Territories when there were too few people. This right of self-government don't attach to each individual who may stay upon the public lands. It is not attaching to every intruder upon the public domain. It only applies to communities and not to individuals. It is a political right, which is called into being when those individuals are organized into political communities. It is not an individual right but a political right, pertaining to the community, as such, and not to the individual. Hence if you are not willing that they shall exercise that political right of self-government, vote against organizing the Territory, but do not invade the right of self-government after you have created them a distinct political community.

We are told by the Republicans on every stump that this doctrine of popular sovereignty is dead. They say Judge Taney killed it [laughter]—that it had its throat cut by the Dred Scott decision—that popular sovereignty has no longer a breath of life in its body; for they tell you that the Supreme Court and the Dred Scott case has decided that the people of a Territory have no right to determine the slavery question for themselves while in a Territory. I have no doubt that you have heard this from the Republicans on every stump in the State, but that not one of them undertook to prove it true. There is not one word of truth in the whole statement. The Supreme Court have decided no such thing. It has not decided that slavery existed in the Territory by virtue of the Constitution of the United States. It is true the President of the United States fell into the error of making that statement in his message communicating the Lecompton Constitution to Congress. But the Supreme Court have not sanctioned the doctrine. It has declared that the right of property in slaves is distinctly recognized in the Constitution of the United States; that the faith of the United States is pledged to protect it in all future time if the slave escapes from his owner; that the only power conferred is the power coupled with the duty of guarding and protecting the rights of the owner when the slave escapes. This is the power Congress has— to provide for the return of the fugitive slave when he runs away. The Court then goes on to say that, in all other respects, slave property stands on precisely the same footing with all other property. It says that there is no word in the Constitution which confers upon Congress greater power over slave property, or entitles that property to less protection than any other kind of property; and that inasmuch as the Constitution has made no distinction between it and all other property, therefore no department of the government can make any such distinction. Now I affirm all that doctrine that the Court has held. I affirm each one of the propositions, that slavery stands on an equal footing with all other property and that Congress has no more or less power over it.

Well now, upon what footing does other property stand in the Territories? Has Congress the right to interfere with your horses, your cattle, your wagons, your plows, your merchandise, or your wheat in the Territories? Did Congress ever yet pass a law creating a criminal code for any Territory of the United States? If your horse is stolen in a Territory, do you apply to the federal courts to punish the thief? Never! If your horse is stolen in a Territory, you go to the Territorial courts, and the man is punished under the Territorial law, and not under the Act of Congress. If a horse is stolen in Ohio, you cannot sue in the federal court because it is a local offense, punishable under the local law in the local courts. And so it is in the Territory— murder, rape, arson, robbery, all the crimes that stain the records of the court, are punishable in the Territory under the local law. Every description of property in all the Territories of the United States is dependent upon the local law for its protection. Life, liberty, and property in the Territory are all under the protection and guardianship of the local law, to be administered and enforced by the local authority. Then if Congress cannot interfere with any other kind of property in the Territories, either to exclude it, prohibit it, or protect it, how can it interfere with slave property in the Territories? According to the Dred Scott decision the federal government cannot interfere in the Territory with slavery, either for it or against it, and that is the affirmance precisely of my doctrine and your doctrine and the Democratic doctrine of popular sovereignty.

Yet, it is true that I have been represented by my enemies as having attacked the Supreme Court and the Dred Scott decision in my advocacy of popular sovereignty. I do not often notice these attacks, but I will give one moment to an assault recently made out of respect for the high authority from which it is said to have come. In the cars this morning, a friend handed me a pamphlet entitled, "Observations on Senator Douglas' Views on Popular Sovereignty, as Expressed in *Harper's Magazine* for September, 1859." The pamphlet is anonymous, but the newspapers, especially the *New York Herald,* published it as written by Jerry Black, the same man who last year wrote letters to Illinois urging federal officeholders to support abolitionists to office in preference to the regular Democratic ticket. ["Shame on him," "He's a renegade," etc.] Whether he is the author or not I have no means of knowing, except the fact that it is so stated in the newspapers, and the additional fact that the gentleman who furnished the pamphlet to me received it under Jerry Black's frank. I will read the last sentence of his pamphlet first:

We are called upon to make a contest, at once unnecessary and hopeless, with the judicial authority of the nation. We object to it. We will not obey Mr. Douglas when he commands us to assault the Supreme Court of the United States. We believe the Court to be right, and Mr. Douglas wrong.

Again he says:

In case he is elected President he must see the laws faithfully executed. Does he think he can keep that oath by fighting the Judiciary?

This, bear it in mind, pretends to be a review of my exposition of popular sovereignty in *Harper's Magazine.* As we rode through the streets I saw the boys circulating that article by the hundred and perhaps by the thousand, and I invite you to look into it and see if there is a word of censure of the Supreme Court or its decision. Not one word. The author of the pamphlet knew when he made the charge against me that

it was an infamous falsehood. I care not who he is.
There is no man in America who has made as many
speeches in defense of the Court against the assaults of
the Republican party as I have.

Last year, in the Illinois canvass, I made just one
hundred and thirty speeches, in every one of which I
vindicated the Court. [Cheers.] The man does not live
who can meet me, look me in the eye, and pretend
to be honest, and assert what is insinuated in that
paper. The author knows it to be false. If you look at
the article in *Harper's Magazine,* which he pretends to
review, you will find that so far from assailing the
Supreme Court or the Dred Scott decision, I quote
that decision to prove that my doctrine of popular
sovereignty is the true doctrine of the Constitution,
and I do prove it; and yet the author of this pamphlet
dare not quote a word to show that his charge that I
assailed the Court is true. What can be thought of the
man who will prostitute a high government office by
writing deliberate falsehoods to mislead the American
people. No wonder he made it anonymous. [Laughter.]
No wonder he did not sign his name to it. When I
write I write my own name, and when I speak I speak
in language that cannot be misunderstood, and everyone knows that I am responsible for what I say. I do
not assault personal enemies through anonymous pam-
phlets. I do not say who the author is; but whoever
he is, he is a calumniator and knew that what he was
writing was a tissue of falsehoods from beginning to
end.

I will notice another statement in this pamphlet for
I understand that Ohio and the Northwestern States

are to be flooded with it. Speaking of me again he says:

He claims for the Territorial government the right of confiscating private property on the ground that *those governments* ARE *sovereign*—have an uncontrollable and independent power over all their internal affairs.

Now, this is a deliberate falsehood. I never claimed that a Territory possessed the power of confiscating private property. I deny that private property can be confiscated either by a Territory or by a State or by the federal government. It cannot be confiscated under our Constitution by any power on earth except it is taken away by due process of law. This statement contains a double falsehood: first, that I advocate confiscation of private property; secondly, that I justify it on the ground that a Territory was a sovereign power. I never said that a Territory was a sovereign power. I never uttered such a piece of nonsense in any speech or report that I ever made or wrote, and the author of this statement knows that I never did, for he occupied the last two pages in proving that I have said over and over again that the Territory was not a sovereign power. [Laughter and applause.] He quotes from my report as Chairman of the Committee on Territories in the Senate in 1856, the following:

The sovereignty of a Territory remains in *abeyance, suspended* in the United States, *in trust for the people until they shall be admitted into the Union as a State. In the meantime* they are admitted to enjoy and exercise all the rights and privileges of self-government *in subordination to the Constitution* of the United States, and IN OBEDIENCE TO THE ORGANIC LAW, passed by Congress

in pursuance of that instrument. These rights and privileges are *all* derived from the Constitution *through the
act of Congress,* and must be exercised and enjoyed in
subjection to all the limitations and restrictions which that
Constitution imposes.

I affirm every word of that extract now. The Territory is no more sovereign than were the Colonies sovereign before the Revolution; but while the Territories
are not sovereign, they have the inalienable right of
self-government—of managing their own affairs and domestic institutions the same as the Colonies had prior
to the Revolution. Thus you see that there has been
a deliberate attempt to misrepresent my position, the
author of the article knowing that I did not hold the
opinions he attributed to me.

After accusing me of a desire to confiscate private
property he goes on to say:

. . . On the other hand, the President, the Judges of the
Supreme Court, nearly all the Democratic members of
Congress, the whole of the party South, and a very large
majority North are penetrated with a conviction that no
such power is vested in a Territorial legislature, and that
those who desire to confiscate private property of any
kind must wait until they get a constitutional convention
or the machinery of a State government in their hands.

According to this new doctrine, before you can confiscate private property you must wait until you have
a State government; and the inference is that when you
have a State government you may confiscate it. Do
you admit that the State government of Ohio can
confiscate any man's private property in the State? I

deny this heresy that you can confiscate property when
a Territory becomes a State any more than you can
when it is in a Territory, or that you can do it in
either. But these misrepresentations have been made
for the purpose of attacking me and breaking the force
of the position occupied by the Democratic party.

I would be sorry to be under the necessity of replying
to an attack made on myself, and if that attack was
only intended for me I would not have noticed it. But
it is made at me and through me at all the friends of
popular sovereignty throughout the country. It is intended to hit my friend Judge Ranney who stands on
the same platform as your candidate for Governor.
[Cheers.] It is intended to reach and strike down the
gallant Dodge, who leads the Democracy of Iowa and
stands on the same platform; it is intended to reach and
strike down the gallant Hobart, who is the Democratic
candidate for Governor of Wisconsin and stands on the
same platform; it is intended to reach and strike down
the indomitable Baker, who leads the indomitable hosts
as candidate for Governor in Minnesota, standing on
the same platform; it is intended to reach and strike
down all the Democratic candidates throughout the
country who maintain the doctrine of popular sovereignty. All I can say is, that when any band or set of
men attempt to declare war against this great doctrine
of popular sovereignty and its advocates, they will have
their hands full. [Applause.] Whenever you have struck
down the champions of popular sovereignty and its
advocates in the Northwest, you have struck down the
entire Democratic party. [Cheers.] If there is one principle on earth which binds the Democracy together with

more unanimity than any others throughout the entire
land, it is this great principle of the right of every
political community, loyal to the Constitution and the
Union, to govern itself in respect to its internal
concerns.

I have not many more words to say. I wish to exhort
all Democrats, all men who regard the peace and harmony of this Union as paramount to partisan success,
to rally around those great principles which alone can
preserve the peace and unanimity of the country. So
long as this doctrine shall prevail that Congress can
interfere with slavery anywhere, there never can be
peace; for so long as the doctrine shall prevail that Congress can and ought to control the question, the antislavery men will demand that it shall be controlled
against slavery, while the proslavery men will demand
that the powers of the government shall be exerted for
slavery. The contest therefore between these jarring
elements, this sectional strife, must last just as long as
the people allow Congress to touch the question. [A
voice, "That's so."]

The agitation can never cease as long as Congress
may act upon it. No matter which way Congress acts,
if it acts at all there will be strife, there will be ill
blood, there will be sectional hate. Suppose the South
should come forward and demand a slave code to be
enacted by Congress to compel the people of Kansas
to have slavery when they did not want it; would you
be satisfied to allow it? ["No."] Then is it any more
satisfactory to the South that the Republicans should
interfere and deprive the people of slavery when they
do want it? We have before us two cases in point await-

ing the meeting of Congress. There is the Territory of New Mexico which was organized in 1850, and refused to maintain and protect slavery until the last year, when it adopted a slave code maintaining and protecting slavery. Now, the Republican party stands pledged by their Philadelphia platform, by all their stump speeches or political sermons that ever disgrace the public, by all their professions to come forward and repeal the slave code which the people have there adopted for themselves. On the other hand the Territory of Kansas which first adopted a slave code establishing and protecting African slavery repealed that code by an act of the Territorial legislature on the 9th of February, 1858, and abolished all laws protecting slavery or the rights of slave property and punishing any man for violating these rights. According to the doctrine of the Southern interventionists, they must interfere and demand that Congress shall now pass a law compelling Kansas to have slavery when she does not want it. The Republicans and the Southern interventionists act on the same principle—a contempt for the rights of the people—in demanding that Congress shall exercise the same power which our fathers resisted when Colonies against the British Parliament. The Democratic party will meet that question just as boldly in New Mexico and Kansas as we have met all similar questions. We shall maintain the doctrine of non-intervention with slavery, either in New Mexico or Kansas. [Cheers.]

I tell you here that every Democrat in America, who is entitled to be deemed a Democrat, holds to the doctrine that if New Mexico wants slavery she has a right to it, and if she wants a slave code that she

has a right to adopt one for herself; and on the other
hand, that if Kansas does not want slavery no person on
earth shall force it on her, and if she does not want a
slave code Congress shall not compel her to have one.
["That's our doctrine," and cheers.] That is what we
mean by popular sovereignty—the right of the people
of Kansas to adopt a slave code when they please and
to repeal it when they get tired of it. We in Illinois
have had some experience on the subject. The old
Ordinance of 1787 told the people of this Northwest
Territory that they should not have slavery if they
wanted it. The Territory of Illinois, notwithstanding
this, passed a slave code, introduced African slavery,
protected and maintained it while in a Territorial condition in spite of the Ordinance. Just so long as Congress said that slavery should not exist in Illinois it
did exist, and the moment the prohibition was withdrawn, and we were left free to do as we pleased, we
abolished it. In the very teeth and face of these facts
Governor Chase comes out to Illinois every year and
makes half a dozen speeches in which he glorifies the
Ordinance of 1787, and tells the people of Illinois that
they would inevitably have been a slave State but for
that Ordinance. Very likely he has told you people of
Ohio, that you derive all the blessings of freedom from
that blessed Ordinance of 1787. Does he tell you so?
[Voices, "Yes! Yes!"] Well, I will tell you what I said
to the people of Illinois when Chase made a few of the
green ones believe that they were made free by the
Ordinance of 1787. I told them that if their freedom
depended upon the compulsory action of an act of
Congress, they did not deserve freedom. [Voices, "That's

it," and applause.] The doctrine of the Republicans is that you are free because you cannot help it. [Laughter and applause.] That you are free because Congress passed an act saying that you should be free. I thought that you were all free because you chose to be free. I thought that you prohibited slavery because you did not want it; but now we are told by the Republicans, "Oh! no; Ohio would be a slave State now but for the Ordinance of 1787, and would always have been a slave State but for that Ordinance." So in Illinois and Indiana and all of the Northwestern States, the people were so depraved that they would have had slavery if Congress had not interfered—this is the Republican doctrine. On the other hand I hold that Ohio derives her freedom from the glorious action of her own citizens, and Ohio will remain free just so long as her own citizens are true to the doctrine of popular sovereignty. [Cheers.] Whenever you become so depraved and degenerate that Congress can force either freedom or slavery on you, you do not deserve to be free any longer.

[A voice, "Is slavery a Christian institution?"] I do not know of any tribunal on earth that can decide the question of the morality of slavery or any other institution. ["Good," and cheers.] I deal with slavery as a political question involving questions of public policy. I deal with slavery under the Constitution, and that is all I have to do with it. Allow me to tell you that when the Constitution was being framed, a party arose in the Convention demanding the instant prohibition of the African slave trade upon moral and religious grounds. [A voice, "That does not answer my question."]

My dear sir, I take my own time to answer the question, and you ought to be very thankful that I did not rebuke your impertinence in interrupting me. [Cries of "Good," and applause.] The Convention which framed the Constitution decided that the slave trade might continue until the year 1808, from and after which time it was, and would be, abolished. Thus the moral and religious ground is waived under the Constitution, leaving each State to have it as long as it pleases and abolish it when it pleases. Now, sir, if the people of Ohio declare slavery to be a moral and religious evil, they have a right to decide this question for themselves; and if the people of Kentucky believe that slavery is not a moral and religious evil, they have a right so to decide and so to construe it. You have no right to interfere with Kentucky, nor has Kentucky a right to interfere with you. ["Good."] And permit me to say that both States, having decided that question to suit themselves, let me warn you, judge not Kentucky, lest you be judged yourselves!

My friends, I will not detain you any longer. I have wearied you and wearied myself, as my voice shows. I must, in conclusion, renew to you my profound gratification at what I have witnessed here today and, in fact, wherever I have been in the State of Ohio. I find the Democratic party a unit, determined to rally as one man round your noble leader and win a glorious triumph. [Cheers.] Your principles are tried—your candidates true and reliable—you have everything to encourage—upon you rest the peace and safety of the country. What will become of this great Confederacy if a mere sectional party shall obtain control of the reins of your Government? Why shall we encourage sectional strife between the North and the South? Are we not brethren of a common country? Do we not rejoice in common glories won by our ancestors on the field of battle? Are we not animated by common hopes to transmit our liberty unimpaired to our latest posterity? Why, then, can we not act on these same principles that animated our fathers when they won our liberties? There was no sectional strife in Revolutionary days. There were no sectional jealousies in Washington's camp. On every battlefield North and South—at Camden, Yorktown, Saratoga, and Trenton— Northern and Southern blood flowed in common streams in a common cause. [Cheers.]

On every one of those sacred battlefields, Southern and Northern men gave up their lives in order that this Union might forever remain composed of free States and slave States, with the right either to have slavery or not, as it pleased. Why, then, can we not act as brothers towards our friends in the South. Have the Southern people ever been wanting in fidelity to the Constitution, or their loyalty to the cause of freedom? On every battlefield Southern chivalry has been conspicuous by the side of Northern chivalry; in every war we have had, the South has always been ready to defend the flag, no matter whether it was upon the Southern or Northern frontier. Along the Canada line and among the snows of that region, you will find the bones of Southern soldiers bleaching, who were killed during the War of 1812. Whenever a call has been made upon this Union, there has been no distinction between the patriotism, the gallantry, and the disinter-

estedness of the two sections. Why, then, shall we not
remain at peace? Are there no Southern men here? Is
there no man here whose heart beats at the thought of
a mother's fate in old Virginia? Is there no daughter
here whose hope and last prayer at night is for a mother
or a sister in a slaveholding State? Why, then, I repeat,
can we not recognize our Southern friends as our
brethren and our equals, and grant them every right
which we claim for ourselves and maintain for ourselves
every right which we concede to them. Then, my
friends, all we have to do so, is to maintain the time-
honored principles of the Democratic party, and stand
upon the Cincinnati platform without the interpolation
of a single plank or the abstraction of a single column—
stand by that platform as it was expounded and understood in 1856, when Mr. Buchanan was elected President upon it. Let us stand by the Kansas-Nebraska
Bill—by the Compromise of 1850—by the right of the
people to govern themselves, as stated by Mr. Buchanan
in his letter of acceptance in 1856. In that letter, remember, he told the people that he stood upon the
doctrine that the people of a Territory, like those of a
State, should decide for themselves whether slavery
should or should not exist within their limits. Let us
be true to that doctrine thus defined, thus understood,
and thus ratified by the people in 1856, and we are
sure to win a glorious triumph in 1860.

I appeal to you again. If you wish to win the battle
next year, give a little hope and encouragement to your
sister States by electing the Democratic ticket this year.
["We will," and cheers.] I am satisfied that you are
to win in the great struggle in 1860, and I wish you

now just to make Ohio an offset to some of the Republican triumphs in the old Republican States by redeeming your State and putting her at the head of the Democratic column. Illinois feels rather uncomfortable in her isolated position. She stands the only Northern State which from the beginning has never failed to cast her electoral vote for a Democratic President—the only Northern State that has never been conquered by the unholy combination of Republicanism and its kindred isms. [Laughter.] You left us alone and we maintained the battle last year single-handed. We now say to Ohio, the oldest of the Northwestern States and the one entitled to take the lead, rally, bring yourself into line, and take the command of the entire Northwest. Illinois does not claim the lead, Ohio is entitled to it. Redeem her from Republicanism, Chase-ism, and Giddings-ism, and come back to your first love, the Democracy. [Cheers and laughter.] Whenever you do that Illinois will follow you. If you do not throw off the shackles, we will maintain the fight single-handed and keep the Democratic flag waving in triumph over one Northwestern State at least. [Great applause.]

My friends, I always leave when I talk the best thing for the conclusion, and now I am going to give it to you: I present to you Judge Ranney, the next Democratic Governor of Ohio. [Tremendous shouts of applause, followed by nine cheers for Douglas.]

SPEECH OF ABRAHAM LINCOLN

at Columbus, Ohio, September 16, 1859 [1]

Fellow Citizens of the State of Ohio: I cannot fail to
remember that I appear for the first time before an
audience in this now great State—an audience that is
accustomed to hear such speakers as Corwin, and Chase,
and Wade, and many other renowned men; and, re-
membering this, I feel that it will be well for you, as
for me, that you should not raise your expectations to
that standard to which you would have been justified
in raising them had one of these distinguished men
appeared before you. You would perhaps be only preparing a disappointment for yourselves, and, as a consequence of your disappointment, mortification to me.
I hope, therefore, that you will commence with very
moderate expectations; and perhaps, if you will give me
your attention, I shall be able to interest you to a
moderate degree.

Appearing here for the first time in my life, I have
been somewhat embarrassed for a topic by way of introduction to my speech; but I have been relieved from
that embarrassment by an introduction which the *Ohio
Statesman* newspaper gave me this morning. In this
paper I have read an article, in which, among other
statements, I find the following:

In debating with Senator Douglas during the memorable
contest of last fall, Mr. Lincoln declared in favor of negro

[1] *Illinois State Journal* (Springfield), September 24, 1859.

suffrage, and attempted to defend that vile conception against the Little Giant.

I mention this now, at the opening of my remarks, for the purpose of making three comments upon it. The first I have already announced—it furnishes me an introductory topic; the second is to show that the gentleman is mistaken; thirdly, to give him an opportunity to correct it. [A voice, "That he won't do."]

In the first place, in regard to this matter being a mistake. I have found that it is not entirely safe, when one is misrepresented under his very nose, to allow the misrepresentation to go uncontradicted. I therefore propose, here at the outset, not only to say that this is a misrepresentation, but to show conclusively that it is so; and you will bear with me while I read a couple of extracts from that very "memorable" debate with Judge Douglas last year, to which this newspaper refers. In the first pitched battle which Senator Douglas and myself had, at the town of Ottawa, I used the language which I will now read. Having been previously reading an extract, I continued as follows:

Now, gentlemen, I don't want to read at any greater length, but this is the true complexion of all I have ever said in regard to the institution of slavery and the black race. This is the whole of it; and anything that argues me into his idea of perfect social and political equality with the negro, is but a specious and fantastic arrangement of words, by which a man can prove a horse chestnut to be a chestnut horse. I will say here, while upon this subject, that I have no purpose directly or indirectly to interfere with the institution of slavery in the States where it exists. I believe I have no lawful right to do so, and I have no

inclination to do so. I have no purpose to introduce political and social equality between the white and the black
races. There is a physical difference between the two which,
in my judgment, will probably forever forbid their living
together upon the footing of perfect equality; and inasmuch
as it becomes a necessity that there must be a difference,
I, as well as Judge Douglas, am in favor of the race to
which I belong having the superior position. I have never
said anything to the contrary, but I hold that, notwithstanding all this, there is no reason in the world why the
negro is not entitled to all the natural rights enumerated
in the Declaration of Independence—the right to life, liberty and the pursuit of happiness. I hold that he is as much
entitled to these as the white man. I agree with Judge
Douglas, he is not my equal in many respects—certainly
not in color, perhaps not in moral or intellectual endowments. But in the right to eat the bread, without leave of
anybody else, which his own hand earns, *he is my equal,
and the equal of Judge Douglas, and the equal of every
living man.*

Upon a subsequent occasion, when the reason for
making a statement like this recurred, I said:

While I was at the hotel today an elderly gentleman
called upon me to know whether I was really in favor of
producing perfect equality between the negroes and white
people. While I had not proposed to myself on this occasion to say much on that subject, yet, as the question
was asked me, I thought I would occupy perhaps five minutes in saying something in regard to it. I will say, then,
that I am not, nor ever have been, in favor of bringing
about in any way the social and political equality of the
white and black races; that I am not, nor ever have been,
in favor of making voters or jurors of negroes, nor of
qualifying them to hold office, or intermarry with the white
people; and I will say in addition to this that there is a

physical difference between the white and black races which
I believe will forever forbid the two races living together on
terms of social and political equality. And inasmuch as
they can not so live, while they do remain together there
must be the position of superior and inferior, and I, as
much as any other man, am in favor of having the superior
position assigned to the white race. I say upon this occasion
I do not perceive that because the white man is to have
the superior position, the negro should be denied everything. I do not understand that because I do not want a
negro woman for a slave, I must necessarily want her
for a wife. My understanding is that I can just let her alone.
I am now in my fiftieth year, and I certainly never have
had a black woman for either a slave or a wife. So it
seems to me quite possible for us to get along without
making either slaves or wives of negroes. I will add to this
that I have never seen, to my knowledge, a man, woman,
or child, who was in favor of producing perfect equality,
social and political, between negroes and white men. I
recollect of but one distinguished instance that I ever
heard of so frequently as to be satisfied of its correctness—
and that is the case of Judge Douglas' old friend, Colonel
Richard M. Johnson. I will also add to the remarks I have
made (for I am not going to enter at large upon this subject), that I have never had the least apprehension that
I or my friends would marry negroes, if there was no law
to keep them from it; but as Judge Douglas and his
friends seem to be in great apprehension that they might,
if there were no law to keep them from it, I give him the
most solemn pledge that I will to the very last stand by
the law of the State which forbids the marrying of white
people with negroes.

There, my friends, you have briefly what I have, upon
former occasions, said upon this subject to which this
newspaper, to the extent of its ability [laughter], has
drawn the public attention. In it you not only perceive,

as a probability, that in that contest I did not at any time say I was in favor of negro suffrage, but the absolute proof that twice—once substantially, and once expressly—I declared against it. Having shown you this, there remains but a word of comment upon that newspaper article. It is this: that I presume the editor of that paper is an honest and truth-loving man [a voice, "That's a great mistake."] and that he will be greatly obliged to me for furnishing him thus early an opportunity to correct the misrepresentation he has made, before it has run so long that malicious people can call him a liar. [Laughter and applause.]

The Giant himself has been here recently. [Laughter.] I have seen a brief report of his speech. If it were otherwise unpleasant to me to introduce the subject of the negro as a topic for discussion, I might be somewhat relieved by the fact that he dealt exclusively in that subject while he was here. I shall, therefore, without much hesitation or diffidence, enter upon this subject.

The American people, on the first day of January, 1854, found the African slave trade prohibited by a law of Congress. In a majority of the States of this Union, they found African slavery, or any other sort of slavery, prohibited by State constitutions. They also found a law existing, supposed to be valid, by which slavery was excluded from almost all the territory the United States then owned. This was the condition of the country, with reference to the institution of slavery, on the 1st of January, 1854. A few days after that a bill was introduced into Congress, which ran through its regular course in the two branches of the national legislature and finally passed into a law in the month of May, by which the act of Congress prohibiting slavery from going into the Territories of the United States was repealed. In connection with the law itself, and, in fact, in the terms of the law, the then existing prohibition was not only repealed, but there was a declaration of a purpose on the part of Congress never thereafter to exercise any power that they might have, real or supposed, to prohibit the extension or spread of slavery. This was a very great change; for the law thus repealed was of more than thirty-years' standing. Following rapidly upon the heels of this action of Congress, a decision of the Supreme Court is made by which it is declared that Congress, if it desires to prohibit the spread of slavery into the Territories, has no Constitutional power to do so. Not only so, but that decision lays down principles which, if pushed to their logical conclusion—I say pushed to their logical conclusion—would decide that the constitutions of free States, forbidding slavery, are themselves unconstitutional. Mark me, I do not say the Judge said this, and let no man say I affirm the Judge used these words; but I only say it is my opinion that what they did say, if pressed to its logical conclusion, will inevitably result thus. [Cries of "Good! Good!"]

Looking at these things, the Republican party, as I understand its principles and policy, believe that there is great danger of the institution of slavery being spread out and extended until it is ultimately made alike lawful in all the States of this Union; so believing, to prevent that incidental and ultimate consummation is the original and chief purpose of the Republican organization. I say "chief purpose" of the Republican organization; for it is certainly true that if the national house shall fall into the hands of the Republicans, they will have to attend to all the other matters of national housekeeping, as well as this. This chief and real purpose of the Republican party is eminently conservative. It proposes nothing save and except to restore this government to its original tone in regard to this element of slavery, and there to maintain it, looking for no further change in reference to it than that which the original framers of the government themselves expected and looked forward to.

The chief danger to this purpose of the Republican party is not just now the revival of the African slave trade, or the passage of a Congressional slave code, or the declaring of a second Dred Scott decision making slavery lawful in all the States. These are not pressing us just now. They are not quite ready yet. The authors of these measures know that we are too strong for them; but they will be upon us in due time, and we will be grappling with them hand to hand, if they are not now headed off. They are not now the chief danger to the purpose of the Republican organization; but the most imminent danger that now threatens that purpose is that insidious Douglas Popular Sovereignty. This is the miner and sapper. While it does not propose to revive the African slave trade, nor to pass a slave code, nor to make a second Dred Scott decision, it is preparing us for the onslaught and charge of these ultimate enemies when they shall be ready to come on and the word of command for them to advance shall be given. I say this "Douglas Popular Sovereignty"—for there is a broad distinction, as I now understand it, between that article and a genuine popular sovereignty.

I believe there is a genuine popular sovereignty. I think a definition of genuine popular sovereignty, in the abstract, would be about this: That each man shall do precisely as he pleases with himself and with all those things which exclusively concern him. Applied to government, this principle would be that a general government shall do all those things which pertain to it, and all the local governments shall do precisely as they please in respect to those matters which exclusively concern them. I understand that this government of the United States, under which we live, is based upon this principle; and I am misunderstood if it is supposed that I have any war to make upon that principle.

Now, what is Judge Douglas' popular sovereignty? It is, as a principle, no other than that if one man chooses to make a slave of another man, neither that other man nor anybody else has a right to object. [Cheers and laughter.] Applied in government, as he seeks to apply it, it is this: If, in a new Territory into which a few people are beginning to enter for the purpose of making their homes, they choose to either exclude slavery from their limits or to establish it there, however one or the other may affect the persons to be enslaved, or the infinitely greater number of persons who are afterward to inhabit that Territory, or the other members of the families of communities of which they are but an incipient member, or the general head of the family of States as parent of all—however their action may affect one or the other of these, there is no power or right to interfere. That is Douglas' popular sovereignty applied.

He has a good deal of trouble with his popular sovereignty. His explanations explanatory of explanations
explained are interminable. [Laughter.] The most
lengthy and, as I suppose, the most maturely considered of his long series of explanations is his great essay
in *Harper's Magazine*. [Laughter.] I will not attempt
to enter upon any very thorough investigation of his
argument as there made and presented. I will nevertheless occupy a good portion of your time here in drawing
your attention to certain points in it. Such of you as
may have read this document will have perceived that
the Judge, early in the document, quotes from two persons as belonging to the Republican party, without
naming them, but who can readily be recognized as
being Governor Seward of New York and myself. It
is true, that exactly fifteen months ago this day, I believe, I for the first time expressed a sentiment upon
this subject, and in such a manner that it should get
into print, that the public might see it beyond the
circle of my hearers; and my expression of it at that
time is the quotation that Judge Douglas makes. He has
not made the quotation with accuracy, but justice to
him requires me to say that it is sufficiently accurate not
to change its sense.

The sense of that quotation condensed is this—that
this slavery element is a durable element of discord
among us, and that we shall probably not have perfect
peace in this country with it until it either masters
the free principle in our government, or is so far mastered by the free principle as for the public mind to
rest in the belief that it is going to its end. This sentiment, which I now express in this way, was, at no great
distance of time, perhaps in different language, and

in connection with some collateral ideas, expressed by
Governor Seward. Judge Douglas has been so much
annoyed by the expression of that sentiment that he
has constantly, I believe, in almost all his speeches
since it was uttered, been referring to it. I find he
alluded to it in his speech here, as well as in the copyright essay. [Laughter.] I do not now enter upon this
for the purpose of making an elaborate argument to
show that we were right in the expression of that sentiment. In other words, I shall not stop to say all that
might properly be said upon this point; but I only ask
your attention to it for the purpose of making one or
two points upon it.

If you will read the copyright essay, you will discover
that Judge Douglas himself says a controversy between
the American Colonies and the government of Great
Britain began on the slavery question in 1699, and
continued from that time until the Revolution; and,
while he did not say so, we all know that it has continued with more or less violence ever since the Revolution.

Then we need not appeal to history, to the declarations of the framers of the government, but we know
from Judge Douglas himself that slavery began to be
an element of discord among the white people of this
country as far back as 1699, or one hundred and sixty
years ago, or five generations of men—counting thirty
years to a generation. Now it would seem to me that
it might have occurred to Judge Douglas, or anybody
who had turned his attention to these facts, that there
was something in the nature of that thing, slavery,
somewhat durable for mischief and discord. [Laughter.]

There is another point I desire to make in regard to this matter before I leave it. From the adoption of the Constitution down to 1820 is the precise period of our history when we had comparative peace upon this question—the precise period of time when we came nearer to having peace about it than any other time of that entire one hundred and sixty years, in which he says it began, or of the eighty years of our own Constitution. Then it would be worth our while to stop and examine into the probable reason of our coming nearer to having peace then than at any other time. This was the precise period of time in which our fathers adopted, and during which they followed, a policy restricting the spread of slavery, and the whole Union was acquiescing in it. The whole country looked forward to the ultimate extinction of the institution. It was when a policy had been adopted, and was prevailing, which led all just and right-minded men to suppose that slavery was gradually coming to an end, and that they might be quiet about it, watching it as it expired. I think Judge Douglas might have perceived that too, and whether he did or not, it is worth the attention of fair-minded men, here and elsewhere, to consider whether that is not the truth of the case. If he had looked at these two facts, that this matter has been an element of discord for one hundred and sixty years among this people, and that the only comparative peace we have had about it was when that policy prevailed in this government which he now wars upon, he might then, perhaps, have been brought to a more just appreciation of what I said fifteen months ago—that "a house divided against itself cannot stand. I believe that this government cannot endure permanently half slave and half free. I do not expect the house to fall. I do not expect the Union to dissolve; but I do expect it will cease to be divided. It will become all one thing or all the other. Either the opponents of slavery will arrest the further spread of it, and place it where the public mind will rest in the belief that it is in the course of ultimate extinction; or its advocates will push it forward, until it shall become alike lawful in all the States, old as well as new, north as well as south." That was my sentiment at that time. In connection with it, I said, "We are now, far into the fifth year since a policy was inaugurated with the avowed object and confident promise of putting an end to slavery agitation. Under the operation of the policy, that agitation has not only not ceased, but has constantly augmented." I now say to you here that we are advanced still farther into the sixth year since that policy of Judge Douglas—that popular sovereignty of his, for quieting the slavery question—was made the national policy. Fifteen months more have been added since I uttered that sentiment, and I call upon you, and all other right-minded men, to say whether that fifteen months have belied or corroborated my words. ["Good, good! That's the truth!"]

While I am here upon this subject, I cannot but express gratitude that this true view of this element of discord among us—as I believe it is—is attracting more and more attention. I do not believe that Governor Seward uttered that sentiment because I had done so before, but because he reflected upon this subject and saw the truth of it. Nor do I believe, because Governor Seward or I uttered it, that Mr. Hickman of Penn-

sylvania, in different language, since that time, has
declared his belief in the utter antagonism which exists
between the principles of liberty and slavery. You see
we are multiplying. [Applause and laughter.] Now,
while I am speaking of Hickman, let me say, I know
but little about him. I have never seen him, and know
scarcely anything about the man. But I will say this
much of him: Of all the Anti-Lecompton Democracy
that have been brought to my notice, he alone has
the true, genuine ring of the metal. And now, without
endorsing anything else he has said, I will ask this
audience to give three cheers for Hickman. [The audience responded with three rousing cheers for Hickman.]

Another point in the copyright essay to which I would
ask your attention is rather a feature to be extracted
from the whole thing than from any express declaration
of it at any point. It is a general feature of that document, and, indeed, of all of Judge Douglas' discussions
of this question, that the Territories of the United
States and the States of this Union are exactly alike—
that there is no difference between them at all—that the
Constitution applies to the Territories precisely as it
does to the States—and that the United States Government, under the Constitution, may not do in a State
what it may not do in a Territory, and what it must
do in a State, it must do in a Territory. Gentlemen,
is that a true view of the case? It is necessary for this
squatter sovereignty; but is it true?

Let us consider. What does it depend upon? It depends altogether upon the proposition that the States
must, without the interference of the general government, do all those things that pertain *exclusively* to

themselves—that are local in their nature, that have no connection with the general government. After Judge Douglas has established this proposition, which nobody disputes or ever has disputed, he proceeds to assume, without proving it, that slavery is one of those little, unimportant, trivial matters which are of just about as much consequence as the question would be to me, whether my neighbor should raise horned cattle or plant tobacco [laughter]; that there is no moral question about it, but that it is altogether a matter of dollars and cents; that when a new Territory is opened for settlement, the first man who goes into it may plant there a thing which, like the Canada thistle, or some other of those pests of the soil, cannot be dug out by the millions of men who will come thereafter; that it is one of those little things that is so trivial in its nature that it has no effect upon anybody save the few men who first plant upon the soil; that it is not a thing which in any way affects the family of communities composing these States, nor any way endangers the general government. Judge Douglas ignores altogether the very well-known fact that we have never had a serious menace to our political existence, except it sprang from this thing which he chooses to regard as only upon a par with onions and potatoes. [Laughter.]

Turn it, and contemplate it in another view. He says, that according to his popular sovereignty, the general government may give to the Territories governors, judges, marshals, secretaries, and all the other chief men to govern them, but they must not touch upon this other question. Why? The question of who shall be governor of a Territory for a year or two, and. pass

away, without his track being left upon the soil or
an act which he did for good or for evil being left
behind, is a question of vast national magnitude. It
is so much opposed in its nature to locality that the
nation itself must decide it; while this other matter of
planting slavery upon a soil—a thing which once planted
cannot be eradicated by the succeeding millions who
have as much right there as the first comers or if
eradicated, not without infinite difficulty and a long
struggle—he considers the power to prohibit it as one
of these little, local, trivial things that the nation ought
not to say a word about, that it affects nobody save
the few men who are there.

Take these two things and consider them together,
present the question of planting a State with the
institution of slavery by the side of a question of who
shall be governor of Kansas for a year or two, and is
there a man here—is there a man on earth—who would
not say that the governor question is the little one, and
the slavery question is the great one? I ask any honest
Democrat if the small, the local, and the trivial and
temporary question is not, Who shall be governor?
While the durable, the important, and the mischievous
one is, Shall this soil be planted with slavery?

This is an idea, I suppose, which has arisen in Judge
Douglas' mind from his peculiar structure. I suppose
the institution of slavery really looks small to him. He
is so put up by nature that a lash upon his back would
hurt him, but a lash upon anybody else's back does not
hurt him. [Laughter.] That is the build of the man,
and consequently he looks upon the matter of slavery
in this unimportant light.

Judge Douglas ought to remember when he is endeavoring to force this policy upon the American people that while he is put up in that way a good many are not. He ought to remember that there was once in this country a man by the name of Thomas Jefferson, supposed to be a Democrat—a man whose principles and policy are not very prevalent amongst Democrats today, it is true; but that man did not take exactly this view of the insignificance of the element of slavery which our friend Judge Douglas does. In contemplation of this thing, we all know he was led to exclaim, "I tremble for my country when I remember that God is just!" We know how he looked upon it when he thus expressed himself. There was danger to this country—danger of the avenging justice of God in that little, unimportant popular sovereignty question of Judge Douglas. He supposed there was a question of God's eternal justice wrapped up in the enslaving of any race of men, or any man, and that those who did so braved the arm of Jehovah—that when a nation thus dared the Almighty every friend of that nation had cause to dread His wrath. Choose ye between Jefferson and Douglas as to what is the true view of this element among us. [Applause.]

There is another little difficulty about this matter of treating the Territories and States alike in all things to which I ask your attention, and I shall leave this branch of the case. If there is no difference between them, why not make the Territories States at once? What is the reason that Kansas was not fit to come into the Union when it was organized into a Territory, in Judge Douglas' view? Can any of you tell any reason why it should not have come into the Union at once? They are fit, as he thinks, to decide upon the slavery question—the largest and most important with which they could possibly deal—what could they do by coming into the Union that they are not fit to do, according to his view, by staying out of it? Oh, they are not fit to sit in Congress and decide upon the rates of postage, or questions of ad valorem or specific duties on foreign goods, or live oak timber contracts [laughter]; they are not fit to decide these vastly important matters, which are national in their import, but they are fit, "from the jump," to decide this little negro question. But, gentlemen, the case is too plain; I occupy too much time on this head, and I pass on.

Near the close of the copyright essay, the Judge, I think, comes very near kicking his own fat into the fire. [Laughter.] I did not think, when I commenced these remarks, that I would read from that article, but I now believe I will:

This exposition of the history of these measures shows conclusively that the authors of the Compromise Measures of 1850 and of the Kansas-Nebraska Act of 1854, as well as the members of the Continental Congress of 1774 and the founders of our system of government subsequent to the Revolution, regarded the people of the Territories and Colonies as political communities which were entitled to a free and exclusive power of legislation in their Provincial legislatures, where their representation could alone be preserved, in all cases of taxation and internal polity.

When the Judge saw that putting in the word "slavery" would contradict his own history, he put in what he knew would pass as synonymous with it, "internal polity." Whenever we find *that* in one of his speeches, the substitute is used in this manner; and I can tell you the reason. It would be too bald a contradiction to say slavery, but "internal polity" is a general phrase, which would pass in some quarters, and which he hopes will pass with the reading community, for the same thing.

This right pertains to the people collectively, as a law-abiding and peaceful community, and not to the isolated individuals who may wander upon the public domain in violation of the law. It can only be exercised where there are inhabitants sufficient to constitute a government, and capable of performing its various functions and duties— a fact to be ascertained and determined by ———

Who do you think? Judge Douglas says "by Congress"! [Laughter.]

Whether the number shall be fixed at ten, fifteen, or twenty thousand inhabitants does not affect the principle.

Now I have only a few comments to make. Popular sovereignty, by his own words, does not pertain to the few persons who wander upon the public domain in violation of law. We have his words for that. When it does pertain to them is when they are sufficient to be formed into an organized political community, and he fixes the minimum for that at 10,000, and the maximum at 20,000. Now I would like to know what is to be done with the 9,000? Are they all to be treated, until they are large enough to be organized into a political community, as wanderers upon the public land in violation of law? And if so treated and driven out, at what point of time would there ever be 10,000? [Great laughter.] If they were not driven out, but remained there as trespassers upon the public land in violation of the law, can they establish slavery there? No—the Judge says popular sovereignty don't pertain to them then. Can they exclude it then? No, popular sovereignty don't pertain to them then. I would like to know, in the case covered by the essay, what condition the people of the Territory are in before they reach the number of 10,000?

But the main point I wish to ask attention to is that the question as to when they shall have reached a sufficient number to be formed into a regular organized community is to be decided "by Congress." Judge Douglas says so. Well, gentlemen, that is about all we want. [Here some one in the crowd made a remark inaudible to the reporter, whereupon Mr. Lincoln continued.] No, that is all the Southerners want. That is what all those who are for slavery want. They do not want Congress to prohibit slavery from coming into the new Territories, and they do not want popular sovereignty to hinder it; and as Congress is to say when they are ready to be organized, all that the South has to do is to get Congress to hold off. Let Congress hold off until they are ready to be admitted as a State, and the South has all it wants in taking slavery into and planting it in all the Territories that we now have, or hereafter may have. In a word, the whole thing, at a dash of the pen, is at last put in the power of Congress; for if they do not have this popular sovereignty until Congress organizes them, I ask if it at last does not come from Congress? If, at last, it amounts to anything

at all, Congress gives it to them. I submit this rather
for your reflection than for comment. After all that is
said, at last by a dash of the pen, everything that has
gone before is undone, and he puts the whole question
under the control of Congress. After fighting through
more than three hours, if you undertake to read it, he
at last places the whole matter under the control of
that power which he had been contending against, and
arrives at a result directly contrary to what he had been
laboring to do. He at last leaves the whole matter to
the control of Congress.

There are two main objects, as I understand it, of
this *Harper's Magazine* essay. One was to show, if possible, that the men of our Revolutionary times were
in favor of his popular sovereignty; and the other was
to show that the Dred Scott decision had not entirely
squelched out this popular sovereignty. I do not propose, in regard to this argument drawn from the history of former times, to enter into a detailed examination of the historical statements he has made. I have
the impression that they are inaccurate in a great many
instances. Sometimes in positive statement, but very
much more inaccurate by the suppression of statements
that really belong to the history. But I do not propose
to affirm that this is so to any very great extent, or
to enter into a very minute examination of his historical statements. I avoid doing so upon this principle—that if it were important for me to pass out of
this lot in the least period of time possible, and I came
to that fence and saw by a calculation of my known
strength and agility that I could clear it at a bound,
it would be folly for me to stop and consider whether

I could or not crawl through a crack. [Laughter.] So I say of the whole history, contained in his essay, where he endeavored to link the men of the Revolution to popular sovereignty. It only requires an effort to leap out of it—a single bound to be entirely successful. If you read it over you will find that he quotes here and there from documents of the Revolutionary times, tending to show that the people of the Colonies were desirous of regulating their own concerns in their own way, that the British government should not interfere; that at one time they struggled with the British government to be permitted to exclude the African slave trade, if not directly, to be permitted to exclude it indirectly by taxation sufficient to discourage and destroy it. From these and many things of this sort, Judge Douglas argues that they were in favor of the people of our own Territories excluding slavery if they wanted to, or planting it there if they wanted to, doing just as they pleased from the time they settled upon the Territory. Now, however his history may apply, and whatever of his argument there may be that is sound and accurate or unsound and inaccurate, if we can find out what these men did themselves do upon this very question of slavery in the Territories, does it not end the whole thing? If, after all this labor and effort to show that the men of the Revolution were in favor of his popular sovereignty and his mode of dealing with slavery in the Territories, we can show that these very men took hold of that subject and dealt with it, we can see for ourselves *how* they dealt with it. It is not a matter of argument or inference, but we know what they thought about it.

It is precisely upon that part of the history of the country that one important omission is made by Judge Douglas. He selects parts of the history of the United States upon the subject of slavery, and treats it as the whole, omitting from his historical sketch the legislation of Congress in regard to the admission of Missouri, by which the Missouri Compromise was established, and slavery excluded from a country half as large as the present United States. All this is left out of his history, and in no wise alluded to by him, so far as I remember, save once when he makes a remark that upon his principle the Supreme Court were authorized to pronounce a decision that the act called the Missouri Compromise was unconstitutional. All that history has been left out. But this part of the history of the country was not made by the men of the Revolution.

There was another part of our political history made by the very men who were the actors in the Revolution, which has taken the name of the Ordinance of 1787. Let me bring that history to your attention. In 1784, I believe, this same Mr. Jefferson drew up an ordinance for the government of the country upon which we now stand—or rather a frame or draft of an ordinance for the government of this country here in Ohio, our neighbors in Indiana, us who live in Illinois, our neighbors in Wisconsin and Michigan. In that ordinance, drawn up not only for the government of that Territory, but for the Territories south of the Ohio River, Mr. Jefferson expressly provided for the prohibition of slavery. Judge Douglas says, and perhaps is right, that that provision was lost from that ordinance. I believe that is true. When the vote was taken upon it, a majority of all present in the Congress of the Confederation voted for it; but there were so many absentees that those voting for it did not make the clear majority necessary, and it was lost. But three years after that the Congress of the Confederation were together again, and they adopted a new ordinance for the government of this northwest territory, not contemplating territory south of the river, for the States owning that territory had hitherto refrained from giving it to the general government; hence they made the ordinance to apply only to what the government owned. In that, the provision excluding slavery *was inserted and passed unanimously,* or at any rate it passed and became a part of the law of the land. Under that ordinance we live. First here in Ohio you were a Territory, then an enabling act was passed authorizing you to form a constitution and State government, provided it was republican and not in conflict with the Ordinance of 1787. When you framed your constitution and presented it for admission, I think you will find the legislation upon the subject, it will show that, "whereas you had formed a constitution that was republican and not in conflict with the Ordinance of 1787," therefore you were admitted upon equal footing with the original States. The same process in a few years was gone through with in Indiana, and so with Illinois, and the same substantially with Michigan and Wisconsin.

Not only did that Ordinance prevail, but it was constantly looked to whenever a step was taken by a new Territory to become a State. Congress always turned their attention to it, and in all their movements upon this subject, they traced their course by that

Ordinance of 1787. When they admitted new States they advertised them of this Ordinance as a part of the legislation of the country. They did so because they had traced the Ordinance of 1787 throughout the history of this country. Begin with the men of the Revolution, and go down for sixty entire years, and until the last scrap of that Territory comes into the Union in the form of the State of Wisconsin—everything was made to conform with the Ordinance of 1787 excluding slavery from that vast extent of country.

I omitted to mention in the right place that the Constitution of the United States was in process of being framed when that Ordinance was made by the Congress of the Confederation; and one of the first acts of Congress itself under the new Constitution itself was to give force to that Ordinance by putting power to carry it out into the hands of the new officers under the Constitution, in place of the old ones who had been legislated out of existence by the change in the government from the Confederation to the Constitution. Not only so, but I believe Indiana once or twice, if not Ohio, petitioned the general government for the privilege of suspending that provision and allowing them to have slaves. A report made by Mr. Randolph of Virginia, himself a slaveholder, was directly against it, and the action was to refuse them the privilege of violating the Ordinance of 1787.

This period of history which I have run over briefly is, I presume, as familiar to most of this assembly as any other part of the history of our country. I suppose that few of my hearers are not as familiar with that part of history as I am, and I only mention it to re-

call your attention to it at this time. And hence I ask
how extraordinary a thing it is that a man who has
occupied a position upon the floor of the Senate of the
United States, who is now in his third term, and who
looks to see the government of this whole country fall
into his own hands, pretending to give a truthful and
accurate history of the slavery question in this country,
should so entirely ignore the whole of that portion of
our history—the most important of all. Is it not a most
extraordinary spectacle that a man should stand up
and ask for any confidence in his statements who sets
out as he does with portions of history, calling upon the
people to believe that it is a true and fair representation, when the leading part and controlling feature of
the whole history is carefully suppressed.

But the mere leaving out is not the most remarkable
feature of this most remarkable essay. His proposition
is to establish that the leading men of the Revolution
were for his great principle of non-intervention by the
government in the question of slavery in the Territories, while history shows that they decided in the cases
actually brought before them in exactly the contrary
way, and he knows it. Not only did they so decide at
that time, but they stuck to it during sixty years,
through thick and thin, as long as there was one of
the Revolutionary heroes upon the stage of political
action. Through their whole course, from first to last,
they clung to freedom. And now he asks the community
to believe that the men of the Revolution were in favor
of his great principle, when we have the naked history
that they themselves dealt with this very subject matter of his principle, and utterly repudiated his prin-

ciple, acting upon a precisely contrary ground. It is as impudent and absurd as if a prosecuting attorney should stand up before a jury, and ask them to convict A as the murderer of B, while B was walking alive before them. [Cheers and laughter.]

I say again, if Judge Douglas asserts that the men of the Revolution acted upon principles by which, to be consistent with themselves, they ought to have adopted his popular sovereignty, then, upon a consideration of his own argument, he had a right to make you believe that they understood the principles of government, but misapplied them—that he has arisen to enlighten the world as to the just application of this principle. He has a right to try to persuade you that he understands their principles better than they did, and therefore he will apply them now, not as they did, but as they ought to have done. He has a right to go before the community and try to convince them of this; but he has no right to attempt to impose upon anyone the belief that these men themselves approved of his great principle. There are two ways of establishing a proposition. One is by trying to demonstrate it upon reason; and the other is to show that great men in former times have thought so and so, and thus to pass it by the weight of pure authority. Now, if Judge Douglas will demonstrate somehow that this is popular sovereignty—the right of one man to make a slave of another, without any right in that other, or anyone else, to object—demonstrate it as Euclid demonstrated propositions—there is no objection. But when he comes forward, seeking to carry a principle by bringing to it the authority of men who themselves utterly repudiate that principle, I ask that he shall not be permitted to do it. [Applause.]

I see, in the Judge's speech here, a short sentence in these words, "Our fathers, when they formed this government under which we live, understood this question just as well and even better than we do now." That is true; I stick to that. [Great cheers and laughter.] I will stand by Judge Douglas in that to the bitter end. [Renewed laughter.] And now, Judge Douglas, come and stand by me, and truthfully show how they acted, understanding it better than we do. All I ask of you, Judge Douglas, is to stick to the proposition that the men of the Revolution understood this proposition, that the men of the Revolution understood this subject better than we do now, *and with that better understanding they acted better than you are trying to act now.* [Applause and laughter.]

I wish to say something now in regard to the Dred Scott decision, as dealt with by Judge Douglas. In that "memorable debate" between Judge Douglas and myself last year, the Judge thought fit to commence a process of catechising me, and at Freeport I answered his questions, and propounded some to him. Among others propounded to him was one that I have here now. The substance, as I remember it, is, "Can the people of the United States Territory, under the Dred Scott decision, in any lawful way, against the wish of any citizen of the United States, exclude slavery from its limits prior to the formation of a State constitution?" He answered that they could lawfully exclude slavery from the United States Territories, notwithstanding the Dred Scott decision. There was something about that answer that has probably been a trouble to the Judge ever since. [Laughter.]

The Dred Scott decision expressly gives every citizen of the United States a right to carry his slaves into the United States Territories. And now there was some inconsistency in saying that the decision was right, and saying too, that the people of the Territory could lawfully drive slavery out again. When all the trash, the words, the collateral matter, was cleared away from it, all the chaff was fanned out of it, it was a bare absurdity—*no less than a thing may be lawfully driven away from where it has a lawful right to be.* [Cheers and laughter.] Clear it of all the verbiage, and that is the naked truth of his proposition—that a thing may be lawfully driven from the place where it has a lawful right to stay. Well, it was because the Judge couldn't help seeing this that he has had so much trouble with it; and what I want to ask your especial attention to, just now, is to remind you, if you have not noticed the fact, that the Judge does not any longer say that the people can exclude slavery. He does not say so in the copyright essay; he did not say so in the speech that he made here, and, so far as I know, since his re-election to the Senate, he has never said, as he did at Freeport, that the people of the Territories can exclude slavery. He desires that you, who wish the Territories to remain free, should believe that he stands by that position; but he does not say it himself. He escapes to some extent the absurd position I have stated by changing his language entirely. What he says now is something different in language, and we will consider whether it is not different in sense too. It is now that the Dred Scott decision, or rather the Constitution under that decision, does not carry slavery into the Territories beyond the power of the people of the Territories *to control it as other property.* He does not say the people can drive it out, but they can control it as other property. The language is different; we should consider whether the sense is different. Driving a horse out of this lot is too plain a proposition to be mistaken about; it is putting him on the other side of the fence. [Laughter.] Or it might be a sort of exclusion of him from the lot if you were to kill him and let the worms devour him; but neither of these things is the same as "controlling him as other property." That would be to feed him, to pamper him, to ride him, to use and abuse him, to make the most money out of him "as other property"; but, please you, what do the men who are in favor of slavery want more than this? [Laughter and applause.] What do they really want, other than that slavery being in the Territories shall be controlled as other property. [Renewed applause.]

If they want anything else, I do not comprehend it. I ask your attention to this, first for the purpose of pointing out the change of ground the Judge has made; and, in the second place, the importance of the change— that that change is not such as to give you gentlemen who want his popular sovereignty the power to exclude the institution or drive it out at all. I know the Judge sometimes squints at the argument that in controlling it as other property by unfriendly legislation they may control it to death, as you might in the case of a horse, perhaps, feed him so lightly and ride him so much that he would die. [Cheers and laughter.] But when you

come to legislative control, there is something more
to be attended to. I have no doubt, myself, that if the
people of the Territories should undertake to control
slave property as other property—that is, control it in
such a way that it would be the most valuable as
property, and make it bear its just proportion in the
way of burdens as property—really deal with it as property—the Supreme Court of the United States will say,
"Godspeed you and amen." But I undertake to give
the opinion, at least, that if the Territories attempt by
any direct legislation to drive the man with his slave
out of the Territory, or to decide that his slave is free
because of his being taken in there, or to tax him
to such an extent that he cannot keep him there, the
Supreme Court will unhesitatingly decide all such legislation unconstitutional, as long as that Supreme Court
is constructed as the Dred Scott Supreme Court is. The
first two things they have already decided, except that
there is a little quibble among lawyers between the
words *dicta* and decision. They have already decided a
negro cannot be made free by Territorial legislation.

What is that Dred Scott decision? Judge Douglas
labors to show that it is one thing, while I think it is
altogether different. It is a long opinion, but it is all
embodied in this short statement: "The Constitution of
the United States forbids Congress to deprive a man
of his property, without due process of law; the right
of property in slaves is distinctly and expressly affirmed
in that Constitution; therefore, if Congress shall undertake to say that a man's slave is no longer his slave
when he crosses a certain line into a Territory, that is
depriving him of his property without due process of

law, and is unconstitutional." There is the whole Dred
Scott decision. They add that if Congress cannot do
so itself, Congress cannot confer any power to do so,
and hence any effort by the Territorial legislature to
do either of these things is absolutely decided against.
It is a foregone conclusion by that court.

Now, as to this indirect mode by "unfriendly legislation," all lawyers here will readily understand that
such a proposition cannot be tolerated for a moment,
because a legislature cannot indirectly do that which it
cannot accomplish directly. Then I say any legislation
to control this property, as property, for its benefit as
property, would be hailed by this Dred Scott Supreme
Court and fully sustained; but any legislation driving
slave property out, or destroying it as property, directly
or indirectly, will most assuredly, by that court, be held
unconstitutional.

Judge Douglas says if the Constitution carries slavery
into the Territories, beyond the power of the people
of the Territories to control it as other property, then
it follows logically that everyone who swears to support the Constitution of the United States must give
that support to that property which it needs. And if
the Constitution carries slavery into the Territories,
beyond the power of the people to control it as other
property, then it also carries it into the States, because
the Constitution is the supreme law of the land. Now,
gentlemen, if it were not for my excessive modesty, I
would say that I told that very thing to Judge Douglas
quite a year ago. This argument is here in print, and
if it were not for my modesty, as I said, I might call
your attention to it. If you read it, you will find that

I not only made that argument, but made it better than he has made it since. [Laughter.]

There is, however, this difference. I say now, and said then, there is no sort of question that the Supreme Court *has* decided that it is the right of the slaveholder to take his slave and hold him in the Territory; and saying this, Judge Douglas himself admits the conclusion. He says if that is so, this consequence will follow; and because this consequence would follow, his argument is, the decision cannot, therefore, be that way—"that would spoil my popular sovereignty, and it cannot be possible that this great principle has been squelched out in this extraordinary way. It might be, if it were not for the extraordinary consequence of spoiling my humbug." [Cheers and laughter.]

Another feature of the Judge's argument about the Dred Scott case is an effort to show that that decision deals altogether in declarations of negatives; that the Constitution does not affirm anything as expounded by the Dred Scott decision, but it only declares a want of power—a total absence of power—in reference to the Territories. It seems to be his purpose to make the whole of that decision to result in a mere negative declaration of a want of power in Congress to do anything in relation to this matter in the Territories. I know the opinion of the Judges states that there is a total absence of power; but that is, unfortunately, not all it states, for the Judges add that the right of property in a slave is distinctly and expressly affirmed in the Constitution. It does not stop at saying that the right of property in a slave is recognized in the Constitution, is declared to exist somewhere in the Constitution, but says it is *affirmed* in the Constitution. Its language is equivalent to saying that it is embodied and so woven into that instrument that it cannot be detached without breaking the Constitution itself. In a word, it is part of the Constitution.

Douglas is singularly unfortunate in his effort to make out that decision to be altogether negative, when the express language at the vital part is that this is distinctly affirmed in the Constitution. I think myself, and I repeat it here, that this decision does not merely carry slavery into the Territories, but by its logical conclusion it carries it into the States in which we live. One provision of that Constitution is that it shall be the supreme law of the land—I do not quote the language—any constitution or law of any State to the contrary notwithstanding. This Dred Scott decision says that the right of property in a slave is affirmed in that Constitution, which is the supreme law of the land, any State constitution or law notwithstanding. Then I say that to destroy a thing which is distinctly affirmed and supported by the supreme law of the land, even by a State constitution or law, is a violation of that supreme law, and there is no escape from it. In my judgment there is no avoiding that result, save that the American people shall see that constitutions are better construed than our Constitution is construed in that decision. They must take care that it is more faithfully and truly carried out than it is there expounded.

I must hasten to a conclusion. Near the beginning of my remarks, I said that this insidious Douglas Popular Sovereignty is the measure that now threatens the purpose of the Republican party, to prevent slavery from being nationalized in the United States. I propose to ask your attention for a little while to some propositions in affirmance of that statement. Take it just as it stands, and apply it as a principle; extend and apply that principle elsewhere and consider where it will lead you. I now put this proposition, that Judge Douglas' popular sovereignty applied will reopen the African slave trade; and I will demonstrate it by any variety of ways in which you can turn the subject or look at it.

The Judge says that the people of the Territories have the right, by his principle, to have slaves, if they want them. Then I say that the people of Georgia have the right to buy slaves in Africa, if they want them, and I defy any man on earth to show any distinction between the two things—to show that the one is either more wicked or more unlawful; to show, on original principles, that one is better or worse than the other; or to show, by the Constitution, that one differs a whit from the other. He will tell me, doubtless, that there is no Constitutional provision against people taking slaves into the new Territories, and I tell him that there is equally no Constitutional provision against buying slaves in Africa. He will tell you that a people, in the exercise of popular sovereignty, ought to do as they please about that thing, and have slaves if they want them; and I tell you that the people of Georgia are as much entitled to popular sovereignty and to buy slaves in Africa, if they want them, as the people of the Territory are to have slaves, if they want them. I ask any man, dealing honestly with himself, to point out a distinction.

I have recently seen a letter of Judge Douglas' in

which, without stating that to be the object, he doubtless endeavors to make a distinction between the two.
He says he is unalterably opposed to the repeal of the
laws against the African slave trade. And why? He then
seeks to give a reason that would not apply to his
popular sovereignty in the Territories. What is that
reason? "The abolition of the African slave trade is a
compromise of the Constitution." I deny it. There is
no truth in the proposition that the abolition of the
African slave trade is a compromise of the Constitution.
No man can put his finger on anything in the Constitution, or on the line of history, which shows it. It
is a mere barren assertion, made simply for the purpose
of getting up a distinction between the revival of the
African slave trade and his "great principle."

At the time the Constitution of the United States
was adopted it was expected that the slave trade would
be abolished. I should assert, and insist upon, that if
Judge Douglas denied it. But I know that it was equally
expected that slavery would be excluded from the Territories, and I can show by history that in regard to
these two things, public opinion was exactly alike; while
in regard to positive action, there was more done in
the Ordinance of 1787 to resist the spread of slavery
than was ever done to abolish the foreign slave trade.
Lest I be misunderstood, I say again that at the time
of the formation of the Constitution, public expectation
was that the slave trade would be abolished, but no
more so than the spread of slavery in the Territories
should be restrained. They stand alike, except that in
the Ordinance of 1787 there was a mark left by public
opinion showing that it was more committed against

the spread of slavery in the Territories than against the foreign slave trade.

Compromise! What word of compromise was there about it. Why, the public sense was then in favor of the abolition of the slave trade; but there was at the time a very great commercial interest involved in it and extensive capital in that branch of trade. There were doubtless the incipient stages of improvement in the South in the way of farming, dependent on the slave trade, and they made a proposition to the Congress to abolish the trade after allowing it twenty years, a sufficient time for the capital and commerce engaged in it to be transferred to other channels. They made no provision that it should be abolished in twenty years; I do not doubt that they expected it would be; but they made no bargain about it. The public sentiment left no doubt in the minds of any that it would be done away. I repeat, there is nothing in the history of those times in favor of that matter being a *compromise* of the Constitution. It was the public expectation at the time, manifested in a thousand ways, that the spread of slavery should also be restricted.

Then I say, if this principle is established, that there is no wrong in slavery, and whoever wants it has a right to have it, is a matter of dollars and cents, a sort of question as to how they shall deal with brutes—that between us and the negro here there is no sort of question, but that at the South the question is between the negro and the crocodile. That is all. It is a mere matter of policy; there is a perfect right according to interest to do just as you please—when this is done, where this doctrine prevails, the miners and sappers will have formed public opinion for the slave trade. They will be ready for Jefferson Davis and Stephens and other leaders of that company to sound the bugle for the revival of the slave trade, for the second Dred Scott decision, for the flood of slavery to be poured over the free States, while we shall be here tied down and helpless and run over like sheep.

It is to be a part and parcel of this same idea, to say to men who want to adhere to the Democratic party, who have always belonged to that party, and are only looking about for some excuse to stick to it, but nevertheless hate slavery, that Douglas' popular sovereignty is as good a way as any to oppose slavery. They allow themselves to be persuaded easily, in accordance with their previous dispositions, into this belief that it is about as good a way of opposing slavery as any, and we can do that without straining our old party ties or breaking up old political associations. We can do so without being called negro worshippers. We can do that without being subjected to the jibes and sneers that are so readily thrown out in place of argument where no argument can be found; so let us stick to this popular sovereignty—this insidious popular sovereignty. Now let me call your attention to one thing that has really happened, which shows this gradual and steady debauching of public opinion, this course of preparation for the revival of the slave trade, for the Territorial slave code, and the new Dred Scott decision that is to carry slavery into the free States. Did you ever, five years ago, hear of anybody in the world saying that the negro had no share in the Declaration of National Independence; that it did not mean negroes at all; and when "all men" were spoken of, negroes were not included?

I am satisfied that five years ago that proposition was not put upon paper by any living being anywhere. I have been unable at any time to find a man in an audience who would declare that he had ever known anybody saying so five years ago. But last year there was not a Douglas popular sovereign in Illinois who did not say it. Is there one in Ohio but declares his firm belief that the Declaration of Independence did not mean negroes at all? I do not know how this is; I have not been here much; but I presume you are very much alike everywhere. Then I suppose that all now express the belief that the Declaration of Independence never did mean negroes. I call upon one of them to say that he said it five years ago.

If you think that now, and did not think it then, the next thing that strikes me is to remark that there has been a *change* wrought in you [laughter and applause], and a very significant change it is, being no less than changing the negro, in your estimation, from the rank of a man to that of a brute. They are taking him down, and placing him, when spoken of, among reptiles and crocodiles, as Judge Douglas himself expresses it.

Is not this change wrought in your minds a very important change? Public opinion in this country is everything. In a nation like ours this popular sovereignty and squatter sovereignty have already wrought a change in the public mind to the extent I have stated. There is no man in this crowd who can contradict it.

Now, if you are opposed to slavery honestly, as much

as anybody, I ask you to note that fact, and the like
of which is to follow, to be plastered on, layer after
layer, until very soon you are prepared to deal with
the negro everywhere as with the brute. If public sentiment has not been debauched already to this point, a
new turn of the screw in that direction is all that is
wanting; and this is constantly being done by the
teachers of this insidious popular sovereignty. You need
but one or two turns further until your minds, now
ripening under these teachings, will be ready for all
these things; and you will receive and support, or submit to, the slave trade, revived with all its horrors,
a slave code enforced in our Territories, and a new
Dred Scott decision to bring slavery up into the very
heart of the free North. This, I must say, is but carrying out those words prophetically spoken by Mr. Clay
many, many years ago—I believe more than thirty years
—when he told an audience that if they would repress
all tendencies to liberty and ultimate emancipation,
they must go back to the era of our independence, and
muzzle the cannon which thundered its annual joyous
return on the Fourth of July; they must blow out the
moral lights around us; they must penetrate the human
soul and eradicate the love of liberty; but until they
did these things, and others eloquently enumerated by
him, they could not repress all tendencies to ultimate
emancipation.

I ask attention to the fact that in a pre-eminent
degree these popular sovereigns are at this work: blow-
ing out the moral lights around us; teaching that the
negro is no longer a man but a brute, that the Declaration has nothing to do with him, that he ranks with

the crocodile and the reptile, that man, with body and soul, is a matter of dollars and cents. I suggest to this portion of the Ohio Republicans, or Democrats if there be any present, the serious consideration of this fact that there is now going on among you a steady process of debauching public opinion on this subject. With this, my friends, I bid you adieu.

SPEECH OF ABRAHAM LINCOLN

at Cincinnati, Ohio, September 17, 1859 [1]

My Fellow Citizens of the State of Ohio: This is the first time in my life that I have appeared before an audience in so great a city as this. I therefore—though I am no longer a young man—make this appearance under some degree of embarrassment. But I have found that when one is embarrassed, usually the shortest way to get through with it is to quit talking or thinking about it, and go at something else. [Applause.]

I understand that you have had recently with you my very distinguished friend, Judge Douglas, of Illinois, [laughter] and I understand, without having had an opportunity (not greatly sought to be sure) of seeing a report of the speech that he made here, that he did me the honor to mention my humble name. I suppose that he did so for the purpose of making some objection to some sentiment at some time expressed by me. I should expect, it is true, that Judge Douglas had reminded you, or informed you, if you had never before heard it, that I had once in my life declared it as my opinion that this government cannot "endure permanently, half slave and half free; that a house divided against itself cannot stand," and, as I had expressed it, I did not expect the house to fall; that I did not expect the Union to be dissolved; but that I did expect that it would cease to be divided; that it would become all one thing or all the other; that either the opponents of

[1] *Illinois State Journal* (Springfield), October 7, 1859.

slavery would arrest the further spread of it, and place it where the public mind would rest in the belief that it was in the course of ultimate extinction; or the friends of slavery will push it forward until it becomes alike lawful in all the States, old or new, free as well as slave. I did, fifteen months ago, express that opinion, and upon many occasions Judge Douglas has denounced it, and has greatly, intentionally or unintentionally, misrepresented my purpose in the expression of that opinion.

I presume, without having seen a report of his speech, that he did so here. I presume that he alluded also to that opinion, in different language, having been expressed at a subsequent time by Governor Seward of New York, and that he took the two in a lump and denounced them; that he tried to point out that there was something couched in this opinion which led to the making of an entire uniformity of the local institutions of the various States of the Union, in utter disregard of the different States, which in their nature would seem to require a variety of institutions and a variety of laws, conforming to the differences in the nature of the different States.

Not only so, I presume he insisted that this was a declaration of war between the free and slave States— that it was the sounding to the onset of continual war between the different States, the slave and free States.

This charge, in this form, was made by Judge Douglas on, I believe, the 9th of July, 1858, in Chicago, in my hearing. On the next evening, I made some reply to it. I informed him that many of the inferences he drew from that expression of mine were altogether foreign to any purpose entertained by me, and in so far as he should ascribe those inferences to me, as my purpose, he was entirely mistaken; and in so far as he might argue that whatever might be my purpose, actions, conforming to my views, would lead to these results, he might argue and establish if he could; but, so far as purposes were concerned, he was totally mistaken as to me.

When I made that reply to him—when I told him on the question of declaring war between the different States of the Union, that I had not said I did not expect any peace upon this question until slavery was exterminated; that I had only said I expected peace when that institution was put where the public mind should rest in the belief that it was in course of ultimate extinction; that I believed, from the organization of our government until a very recent period of time, the institution had been placed and continued upon such a basis; that we had had comparative peace upon that question through a portion of that period of time only because the public mind rested in that belief in regard to it; and that when we returned to that position in relation to that matter, I supposed we should again have peace as we previously had. I assured him, as I now assure you, that I neither then had, nor have, or ever had, any purpose in any way of interfering with the institution of slavery, where it exists. [Long continued applause.] I believe we have no power under the Constitution of the United States, or rather under the form of government under which we live, to interfere with the institution of slavery, or any other of the institutions of our sister States, be they free or slave States. [Cries of "Good," and applause.] I declared then, and I now redeclare, that I have as little inclination to so interfere with the institution of slavery where it now exists, through the instrumentality of the general government, or any other instrumentality, as I believe we have no power to do so. [A voice, "You're right."] I accidentally used this expression: I had no purpose of entering into the slave States to disturb the institution of slavery! So, upon the first occasion that Judge Douglas got an opportunity to reply to me, he passed by the whole body of what I had said upon that subject, and seized upon the particular expression of mine, that I had no purpose of entering into the slave States to disturb the institution of slavery! "Oh, no," said he, "he [Lincoln] won't enter into the slave States to disturb the institution of slavery; he is too prudent a man to do such a thing as that; he only means that he will go on to the line between the free and slave States, and shoot over at them. [Laughter.] This is all he means to do. He means to do them all the harm he can, to disturb them all he can, in such a way as to keep his own hide in perfect safety." [Laughter.]

Well, now, I did not think, at that time, that that was either a very dignified or very logical argument; but so it was, I had to get along with it as well as I could.

It has occurred to me here tonight that if I ever do shoot over the line at the people on the other side of the line into a slave State, and purpose to do so, keeping my skin safe, that I have now about the best chance I shall ever have. [Laughter and applause.] I should not wonder that there are some Kentuckians about this

audience; we are close to Kentucky; and whether that
be so or not, we are on elevated ground, and, by speaking distinctly, I should not wonder if some of the Kentuckians would hear me on the other side of the river.
[Laughter.] For that reason I propose to address a portion of what I have to say to the Kentuckians.

I say, then, in the first place, to the Kentuckians,
that I am what they call, as I understand it, a "Black
Republican." [Applause and laughter.] I think slavery
is wrong, morally and politically. I desire that it should
be no further spread in these United States, and I
should not object if it should gradually terminate in
the whole Union. [Applause.] While I say this for myself, I say to you Kentuckians that I understand you
differ radically with me upon this proposition; that
you believe slavery is a good thing; that slavery is right;
that it ought to be extended and perpetuated in this
Union. Now, there being this broad difference between
us, I do not pretend, in addressing myself to you
Kentuckians, to attempt proselyting you; that would
be a vain effort. I do not enter upon it. I only propose
to try to show you that you ought to nominate for the
next Presidency, at Charleston, my distinguished friend
Judge Douglas. [Applause.] In all that there is a difference between you and him, I understand he is as sincerely for you, and more wisely for you, than you are
for yourselves. [Applause.] I will try to demonstrate
that proposition. Understand, now, I say that I believe
he is as sincerely for you, and more wisely for you,
than you are for yourselves.

What do you want more than anything else to make
successful your views of slavery—to advance the out-

spread of it, and to secure and perpetuate the nation-
ality of it? What do you want more than anything
else? What is needed absolutely? What is indispensable
to you? Why! if I may be allowed to answer the question, it is to retain a hold upon the North—it is to
retain support and strength from the free States. If you
can get this support and strength from the free States,
you can succeed. If you do not get this support and
this strength from the free States, you are in the minority, and you are beaten at once.

If that proposition be admitted—and it is undeniable
—then the next thing I say to you is that Douglas, of
all the men in this nation, is the only man that affords
you any hold upon the free States; that no other man
can give you any strength in the free States. This being
so, if you doubt the other branch of the proposition,
whether he is for you—whether he is really for you as
I have expressed it—I propose asking your attention
for awhile to a few facts.

The issue between you and me, understand, is that
I think slavery is wrong and ought not to be outspread,
and you think it is right and ought to be extended and
perpetuated. [A voice, "Oh, Lord."] That is my Kentuckian I am talking to now. [Applause.]

I now proceed to try to show you that Douglas is
as sincerely for you and more wisely for you than you
are for yourselves.

In the first place, we know that in a government
like this, in a government of the people, where the
voice of all the men of the country, substantially,
enter into the execution—or administration, rather—of
the government—in such a government, what lies at
the bottom of all of it is public opinion. I lay down

the proposition that Douglas is not only the man that promises you in advance a hold upon the North, and support in the North, but that he constantly molds public opinion to your ends; that in every possible way he can, he constantly molds the public opinion of the North to your ends; and if there are a few things in which he seems to be against you—a few things which he says that appear to be against you, and a few that he forbears to say which you would like to have him say—you ought to remember that the saying of the one, or the forbearing to say the other, would loose his hold upon the North, and, by consequence, would lose his capacity to serve you. [A voice, "That is so."]

Upon this subject of molding public opinion, I call your attention to the fact—for a well-established fact it is—that the Judge never says your institution of slavery is wrong; he never says it is right, to be sure, but he never says it is wrong. [Laughter.] There is not a public man in the United States, I believe, with the exception of Senator Douglas, who has not, at some time in his life, declared his opinion whether the thing is right or wrong; but Senator Douglas never declares it is wrong. He leaves himself at perfect liberty to do all in your favor which he would be hindered from doing if he were to declare the thing to be wrong. On the contrary, he takes all the chances that he has for inveigling the sentiment of the North, opposed to slavery, into your support, by never saying it is right. [Laughter.] This you ought to set down to his credit. [Laughter.] You ought to give him full credit for this much, little though it be, in comparison to the whole which he does for you.

Some other things I will ask your attention to. He

said upon the floor of the United States Senate, and he has repeated it, as I understand, a great many times, that he does not care whether slavery is "voted up or voted down." This again shows you, or ought to show you if you would reason upon it, that he does not believe it to be wrong; for a man may say, when he sees nothing wrong in a thing, that he does not care whether it be voted up or voted down, but no man can logically say that he cares not whether a thing goes up or goes down, which to him appears to be wrong. You therefore have a demonstration in this that to Douglas' mind your favorite institution, which you would have spread out and made perpetual, is no wrong.

Another thing he tells you, in a speech made at Memphis in Tenesseee, shortly after the canvass in Illinois, last year. He there distinctly told the people that there was a "line drawn by the Almighty across this continent, on the one side of which the soil must always be cultivated by slaves," that he did not pretend to know exactly where that line was [laughter and applause], but that there was such a line. I want to ask your attention to that proposition again: that there is one portion of this continent where the Almighty has designed the soil shall always be cultivated by slaves; that its being cultivated by slaves at that place is right; that it has the direct sympathy and authority of the Almighty. Whenever you can get these Northern audiences to adopt the opinion that slavery is right on the other side of the Ohio; whenever you can get them, in pursuance of Douglas' views, to adopt that sentiment, they will very readily make the other argument, which is perfectly logical, that that which is right on that side of the Ohio cannot be wrong on this [laughter], and that if you have that property on that side of the Ohio, under the seal and stamp of the Almighty, when by any means it escapes over here, it is wrong to have constitutions and laws "to devil" you about it. So Douglas is molding the public opinion of the North, first to say that the thing is right in your State over the Ohio River, and hence to say that that which is right there is not wrong here [at this moment the cannon was fired to the great injury of sundry panes of glass in the vicinity], and that all laws and constitutions here, recognizing it as being wrong, are themselves wrong, and ought to be repealed and abrogated. He will tell you, men of Ohio, that if you choose here to have laws against slavery, it is in conformity to the idea that your climate is not suited to it, that your climate is not suited to slave labor, and therefore you have constitutions and laws against it.

Let us attend to that argument for a little while and see if it be sound. You do not raise sugar cane (except the new-fashioned sugar cane, and you won't raise that long), but they do raise it in Louisiana. You don't raise it in Ohio because you can't raise it profitably, because the climate don't suit it. [Here again the cannon interrupted; its report was followed by another fall of window glass.] They do raise it in Louisiana because there it is profitable. Now, Douglas will tell you that is precisely the slavery question. That they do have slaves there because they are profitable, and you don't have them here because they are not profitable. If that is so, then it leads to dealing with the one precisely as with the other. Is there, then, anything in the constitution or laws of Ohio against raising sugar cane? Have you found it necessary to put any such provision in your law? Surely not! No man desires to raise sugar cane in Ohio; but, if any man did desire to do so, you would say it was a tyrannical law that forbid his doing so; and whenever you shall agree with Douglas, whenever your minds are brought to adopt his argument, as surely you will have reached the conclusion that although slavery is not profitable in Ohio, if any man wants it, it is wrong to him not to let him have it.

In this matter Judge Douglas is preparing the public mind for you of Kentucky to make perpetual that good thing in your estimation, about which you and I differ.

In this connection let me ask your attention to another thing. I believe it is safe to assert that five years ago no living man had expressed the opinion that the negro had no share in the Declaration of Independence. Let me state that again: five years ago no living man had expressed the opinion that the negro had no share in the Declaration of Independence. If there is in this large audience any man who ever knew of that opinion being put upon paper as much as five years ago, I will be obliged to him now or at a subsequent time to show it.

If that be true I wish you then to note the next fact; that within the space of five years Senator Douglas, in the argument of this question, has got his entire party, so far as I know, without exception, to join in saying that the negro has no share in the Declaration of Independence. If there be now in all these United States, one Douglas man that does not say this, I have

been unable upon any occasion to scare him up. Now,
if none of you said this five years ago, and all of you
say it now, that is a matter that you Kentuckians ought
to note. That is a vast change in the Northern public
sentiment upon that question.

Of what tendency is that change? The tendency of
that change is to bring the public mind to the conclusion that when men are spoken of, the negro is not
meant; that when negroes are spoken of, brutes alone
are contemplated. That change in public sentiment has
already degraded the black man in the estimation of
Douglas and his followers from the condition of a man
of some sort, and assigned him to the condition of a
brute. Now, you Kentuckians ought to give Douglas
credit for this. That is the largest possible stride that
can be made in regard to the perpetuation of your thing
of slavery. [A voice, "Speak to Ohio men, and not to
Kentuckians!"] I beg permission to speak as I please.
[Laughter.]

In Kentucky perhaps, in many of the slave States
certainly, you are trying to establish the rightfulness
of slavery by reference to the Bible. You are trying to
show that slavery existed in the Bible times by Divine
ordinance. Now Douglas is wiser than you, for your
own benefit, upon that subject. Douglas knows that
whenever you establish that slavery was right by the
Bible, it will occur that that slavery was the slavery
of the *white* man—of men without reference to color—
and he knows very well that you may entertain that idea
in Kentucky as much as you please, but you will never
win any Northern support upon it. He makes a wiser
argument for you: he makes the argument that the

slavery of the *black* man, the slavery of the man who has a skin of a different color from your own, is right. He thereby brings to your support Northern voters who could not for a moment be brought by your own argument of the Bible-right of slavery. Will you not give him credit for that? Will you not say that in this matter he is more wisely for you than you are for yourselves?

Now, having established with his entire party this doctrine, having been entirely successful in that branch of his efforts in your behalf, he is ready for another.

At this same meeting at Memphis, he declared that while in all contests between the negro and the white man, he was for the white man, but that in all questions between the negro and the crocodile he was for the negro. [Laughter.] He did not make that declaration accidentally at Memphis. He made it a great many times in the canvass in Illinois last year (though I don't know that it was reported in any of his speeches there), but he frequently made it. I believe he repeated it at Columbus, and I should not wonder if he repeated it here. It is, then, a deliberate way of expressing himself upon that subject. It is a matter of mature deliberation with him thus to express himself upon that point of his case. It therefore requires some deliberate attention.

The first inference seems to be that if you do not enslave the negro you are wronging the white man in some way or other, and that whoever is opposed to the negro being enslaved is in some way or other against the white man. Is not that a falsehood? If there was a necessary conflict between the white man and the negro, I should be for the white man as much as Judge

Douglas; but I say there is no such necessary conflict. I say that there is room enough for us all to be free [loud manifestations of applause], and that it not only does not wrong the white man that the negro should be free, but it positively wrongs the mass of the white men that the negro should be enslaved—that the mass of white men are really injured by the effect of slave labor in the vicinity of the fields of their own labor. [Applause.]

But I do not desire to dwell upon this branch of the question more than to say that this assumption of his is false; and I do hope that that fallacy will not long prevail in the minds of intelligent white men. At all events, you Kentuckians ought to thank Judge Douglas for it. It is for your benefit it is made.

The other branch of it is, that in a struggle between the negro and the crocodile, he is for the negro. Well, I don't know that there is any struggle between the negro and the crocodile, either. [Laughter.] I suppose that if a crocodile (or as we old Ohio River boatmen used to call them, alligators) should come across a white man, he would kill him if he could, and so he would a negro. But what, at last, is this proposition? I believe it is a sort of proposition in proportion, which may be stated thus: As the negro is to the white man, so is the crocodile to the negro; and as the negro may rightfully treat the crocodile as a beast or reptile, so the white man may rightfully treat the negro as a beast or a reptile. [Applause.] That is really the "knip" of all that argument of his.

Now, my brother Kentuckians, who believe in this, you ought to thank Judge Douglas for having put that in a much more taking way than any of yourselves have done. [Applause.]

Again, Douglas' *great principle,* "Popular Sovereignty," as he calls it, gives you, by natural consequence, the revival of the slave trade whenever you want it. If you question this, listen awhile, consider awhile what I shall advance in support of that proposition.

He says that it is the sacred right of the man who goes into the Territories to have slavery if he wants it. Grant that for argument's sake. Is it not the sacred right of the man that don't go there equally to buy slaves in Africa, if he wants them? Can you point out the difference? The man who goes into the Territories of Kansas and Nebraska, or any other new Territory, with the sacred right of taking a slave there which belongs to him, would certainly have no more right to take one there than I would who own no slave, but who would desire to buy one and take him there. You will not say—you, the friends of Douglas—but that the man who does not own a slave has an equal right to buy one and take him to the Territory as the other does?

[A voice, "I want to ask a question. Don't foreign nations interfere with the slave trade?"] Well! I understand it to be a principle of Democracy to whip foreign nations whenever they interfere with us. [Laughter and applause.] [Voice, "I only asked for information. I am a Republican myself."] You and I will be on the best terms in the world, but I do not wish to be diverted from the point I was trying to press.

I say that Douglas Popular Sovereignty, establishing a sacred right in the people, if you please, if carried to its logical conclusion gives equally the sacred right to the people of the States or the Territories themselves to buy slaves wherever they can buy them cheapest; and if any man can show a distinction, I should like to hear him try it. If any man can show how the people of Kansas have a better right to slaves because they want them than the people of Georgia have to buy them in Africa, I want him to do it. I think it cannot be done. If it is popular sovereignty for the people to have slaves because they want them, it is popular sovereignty for them to buy them in Africa because they desire to do so.

I know that Douglas has recently made a little effort—not seeming to notice that he had a different theory—has made an effort to get rid of that. He has written a letter addressed to somebody, I believe, who resides in Iowa, declaring his opposition to the repeal of the laws that prohibit the African slave trade. He bases his opposition to such repeal upon the ground that these laws are themselves one of the compromises of the Constitution of the United States. Now it would be very interesting to see Judge Douglas or any of his friends turn to the Constitution of the United States and point out that compromise, to show where there is any compromise in the Constitution, or provision in the Constitution, express or implied, by which the administrators of that Constitution are under any obligation to repeal the African slave trade. I know, or at least I think I know, that the framers of that Constitution did expect that the African slave trade would be abolished at the end of twenty years, to which time their prohibition against its being abolished extended. I think there is abundant contemporaneous history to show that the framers of the Constitution expected it to be abolished. But while they so expected, they gave nothing for that expectation, and they put no provision in the Constitution requiring it should be so abolished. The migration or importation of such persons as the States shall see fit to admit shall not be prohibited, but a certain tax might be levied upon such importation. But what was to be done after that time? The Constitution is as silent about that as it is silent personally about myself. There is absolutely nothing in it about that subject—there is only the expectation of the framers of the Constitution that the slave trade would be abolished at the end of that time; and they expected it would be abolished, owing to public sentiment, before that time; and they put that provision in, in order that it should not be abolished before that time, for reasons which I suppose they thought to be sound ones, but which I will not now try to enumerate before you.

But while they expected the slave trade would be abolished at that time, they expected that the spread of slavery into the new Territories should also be restricted. It is as easy to prove that the framers of the Constitution of the United States expected that slavery should be prohibited from extending into the new Territories as it is to prove that it was expected that the slave trade should be abolished. Both these things were expected. One was no more expected than the other, and one was no more a compromise of the Constitution than the other. There was nothing said in the Constitution in regard to the spread of slavery into the Territory. I grant that; but there was something very important said about it by the same generation of men in the adoption of the old Ordinance of 1787, through the influence of which you here in Ohio, our neighbors in Indiana, we in Illinois, our neighbors in Michigan and Wisconsin are happy, prosperous, teeming millions of free men. [Continued applause.] That generation of men, though not to the full extent members of the Convention that framed the Constitution, were to some extent members of that Convention, holding seats at the same time in one body and the other, so that if there was any compromise on either of these subjects, the strong evidence is that that compromise was in favor of the restriction of slavery from the new Territories.

But Douglas says that he is unalterably opposed to the repeal of those laws because, in his view, it is a compromise of the Constitution. You Kentuckians, no doubt, are somewhat offended with that! You ought not to be! You ought to be patient! You ought to know that if he said less than that, he would lose the power of "lugging" the Northern States to your support. Really, what you would push him to do would take from him his entire power to serve you. And you ought to remember how long, by precedent, Judge Douglas holds himself obliged to stick by compromises. You ought to remember that by the time you yourselves think you are ready to inaugurate measures for the revival of the African slave trade, that sufficient time will have arrived, by precedent, for Judge Douglas to break through that compromise. He says now nothing more strong than he said in 1849 when he declared in favor of the Missouri Compromise—that precisely four years and a quarter after he declared that Compromise to be a sacred thing, which "no ruthless hand would ever dare to touch," he himself brought forward the measure ruthlessly to destroy it. [A voice, "Hit him again!" and applause.] By a mere calculation of time it will only be four years more until he is ready to take back his profession about the sacredness of the Compromise abolishing the slave trade. Precisely as soon as you are ready to have his services in that direction, by fair calculation, you may be sure of having them. [Applause and laughter.]

But you remember and set down to Judge Douglas' debit, or discredit, that he, last year, said the people of the Territories can, in spite of the Dred Scott decision, exclude your slaves from those Territories; that he declared, by "unfriendly legislation" the extension of your property into the new Territories may be cut off in the teeth of the decision of the Supreme Court of the United States.

He assumed that position at Freeport on the 27th of August, 1858. He said that the people of the Territories can exclude slavery in so many words. You ought, however, to bear in mind that he has never said it since. [Laughter.] You may hunt in every speech that he has since made, and he has never used that expression once. He has never seemed to notice that he is stating his views differently from what he did then; but by some sort of accident, he has always really stated it differently. He has always since then declared that "the Constitution does not carry slavery into the Territories of the United States beyond the power of the people legally to control

it as other property." Now, there is a difference in the
language used upon that former occasion and in this
latter day. There may or may not be a difference in
the meaning, but it is worth while considering whether
there is not also a difference in meaning.

What is it to exclude? Why, it is to drive it out. It
is in some way to put it out of the Territory. It is
to force it across the line, or change its character, so
that as property it is out of existence. But what is the
controlling of it "as other property"? Is controlling it
as other property the same thing as destroying it, or
driving it away? I should think not. I should think the
controlling of it as other property would be just about
what you in Kentucky should want. I understand the
controlling of property means the controlling of it
for the benefit of the owner of it. While I have no
doubt the Supreme Court of the United States would
say "Godspeed" to any of the Territorial legislatures
that should thus control slave property, they would sing
quite a different tune if, by the pretense of controlling
it, they were to undertake to pass laws which virtually
excluded it—and that upon a very well-known principle
to all lawyers, that what a legislature cannot directly
do, it cannot do by indirection; that, as the legislature
has not the power to drive slaves out, they have no
power by indirection, by tax, or by imposing burdens
in any way on that property, to effect the same end,
and that any attempt to do so would be held by the
Dred Scott court unconstitutional.

Douglas is not willing to stand by his first proposition that they can exclude it, because we have seen
that that proposition amounts to nothing more nor less

than the naked absurdity that you may lawfully drive
out that which has a lawful right to remain. He admitted at first that the slave might be lawfully taken
into the Territories under the Constitution of the
United States, and yet asserted that he might be lawfully driven out. That being the proposition, it is
the absurdity I have stated. He is not willing to stand
in the face of that direct, naked, and impudent absurdity; he has, therefore, modified his language into
that of being *"controlled as other property."*

The Kentuckians don't like this in Douglas! I will
tell you where it will go. He now swears by the Court.
He was once a leading man in Illinois to break down
a court because it had made a decision he did not like.
But he now not only swears by the Court, the courts
having got to working for you, but he denounces all
men that do not swear by the courts as unpatriotic,
as bad citizens. When one of these acts of unfriendly
legislation shall impose such heavy burdens as to, in
effect, destroy property in slaves in a Territory and
show plainly enough that there can be no mistake in
the purpose of the legislature to make them so burden-
some, this same Supreme Court will decide that law to
be unconstitutional, and he will be ready to say for
your benefit, "I swear by the Court; I give it up"; and
while that is going on he has been getting all his men
to swear by the courts, and to give it up with him. In
this again he serves you faithfully, and, as I say, more
wisely than you serve yourselves.

Again: I have alluded in the beginning of these remarks to the fact that Judge Douglas has made great
complaint of my having expressed the opinion that this

Government "cannot endure permanently, half slave and half free." He has complained of Seward for using different language and declaring that there is an "irrepressible conflict" between the principles of free and slave labor. [A voice, "He says it is not original with Seward. That is original with Lincoln."] I will attend to that immediately, sir. Since that time, Hickman, of Pennsylvania, expressed the same sentiment. He has never denounced Mr. Hickman: Why? There is a little chance, notwithstanding that opinion in the mouth of Hickman, that he may yet be a Douglas man. That is the difference! It is not unpatriotic to hold that opinion if a man is a Douglas man.

But neither I, nor Seward, nor Hickman is entitled to the enviable or unenviable distinction of having first expressed that idea. That same idea was expressed by the Richmond *Enquirer* in Virginia, in 1856—quite two years before it was expressed by the first of us. And while Douglas was pluming himself that in his conflict with my humble self, last year, he had "squelched out" that fatal heresy, as he delighted to call it, and had suggested that if he only had had a chance to be in New York and meet Seward he would have "squelched" it there also, it never occurred to him to breathe a word against Pryor. I don't think that you can discover that Douglas ever talked of going to Virginia to "squelch" out that idea there. No. More than that. That same Roger A. Pryor was brought to Washington city, and made the editor of the par excellence Douglas paper, after making use of that expression, which, in us, is so unpatriotic and heretical. From all this, my Kentucky friends may see that this opinion is heretical in his view

only when it is expressed by men suspected of a desire
that the country shall all become free, and not when
expressed by those fairly known to entertain the desire
that the whole country shall become slave. When expressed by that class of men, it is in no wise offensive
to him. In this again, my friends of Kentucky, you have
Judge Douglas with you.

There is another reason why you Southern people
ought to nominate Douglas at your convention at
Charleston. That reason is the wonderful capacity of
the man [laughter]—the power he has of doing what
would seem to be impossible. Let me call your attention
to one of these apparently impossible things.

Douglas had three or four very distinguished men
of the most extreme antislavery views of any men in
the Republican party expressing their desire for his
re-election to the Senate last year. That would, of itself,
have seemed to be a little wonderful; but that wonder
is heightened when we see that Wise of Virginia, a man
exactly opposed to them, a man who believes in the
divine right of slavery, was also expressing his desire
that Douglas should be re-elected, and that another
man that may be said to be kindred to Wise, Mr.
Breckinridge, the Vice-President, and of your own State,
was also agreeing with the antislavery men in the North
that Douglas ought to be re-elected. Still, to heighten
the wonder, a Senator from Kentucky, whom I have
always loved with an affection as tender and endearing
as I have ever loved any man, who was opposed to the
antislavery men for reasons which seemed sufficient to
him and equally opposed to Wise and Breckinridge,
was writing letters into Illinois to secure the re-election

of Douglas. Now, that all these conflicting elements
should be brought, while at daggers' points with one
another, to support him is a feat that is worthy for
you to note and consider. It is quite probable that
each of these classes of men thought, by the re-election
of Douglas, their peculiar views would gain something:
it is probable that the antislavery men thought their
views would gain something; that Wise and Breckinridge thought so too, as regards their opinions; that
Mr. Crittenden thought that his views would gain something, although he was opposed to both these other
men. It is probable that each and all of them thought
that they were using Douglas, and it is yet an unsolved
problem whether he was not using them all. If he was,
then it is for you to consider whether that power to
perform wonders is one for you lightly to throw away.

There is one other thing that I will say to you in
this relation. It is but my opinion, I give it to you
without a fee. It is my opinion that it is for you to take
him or be defeated; and that if you do take him you
may be beaten. You will surely be beaten if you do not
take him. We, the Republicans and others forming the
Opposition of the country, intend to "stand by our
guns," to be patient and firm, and in the long run to
beat you whether you take him or not. [Applause.]
We know that before we fairly beat you, we have to
beat you both together. We know that you are "all of a
feather" [loud applause], and that we have to beat you
all together, and we expect to do it. [Applause.] We don't
intend to be very impatient about it. We mean to be
as deliberate and calm about it as it is possible to be,
but as firm and resolved as it is possible for men to

be. When we do as we say, beat you, you perhaps want
to know what we will do with you. [Laughter.]

I will tell you, so far as I am authorized to speak
for the Opposition, what we mean to do with you. We
mean to treat you, as near as we possibly can, like Washington, Jefferson, and Madison treated you. [Cheers.]
We mean to leave you alone, and in no way to interfere with your institution, to abide by all and every
compromise of the Constitution, and, in a word, coming
back to the original proposition, to treat you, so far
as degenerated men (if we have degenerated) may,
according to the examples of those noble fathers—Washington, Jefferson, and Madison. [Applause.] We mean
to remember that you are as good as we; that there is
no difference between us other than the difference of
circumstances. We mean to recognize and bear in mind
always that you have as good hearts in your bosoms as
other people, or as we claim to have, and treat you
accordingly. We mean to marry your girls when we
have a chance—the white ones I mean [laughter]—and
I have the honor to inform you that I once did have a
chance in that way. [A voice, "Good for you," and applause.]

I have told you what we mean to do. I want to know,
now, when that thing takes place, what you mean to
do. I often hear it intimated that you mean to divide
the Union whenever a Republican, or anything like it,
is elected President of the United States. [A voice,
"That is so."] "That is so," one of them says. I wonder
if he is a Kentuckian? [A voice, "He is a Douglas man."]
Well, then, I want to know what you are going to do
with your half of it? [Applause and laughter.] Are
you going to split the Ohio down through, and push

your half off a piece? Or are you going to keep it right alongside of us outrageous fellows? Or are you going to build up a wall some way between your country and ours, by which that moveable property of yours can't come over here any more, to the danger of your losing it? Do you think you can better yourselves on that subject by leaving us here under no obligation whatever to return those specimens of your moveable property that come hither? You have divided the Union because we would not do right with you, as you think, upon that subject; when we cease to be under obligations to do anything for you, how much better off do you think you will be? Will you make war upon us and kill us all? Why, gentlemen, I think you are as gallant and as brave men as live; that you can fight as bravely in a good cause, man for man, as any other people living; that you have shown yourselves capable of this upon various occasions; but, man for man, you are not better than we are, and there are not so many of you as there are of us. [Loud cheering.] You will never make much of a hand at whipping us. If we were fewer in numbers than you, I think that you could whip us; if we were equal, it would likely be a drawn battle; but being inferior in numbers, you will make nothing by attempting to master us.

But perhaps I have addressed myself as long, or longer, to the Kentuckians than I ought to have done, inasmuch as I have said that whatever course you take we intend in the end to beat you. I propose to address a few remarks to our friends by way of discussing with them the best means of keeping that promise that I have in good faith made. [Long continued applause.]

It may appear a little episodical for me to mention

the topic of which I shall speak now. It is a favorite proposition of Douglas' that the interference of the general government, through the Ordinance of 1787, or through any other act of the general government, never has made or ever can make a free State; that the Ordinance of 1787 did not make free States of Ohio, Indiana, or Illinois. That these States are free upon his "great principle" of popular sovereignty because the people of those several States have chosen to make them so. At Columbus, and probably here, he undertook to compliment the people that they themselves have made the State of Ohio free and that the Ordinance of 1787 was not entitled in any degree to divide the honor with them. I have no doubt that the people of the State of Ohio did make her free according to their own will and judgment, but let the facts be remembered.

In 1802, I believe, it was you who made your first constitution, with the clause prohibiting slavery, and you did it, I suppose, very nearly unanimously. But you should bear in mind that you—speaking of you as one people—that you did so unembarrassed by the actual presence of the institution amongst you; that you made it a free State, not with the embarrassment upon you of already having among you many slaves, which, if they had been here, and you had sought to make a free State, you would not know what to do with. If they had been among you, embarrassing difficulties, most probably, would have induced you to tolerate a slave constitution instead of a free one, as indeed these very difficulties have constrained every people on this continent who have adopted slavery.

Pray what was it that made you free? What kept you free? Did you not find your country free when you came to decide that Ohio should be a free State? It is important to enquire by what reason you found it so? Let us take an illustration between the States of Ohio and Kentucky. Kentucky is separated by this river Ohio, not a mile wide. A portion of Kentucky, by reason of the course of the Ohio, is further north than this portion of Ohio in which we now stand. Kentucky is entirely covered with slavery—Ohio is entirely free from it. What made that difference? Was it climate? No! A portion of Kentucky was further north than this portion of Ohio. Was it soil? No! There is nothing in the soil of the one more favorable to slave labor than the other. It was not climate or soil that caused one side of the line to be entirely covered with slavery and the other side free of it. What was it? Study over it. Tell us, if you can, in all the range of conjecture, if there be anything you can conceive of that made that difference, other than that there was no law of any sort keeping it out of Kentucky, while the Ordinance of 1787 kept it out of Ohio. If there is any other reason than this, I confess that it is wholly beyond my power to conceive of it. This, then, I offer to combat the idea that that Ordinance has never made any State free.

I don't stop at this illustration. I come to the State of Indiana; and what I have said as between Kentucky and Ohio, I repeat as between Indiana and Kentucky; it is equally applicable. One additional argument is applicable also to Indiana. In her Territorial condition she more than once petitioned Congress to abrogate the Ordinance entirely, or at least so far as to suspend its operation for a time, in order that they should exercise the "popular sovereignty" of having slaves if they wanted them. The men then controlling the general government, imitating the men of the Revolution, refused Indiana that privilege. And so we have the evidence that Indiana supposed she could have slaves if it were not for that Ordinance; that she besought Congress to put that barrier out of the way; that Congress refused to do so; and it all ended at last in Indiana being a free State. Tell me not, then, that the Ordinance of 1787 had nothing to do with making Indiana a free State, when we find some men chafing against, and only restrained by, that barrier.

Come down again to our State of Illinois. The great Northwest Territory, including Ohio, Indiana, Illinois, Michigan, and Wisconsin, was acquired first, I believe, by the British government, in part, at least, from the French. Before the establishment of our independence it became a part of Virginia, enabling Virginia afterwards to transfer it to the general government. There were French settlements in what is now Illinois, and at the same time there were French settlements in what is now Missouri—in the tract of country that was not purchased till about 1803. In these French settlements negro slavery had existed for many years—perhaps more than a hundred, if not as much as two hundred years—at Kaskaskia, in Illinois, and at St. Genevieve, or Cape Girardeau, perhaps, in Missouri. The number of slaves was not very great, but there was about the same number in each place. They were there when we acquired the Territory. There was no effort made to break up the relation of master and slave, and even the Ordinance of 1787 was not so enforced as to destroy that slavery in Illinois; nor did the Ordinance apply to Missouri at all.

What I want to ask your attention to, at this point, is that Illinois and Missouri came into the Union about the same time, Illinois in the latter part of 1818, and Missouri, after a struggle, I believe some time in 1820. They had been filling up with American people about the same period of time, their progress enabling them to come into the Union at about the same time. At the end of that ten years in which they had been so preparing (for it was about that period of time), the number of slaves in Illinois had actually decreased, while in Missouri, beginning with very few, at the end of that ten years there were about ten thousand. This being so, and it being remembered that Missouri and Illinois are, to a certain extent, in the same parallel of latitude—that the Northern half of Missouri and the Southern half of Illinois are in the same parallel of latitude—so that climate would have the same effect upon one as upon the other, and that in the soil there is no material difference so far as bears upon the question of slavery being settled upon one or the other—there being none of those natural causes to produce a difference in filling them, and yet there being a broad difference in their filling up, we are led again to inquire what was the cause of that difference.

It is most natural to say that in Missouri there was no law to keep that country from filling up with slaves, while in Illinois there was the Ordinance of 1787. The Ordinance being there, slavery decreased during that ten years—the Ordinance not being in the other, it increased from a few to ten thousand. Can anybody doubt the reason of the difference?

I think all these facts most abundantly prove that

my friend Judge Douglas' proposition that the Ordinance of 1787, or the national restriction of slavery, never had a tendency to make a free State is a fallacy— a proposition without the shadow or substance of truth about it.

Douglas sometimes says that all the States (and it is part of this same proposition I have been discussing) that have become free have become so upon his "great principle"—that the State of Illinois itself came into the Union as a slave State, and that the people, upon the "great principle" of popular sovereignty, have since made it a free State. Allow me but a little while to state to you what facts there are to justify him in saying that Illinois came into the Union as a slave State.

I have mentioned to you that there were a few old French slaves there. They numbered, I think, one or two hundred. Besides that there had been a Territorial law for indenturing black persons. Under that law, in violation of the Ordinance of 1787, but without any enforcement of the Ordinance to overthrow the system, there had been a small number of slaves introduced as indentured persons. Owing to this, the clause for the prohibition of slavery was slightly modified. Instead of running like yours, that neither slavery nor involuntary servitude, except for crime of which the party shall have been duly convicted, should exist in the State, they said that neither slavery nor involuntary servitude should thereafter be introduced, and that the children of indentured servants should be born free; and nothing was said about the few old French slaves. Out of this fact, that the clause for prohibiting slavery was modified because of the actual presence of it,

Douglas asserts again and again that Illinois came into the Union as a slave State. How far the facts sustain the conclusion that he draws, it is for intelligent and impartial men to decide. I leave it with you, with these remarks worthy of being remembered, that that little thing, those few indentured servants being there, was of itself sufficient to modify a constitution made by a people ardently desiring to have a free constitution— showing the power of the actual presence of the institution of slavery to prevent any people, however anxious to make a free State, from making it perfectly so.

I have been detaining you longer perhaps than I ought to do. [Long and repeated cries of "Go on."]

I am in some doubt whether to introduce another topic upon which I could talk awhile. [Cries of "Go on," and "Give us it."] It is this, then. Douglas Popular Sovereignty, as a principle, is simply this: If one man chooses to make a slave of another man, neither that other man or anybody else has a right to object. [Cheers and laughter.] Apply it to government, as he seeks to apply it, and it is this: If, in a new Territory, into which a few people are beginning to enter for the purpose of making their homes, they choose to either exclude slavery from their limits or to establish it there, however one or the other may affect the persons to be enslaved, or the infinitely greater number of persons who are afterwards to inhabit that Territory, or the other members of the family of communities of which they are but an incipient member, or the general head of the family of States as parent of all—however their action may affect one or the other of these, there is no power or right to interfere. That is Douglas

Popular Sovereignty applied. Now, I think that there is a real popular sovereignty in the world. I think a definition of popular sovereignty, in the abstract, would be about this—that each man shall do precisely as he pleases with himself and with all those things which exclusively concern him. Applied in government, this principle would be—that a general government shall do all those things which pertain to it, and all the local governments shall do precisely as they please in respect to those matters which exclusively concern them.

Douglas looks upon slavery as so insignificant that the people must decide that question for themselves; and yet they are not fit to decide who shall be their governor, judge, or secretary, or who shall be any of their officers. These are vast national matters in his estimation; but the little matter in his estimation is that of planting slavery there. That is purely of local interest, which nobody should be allowed to say a word about. [Applause.]

Labor is the great source from which nearly all, if not all, human comforts and necessities are drawn. There is a difference in opinion about the elements of labor in society. Some men assume that there is a necessary connection between capital and labor, and that connection draws within it the whole of the labor of the community. They assume that nobody works unless capital excites them to work. They begin next to consider what is the best way. They say that there are but two ways: one is to hire men and to allure them to labor by their consent; the other is to buy the men and drive them to it, and that is slavery. Having assumed that, they proceed to discuss the question of whether the laborers themselves are better off in the condition of slaves or of hired laborers, and they usually decide that they are better off in the condition of slaves.

In the first place, I say that the whole thing is a mistake. That there is a certain relation between capital and labor, I admit. That it does exist, and rightfully exists, I think is true. That men who are industrious, and sober, and honest in the pursuit of their own interests should after a while accumulate capital, and after that should be allowed to enjoy it in peace, and also, if they should choose, when they have accumulated it, to use it to save themselves from actual labor and hire other people to labor for them, is right. In doing so they do not wrong the man they employ, for they find men who have not of their own land to work upon or shops to work in, and who are benefited by working for others—hired laborers, receiving their capital for it. Thus a few men that own capital hire a few others, and these establish the relation of capital and labor rightfully. A relation of which I make no complaint. But I insist that that relation, after all, does not embrace more than one-eighth of the labor of the country.

[The speaker proceeded to argue that the hired laborer, with his ability to become an employer, must have every precedence over him who labors under the inducement of force. He continued:]

I have taken upon myself, in the name of some of you, to say that we expect upon these principles to ultimately beat them. In order to do so, I think we want and must have a national policy in regard to the institution of slavery that acknowledges and deals with that institution as being wrong. [Loud cheering.] Whoever desires the prevention of the spread of slavery and the nationalization of that institution, yields all, when he yields to any policy that either recognizes slavery as being right or as being an indifferent thing. Nothing will make you successful but setting up a policy which shall treat the thing as being wrong. When I say this, I do not mean to say that this general government is charged with the duty of redressing or preventing all the wrongs in the world; but I do think that it is charged with the duty of preventing and redressing all wrongs which are wrongs to itself. This government is expressly charged with the duty of providing for the general welfare. We believe that the spreading out and perpetuity of the institution of slavery impairs the general welfare. We believe—nay, we know—that that is the only thing that has ever threatened the perpetuity of the Union itself. The only thing which has ever menaced the destruction of the government under which we live is this very thing. To repress this thing, we think, is providing for the general welfare. Our friends in Kentucky differ from us. We need not make our argument for them, but we who think it is wrong in all its relations, or in some of them at least, must decide as to our own actions and our own course, upon our own judgment.

I say that we must not interfere with the institution of slavery in the States where it exists because the Constitution forbids it, and the general welfare does not require us to do so. We must not withhold an efficient fugitive slave law, because the Constitution requires us, as I understand it, not to withhold such a law. But we must prevent the outspreading of the institution because neither the Constitution nor general welfare requires us to extend it. We must prevent the revival of the African slave trade and the enacting by Congress of a Territorial slave code. We must prevent each of these things being done by either congresses or courts. The people of these United States are the rightful masters of both congresses and courts [applause], not to overthrow the Constitution, but to overthrow the men who pervert that Constitution. [Applause.]

To do these things we must employ instrumentalities. We must hold conventions; we must adopt platforms, if we conform to ordinary custom; we must nominate candidates; and we must carry elections. In all these things, I think that we ought to keep in view our real purpose, and in none do anything that stands adverse to our purpose. If we shall adopt a platform that fails to recognize or express our purpose, or elect a man that declares himself inimical to our purpose, we not only take nothing by our success, but we tacitly admit that we act upon no other principle than a desire to have "the loaves and fishes," by which, in the end, our apparent success is really an injury to us.

I know that it is very desirable with me, as with everybody else, that all the elements of the Opposition shall unite in the next Presidential election and in all future time. I am anxious that that should be, but there are things seriously to be considered in relation to that matter. If the terms can be arranged, I am in favor of the union. But suppose we shall take up some man, and put him upon one end or the other of the ticket, who declares himself against us in regard to the prevention of the spread of slavery—who turns up his nose and says he is tired of hearing anything more about it, who is more against us than against the enemy —what will be the issue? Why, he will get no slave States after all—he has tried that already until being beat is the rule for him. If we nominate him upon that ground, he will not carry a slave State; and not only so, but that portion of our men who are high-strung upon the principle we really fight for will not go for him, and he won't get a single electoral vote anywhere, except, perhaps, in the State of Maryland. There is no use in saying to us that we are stubborn and obstinate because we won't do some such thing as this. We cannot do it. We cannot get our men to vote it. I speak by the card, that we cannot give the State of Illinois in such case by fifty thousand. We would be flatter down than the "Negro Democracy" themselves have the heart to wish to see us.

After saying this much, let me say a little on the other side. There are plenty of men in the slave States that are altogether good enough for me to be either President or Vice-President, provided they will profess their sympathy with our purpose and will place themselves on the ground that our men, upon principle, can vote for them. There are scores of them, good men in their character for intelligence and talent and integrity. If such a one will place himself upon the right ground, I am for his occupying one place upon the next Republican or Opposition ticket. [Applause.] I will heartily go for him. But unless he does so place himself, I think it a matter of perfect nonsense to attempt to bring about a union upon any other basis; that if a union be made, the elements will scatter so that there can be no success for such a ticket, nor anything like success. The good old maxims of the Bible are applicable, and truly applicable, to human affairs, and in this, as in other things, we may say here that he who is not for us is against us; he who gathereth not with us, scattereth. [Applause.] I should be glad to have some of the many good, and able, and noble men of the South to place themselves where we can confer upon them the high honor of an election upon one or the other end of our ticket. It would do my soul good to do that thing. It would enable us to teach them that, inasmuch as we select one of their own number to carry out our principles, we are free from the charge that we mean more than we say.

But, my friends, I have detained you much longer than I expected to do. I believe I may do myself the compliment to say that you have stayed and heard me with great patience, for which I return you my most sincere thanks.

Date Due